The RHS Encyclopedia of Practical Gardening

ROCK
GARDENING

——————————— DUNCAN LOWE ———————————

MITCHELL BEAZLEY

First published in 1996

ISBN 1 85732 775 6

Edited and designed by Mitchell Beazley, an imprint of Reed Consumer Books Limited
Michelin House, 81 Fulham Road,
London SW3 6RB
and Auckland, Melbourne, Singapore and Toronto
Produced by Mandarin Offset
Printed and bound in Hong Kong

Contents

Introduction

Rock gardening has some things in common with the English parish, which can hold within its boundaries everything from the tiniest cottage to the grandest manor house, and from an historic pile to the latest housing development. The old has not been discarded in giving way to the new and so each stage of change remains, valued and cared for. The rock garden too has its range of styles, from the early to the up-to-date, all of which continue to be used and admired. It can be small enough to fit into a window box or spread over an area large enough to be called a landscape.

In its construction the rock garden may imitate or suggest a natural effect such as an outcrop, cliff or stone-slide. On the other hand it may make no attempt to simulate nature, but simply serve to create a feature of rock or stone to enhance the garden. Whatever its form or style, the rock garden is a home for plants: special plants needing special preparations and treatments to flourish.

We use the term "rock plants" very broadly in modern gardening and there is really no difference between "rock plants" and "alpines". Many do originate from mountains and rocky places but we also include others from moorland, pasture and woodland habitats whose stature and behaviour are in keeping with the theme and scale of the rock garden. To meet the needs of such a variety of plant type we have had to contrive a diversity of structures and arrangements which are not only functional, but also pleasing to the eye.

The designing and making of these are the principal subjects of this book, and in support there is information and guidance on the selection and treatment of plants. The purpose is to provide practical instruction and advice for each stage of the work involved, from the very first thoughts to finishing touches, to fully equip the reader for the creation and enjoyment of a rock garden.

Glossary

Auger Tool for boring holes in wood.

Bark chips Fragmented tree bark.

Bark surfacing Chipped or shredded tree bark used as a mulch on the soil or as surfacing for paths.

Batter The slight backwards tilt of a retaining wall.

Bedding lines Grooves and ledges following the natural strata of rocks.

Bog garden A prepared area where the soil is kept permanently moist but not permanently waterlogged

Bonding Staggering the vertical joints in the alternate courses of a wall to give strength and firmness.

Breeze block Lightweight rectangular building block.

Builder's level Large spirit level, used to check both horizontal and vertical surfaces.

Bulb Globular, usually underground, storage organ composed mainly of fleshy scales.

Bulb frame A prepared bed with adjustable glazed covering to keep dormant bulbs dry.

Bulbil An infant bulb, produced as an off-set from a mature bulb or at a node.

Calcareous With significant lime content.

Cantilever Slabs laid on top of finished walling.

Carpeting plant One with a low, spreading habit.

Chock Block of wood or stone used to wedge an object temporarily in position.

Cleaving Splitting a slab of stone along its natural grain.

Clone A plant, or group of plants produced vegetatively from one original parent plant, all of which are genetically identical.

Cocoa shell The waste husks of cocoa beans, used for mulching.

Coir Peat substitute, produced from processed coconut fibre.

Compost A mixture of materials prepared for potting or seed raising – or decayed organic matter used to improve the soil.

Composted bark Shredded tree bark partially rotted, used for soil improvement and mulching.

Concrete commons Frostproof house bricks made from concrete.

Cotswold limestone A coarse-grained limestone with a warm buff tint.

Course An individual layer of stones, blocks or bricks in a wall.

Crazy paving Slabs of irregular shape fitted together to form the surface of a path or area.

Crevice plant One found growing naturally in rock crevices.

Crown The basal part of a herbaceous plant at soil level from which roots and shoots grow.

Cultivar Variation in a cultivated plant which retains certain characteristics when propagated, as distinct from that in a naturally occurring variety.

Cushion plant One with a compact, domed habit of growth.

Dibber Pointed tool for making holes in soil for the purposes of planting.

Dressed stone Stone cut into rectangular form for walling.

Dwarf Plants, shrubs and trees which are smaller in stature than is normal.

Dwarf wall Of low height, usually less than 60cm (2ft).

Ericaceous Applied to plants belonging to the family *Ericaceae* which usually require soil with a pH of 6 or less.

Fern trowel Narrow-bladed digging trowel.

Freestone Walling stone used as hewn from the quarry, without any subsequent shaping – as in drystone walls.

Fulcrum The support upon which a lever pivots.

Genus A group of plants which have a range of characteristics in common. A genus is subdivided into species.

Glossary 2

Geotextile Woven plastic fabric used in the construction industry.

Glyphosate The active ingredient of certain systemic herbicides.

Granite Hard rock of igneous origin.

Gravel Small stones, rounded or angular in shape, from natural deposits or produced by crushing.

Grit Small angular particles of stone.

Grout To fill the joints of paving with mortar.

Hand cultivator Metal, tined tool for breaking up the soil to create a tilth or for scratching up small weeds.

Hardcore Clean, hard rubble used for the foundation layer in path making.

Hardening off Progressive exposure of young plants raised under cover to outdoor garden conditions.

Heavy soil That which contains a high proportion of clay.

Herbaceous Non-woody plants that die down in autumn and produce new foliage the following spring.

Herbicide Chemical preparation used to kill weeds and other vegetation.

Humus Complex mixture of compounds formed from the remains of decomposed vegetable matter; also used rather loosely to describe the fibrous, spongy, moisture-retaining organic matter in soils.

Hybrid A plant produced by the cross-fertilization of genetically dissimilar plants, eg. two species, usually of the same genus.

Hypertufa An artificial stone made by mixing cement with peat or peat substitute and coarse sand, usually in the proportions of 1 to 1½–2, with water added. Used for making rocks, coating containers and casting troughs.

Indoor rock garden One which is permanently protected by overhead glass.

Knapping Squaring off the end of a rounded stone with a heavy hammer.

Leaf litter The partially decomposed leaves of deciduous trees.

Light soil One which is predominantly sandy, with low clay content and little humus.

Limestone Calcareous sedimentary rock of marine origin.

Liverwort Primitive plants with fleshy ribbon- or plate-like growth, related to the mosses.

Loam Fibrous, high quality soil, rich in humus produced by stacking and rotting down meadow turves for a year or more.

Lump hammer A heavy hammer used for breaking and cutting stone.

Mat-forming plant See Carpeting plant.

Moisture meter Simple electrically actuated gauge for measuring the moisture level in soil.

Mortar A mixture of cement, sand and water used for the bonding of walling components, pointing, grouting and rendering.

Mulch Organic or inorganic substance used to provide a surface covering over soil to retain soil moisture, maintain a cool and even soil temperature and suppress weeds.

Node Point on a stem or shoot from which leaves sprout.

Pan A squat plant pot with a height of half its diameter or less.

Pea gravel Rounded pebbles, usually of flint or quartzite.

Perennial A plant with a lifespan of at least three seasons.

Perlite A lightweight, granular material composed of heat-expanded volcanic mineral.

pH value Used to describe the degree of acidity or alkalinity of a particular soil. Below 7 on the pH scale is acid, above 7 is alkaline.

Pitch A repeated measurement between a number of points.

Plasticizer A liquid additive for mortar mixing which improves the working consistency.

Plunge bed A containment holding sand into which potted plants are sunk to the level of their rims.

Pointing Finishing the joints in walling with neatly applied mortar.

Pointing trowel A small, flat, triangular-shaped trowel used to fill and smooth off joints in walling.

Quartzite A siliceous, fairly hard mineral, common in gravels and grits.

Random stone See Freestone.

Retaining wall A wall built against a bank of earth to hold it in place.

Rhizome A swollen, usually creeping stem which acts as a storage organ and produces at intervals new shoots.

Rootstock The underground part of a plant, including its root system, from which shoots are produced.

Rosette A circular cluster of leaves growing from more or less the same point.

Run-off The excess water draining from a bed or area of the garden.

Sack truck A two-wheeled hand truck which provides leverage for the take-up of the load.

Sandstone Sedimentary rock, variable in its granular make-up, colour and hardness.

Scree Stone fragments or gravel mixed with a small proportion of soil; it holds little moisture.

Sedge peat The partially decayed remains of bog sedges; it is darker and less acidic than moss peat.

Self-tapping screws Hardened steel screws, used for fastening thin-gauge or soft metals.

Settlement The progressive slumping of soil which occurs after filling in a raised bed or trough.

Setts The rectangular 'cobbles' used to surface streets and roads before the advent of asphalt-based covering.

Sharp sand Coarse-grained sand suitable for horticultural purposes and used in concrete making.

Shreddings The product of prunings and clippings put through a garden shredder.

Slow-release fertilizer A balanced mixture of plant nutrients, in the form of coarse powder or coated granules, which remain active in the soil for months, released at a steady rate.

Soakaway A prepared pit into which excess soil water and runoff drains.

Spent mushroom compost A mixture of peat, straw, manure and a little chalk, used in commercial mushroom growing. Available after some months of use.

Sphagnum peat (also known as moss peat) is the partially decayed remains of sphagnum moss.

Spot plant One placed for special effect.

Stolon A branching shoot usually growing above ground which roots down at its tip.

Stone chippings Angular pebbles produced by crushing stone.

Straightedge A length of wood or metal with a perfectly straight edge used in aligning and levelling work.

Strata The layers in deposited (sedimentary) rocks.

Synthetic stone (also known as reconstituted stone) is an artificial stone made from selected sand and cement, dyed to produce a natural colour.

Tamping Packing down firmly.

Terracing Creating level beds on sloping ground.

Top-dressing A layer of gravel, bark or other material on the soil surface.

Tor A prominent stack of eroded rock.

Trucking The use of hand trucks for the movement of rocks and troughs.

Tuber A swollen underground stem or root acting as a storage organ.

Tufa Accumulated limy deposit in the form of soft porous rock.

Umbel A flat-topped or domed flower head in which the flowers are borne on stalks of more or less equal length all arising from the top of the main stem.

Types of rock garden 1

The desire to build a rock garden can have one of several motives, perhaps the most common of which is the introduction of a prominent feature or centrepiece. This usually takes one of two distinct forms.

The natural effect

Selected rocks are built up in order to create a resemblance to naturally outcropping stone, incorporating a number of well-prepared planting places. The most challenging location for this type of rock garden is on a featureless, level site, for although natural outcrops do occur in such situations, they are few compared with their prevalence in hilly regions. Where the site has moderate changes in level it is much easier to achieve a realistic simulation of exposed bedrock. The primary aim in the building of outcrops is to produce a convincing relationship, rock-to-rock, in the completed structure. Time and trouble taken in finding and obtaining attractively-formed and textured stone will be repaid by ease of building and attaining an authentic finished appearance.

Also in this category are boulder and pebble beds, which mimic the stone piles and torrent shingles of mountains and wildernesses.

The rock feature

Stone is used to produce an artistic form. Like the outcrop it is designed to accommodate plants, but this is less important than the architectural value. Quite often the rockwork is designed to embody water features such as springs, falls or pools. This abstract approach can be helpful where the only rock that is reasonably obtainable is awkward and angular in shape, defying natural-looking arrangement. Even larger pieces of masoned stone from the demolition of old buildings can be utilized for these constructions.

Other types of rock garden are somewhat less concerned with visual qualities and cater primarily for the welfare of the plants.

Specialized beds

The rock is still prominent to give an appropriate setting, but it is secondary to the provision of the best possible growing conditions for the inhabitants. The latter are frequently choice species with particular requirements and need more than normal attention. Scree beds are typical of these purpose-built growing areas, as also are bulb frames and bog gardens.

Raised beds

Basically elevated versions of the above, these provide the first-class drainage so essential to the well-being of many rock garden plants. This asset can also be the solution to the problem of an excessively moist site. Other benefits of the raised growing area are that it brings the plants within easy reach for both tending them and enjoying them, significantly reduces invasions by pests and weeds, and can be a boon to the disabled gardener.

Natural arrangements

Featured rock

By being suitably positioned and filled with a chosen soil mixture, the raised bed becomes, to some extent, independent of the general garden conditions. In more recent years it has been widely adopted in the cultivation of plants that are less than easy to please.

Island beds
Semi-formal in appearance, these serve both as specially prepared growing places for rock plants and as free-standing garden features. They are usually surrounded by lawn or an even expanse of gravel or paving. Like raised beds, they are elevated above the general ground level and so are naturally well-drained.

Boulder and pebble beds
Large boulders set in fairly flat beds covered in pebbles characterize these beds. They can imitate old river beds, with rounded material, or have a rugged character that is suggestive of stony wasteland.

WALLS

Whether existing or planned, walls can be modified to provide homes for plants, especially those native to cliffs and rocky ground. Retaining walls backed by earth or hollow walls filled with soil are useful and complementary extensions to the rock garden.

Rock garden scree

Boulder beds

Raised beds

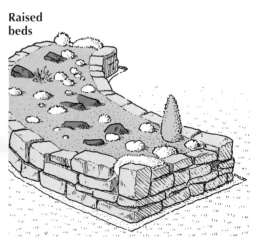

Island beds

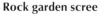

Types of rock garden 2

So far, the forms of rock garden described are free-standing and suited to a more or less flat site. However, a slope or bank in the garden plot offers great potential and in fact is often the reason behind many rock gardens being built in the first place.

Terracing

This is the traditional treatment for a steep incline, producing narrow, level growing areas and access paths. When adopted in rock gardening this method creates what are, in effect, raised beds on a slope by the use of walling or well-matched and close-fitting blocks of stone.

MINIATURE VERSIONS

Many of the rock garden types described are quite feasible for very confined spaces. Little cliffs can be built against the walls of a back yard or town garden, providing near-vertical planting areas to add to the horizontals. Dwarf raised beds will give height and form to the floor of a courtyard or can edge a patio. A trough or large clay pan is capable of holding an entire "Tom Thumb" rock garden, in which the largest stone is no bigger than a clenched fist. These cameos make the very best of limited space. Because so many rock plants are of a small and slow-growing nature the scope and variety that can be housed in tiny plots are remarkable.

Facing

Although it presents more difficulties in handling and construction than terracing, facing can produce dramatic effects. It is inspired by the slabs of exposed rock encountered in mountain terrain, which are often the habitats of choice plants.

Bluffs

Outcrops or crags protruding from a steep slope, these have great visual impact. The labour and skill required in their making are, however, considerable. Also, the need for size and space to obtain the best from them means that their place is in the larger garden.

Cliffs

Cliffs are, understandably, rare in general rock gardening. A major reason for this scarcity is that the contours required to form the basis of their construction are seldom found in the usual run of garden plots. Another constraint is the necessary size and weight of the rocks, which are essential to a satisfactory appearance. These have to be set in place both safely and with complete stability, which requires equipment and handling skills that are usually beyond the means of most amateur gardeners. Nevertheless, a well-contrived cliff can be a very special and lasting asset to a garden landscape, fully deserving inclusion here, if only to encourage those with sufficient enthusiasm, determination and space to make the attempt. The end result forms an unequalled setting for

Terracing on a steep slope

Rock slab facing

plants whose natural habit is to grow in curtains and cascades down rock faces, or send out plumes of flowers from their crevice-dwelling mats and cushions.

Gullies and gorges

Such land forms can be utilized to great effect. By introducing rockwork into the sides of a gully, whether natural or contrived, a small-scale gorge can be created. The treatment is equally valid for a sunken garden path or something approaching the size of a railway cutting.

Pavement plantings

These are very popular, particularly since the patio is such an important element of many garden designs. Existing paved areas or pathways can be altered so as to permit the introduction of plants and bring a softening of edges or patches of colour to brighten drab surfaces. Newly-made pavements have the advantage of allowing planting places to be built in as the work progresses. Taken further, an area may be designed specifically as a pavement garden in which the plants have priority and the stonework is there to provide the right surface for the plants to sprawl upon, at the same time creating an agreeable backcloth for the display. They can be formal or random in style, incorporating crazy paving or rectangular slabs.

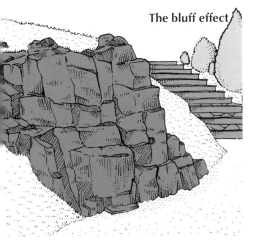

The bluff effect

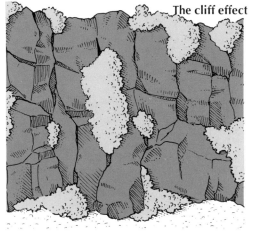

The cliff effect

Miniature rock gardens

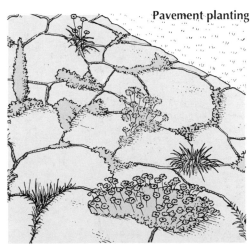

Pavement planting

Types of rock garden 3

Ericaceous and woodland beds
These have had an accepted place in rock gardening for as long as this branch of horiticulture has existed. Although the inhabitants of these beds are not generally of alpine or stony region origins, their size and habit make them suitable for the scale and character of the rock garden and its surroundings. It is not unusual for a mixture of ericaceous and woodland types to be grown in the same bed or prepared area, even though in the natural world they would never meet. What they have in common, however, is a preference for a spongy, fibrous, moisture-retentive soil, and where this is provided they will happily live together. In planning such beds it is important to take account of the local climate. In districts with drier, warmer summers a measure of permanent shading is sometimes a necessity for woodland plants and might even benefit species from moorland or open hillsides. The same plants in cooler, wetter. areas may well do better without any shading, other than in exceptional hot, dry spells, when temporary measures might be called for.

In character these beds are gentler in form and texture than their rock-built counterparts; they can incorporate stones with rounded profiles and time-softened surfaces with very pleasing results. Because of its natural associations, timber, in the form of roughly trimmed logs and other rustic artefacts, is also popular for establishing the basic structure containing planting arrangements.

Indoor rock gardens
This term is used here to present the various types of enclosed or roofed cultivation systems used either for the protection of vulnerable plants or for the protection of the grower. Both offer a more comfortable environment in which to tend the plants when the weather is unpleasant. Cost is the main restriction on the size of these shelters, which rarely enclose an area larger than the average living room. However, their use extends the scope of plants that can be grown and enjoyed beyond that limited by the conditions of the open garden. The most familiar of them is the alpine house, which is essentially a greenhouse with increased ventilation. There are also other forms, all with the main purpose of putting a glass roof over the growing area to provide a sheltered growing environment.

Ericaceous bed

Woodland bed

Indoor rock garden

Choosing the site

If the rock garden is to be successful as a home for plants its position and the conditions prevailing are critical. Of course, you may have a plot where choice is extremely limited, or perhaps, for effect, you want the site in a particular spot, but in all cases you should take into account the following.

Light and shade
In their natural homes mountain plants are accustomed to intense sunlight, reaching them through clear, unpolluted air. They have evolved in this bright atmosphere and in cultivation need the best light that we can give them. Other plants, from lower cliffs and stony places, also favour sunny ledges and crevices. Only a small minority seek a measure of shade. If deprived of sufficient sunlight the plants tend to grow lax and flower poorly, so, when planning your rock feature, concentrate on areas of the garden that are open to full light for the better part of the day. The only possible exception to this might be where the local climate can produce very hot, sultry conditions, in which case look for areas that go into shade from early afternoon onwards. Light shade lasting for most or all of the day is not an alternative; you should *ration* the sunlight, not *dilute* its quality.

If the only location you have is in almost constant shade, however, there are a number of rock plants which will tolerate the shortage of light, some of which have attractive flowers, while others can be grown principally for their foliage effects. Make a careful choice from these sun-shy types and create the right growing conditions for them.

Drainage
Another feature of mountain slopes and rocky terrain is the superb drainage that the plants enjoy. This keeps their root runs free from soggy and stagnant conditions as well as providing them with quick-drying, clean surfaces on which to sit or spread. Because they are used to these effects and are specially adapted to them, they are distressed by prolonged wetness and lingering dampness, becoming weakened and vulnerable to disease. So, whatever the form or style of the rock garden its drainage must be faultless and its surfaces free from prolonged moistness. With this in mind, when selecting the place to build the rock garden take note of any places in the garden that are slow to dry out after rain and areas that are always softer and damper than elsewhere. Look for patches where moss and liverwort are particularly troublesome, indicating lasting dankness and poor drainage. If you have no options because the whole garden, or the only available site in it, is naturally inclined to be over-wet, then you will have to improve matters by installing a drainage system (see pages 20–23).

Problems with trees
In addition to producing shade, nearby trees shed drips for some time after rain has passed. If the branches encroach over the site then not only will their spatterings prolong the dampness below, but the droplets will bring down pests and fungal diseases to blight any plants within range. A further threat of trees is the danger of their roots invading the fabric of the rock garden, so robbing it of moisture in dry periods and carrying away nutrients. At worst, vigorous trees can also undermine the whole structure.

Wind damage
In winter plants can be exposed to icy blasts which they are not equipped to endure. If your site is prone to cold winds you will need to provide protection, for example, by planting a sheltering barrier of shrubs or a low hedge.

> ### UNDERGROUND HAZARDS
> Wherever possible you should avoid building over places known to have electricity supply cables, gas pipes, water pipes or drains running beneath them. You may damage these during construction or have to face the ruination of the rock garden should repairs to them become necessary.

Traffic
Washing lines, children's bicycles, delivery men and pets are all threats to the rock garden and its plants. Make sure you take such things into account when making the decision where to build. It is also important to ensure that you provide adequate access for such things as wheelbarrows, lawnmowers and other garden implements.

Drawing up plans

A basic plan not only guides the work of creating a rock garden but also helps to avoid possible pitfalls.

Your first step is to select a scale for the plan. Measure the maximum length and breadth of the area involved, then compare these with the size of the sheet upon which the plan is to be drawn. Very often a scale of 1 cm=1 m (1:100) is satisfactory and works equally well for either feet or yards, but for the smaller garden scales of 1:50 or 1:25 may be more appropriate.

Next note and measure the positions of important features in the area and draw these on the plan. Take into account:

Direction The aspect of the site.
Gradient Any slope or fall in the ground which might aid drainage or benefit the lie of the rockwork.
Services Any known routes of services below ground; electricity, water, gas, drains and telephone.
Shade The extent of shade cast by adjacent trees or buildings.
Views Any house windows from which the rock garden might be viewed.
Access Existing paths and driveways.

CAUTION
Inspection covers on household drains must not be covered with soil or rocks. Any "disguise" used to hide them has to be easily removable and must not impair the function of the inspection facility.

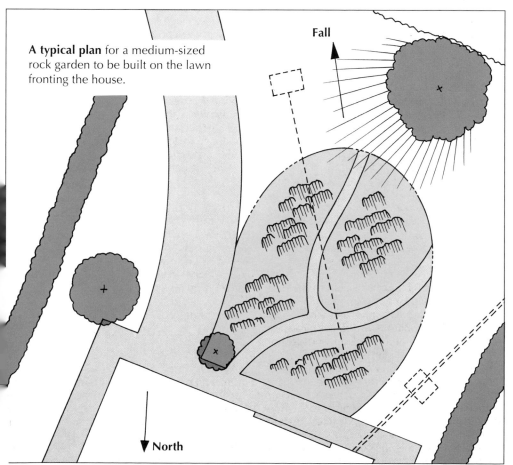

A typical plan for a medium-sized rock garden to be built on the lawn fronting the house.

Fall

North

The raw materials

Rocks and stones for construction

There are varied sources of rock from which to choose depending on where you live. Try and use local stone wherever possible for the most natural effect; for example, do not use limestone in a sandstone area. However, you might well find that local supplies are meagre or non-existent, requiring rock to be imported at considerable expense.

Sandstone is commonly available, both in block and slab form. In general it is supplied freshly quarried with a pleasant, mellow colouring. The blocks are frequently angular in shape, bearing little resemblance to hillside boulders and tors and are very difficult to build into a natural-looking arrangement. In contrast, slabs can emerge from the quarry with figured surfaces and irregular edges which give them an immediate rustic appearance that enhances any paved area or pathway.

York stone is a name used inaccurately nowadays to describe almost any natural sandstone paving slabs. The authentic material is still obtainable, for the greater part second-hand (and none the worse for that), but also fresh from the quarry. In both cases the cost is far higher than that of man-made substitutes.

Limestone, when quarried, is possibly less attractive and more difficult to work with than new sandstone. Its colour is usually very stark and the blocks are sharp-edged and erratic in form. Natural limestone outcrops weather relatively quickly and so have a characteristic rounded, worn appearance, quite unlike the freshly quarried version. Natural water-worn limestone has been long esteemed as the best material for rock garden construction, but is now protected as a conservation drive. Its removal for subsequent sale as rock garden material, or any other use, is strongly opposed. The only really acceptable sources now are where it is being removed from places such as old gardens or public parks for re-use.

Cotswold limestone is of a more granular consistency and warmer colouring than the greyer, harder forms of northern regions. Even as quarried stone it has a softer profile. This attractive, mellow stone is mainly used for building walls.

Granite presents many problems in rock-garden construction; it has a harshness to its shape and a resistance to weathering that defy attempts to produce pleasing constructions at ease with a garden setting. However, in the form of setts or cobbles, as used in bygone road surfacing, it is a useful walling material, thanks to the mason's work in squaring off the awkwardly shaped chunks. These are sometimes available from local council sales and demolition contractors.

Flint has been utilized with great skill in past and present buildings, where knapped, rounded lumps have been bonded by generous mortaring to produce walls, but as a stone for the rock garden it lacks sufficient size. Furthermore, it does not occur naturally as massive rock. Flint pea gravel is widely used in path making, although it is rather harsh in colour for association with more subdued rock and stone.

Slate can be used to form impressive rock features, particularly if large, rough slabs are used. Its rather drab colour can be used to advantage as a foil for brightly coloured flowers and silver or golden foliage.

Tufa is, geologically speaking, not a true rock but a deposit occurring in limestone regions. It has remarkable properties and potential for the rock gardener (see pages 66–7).

In addition to those already mentioned there are localized rock types of limited availability. Examples include Portland stone, Lakeland basalts and Welsh pre-Cambrian forms. It is only by visiting the areas where these rocks occur naturally that supplies of excellent material may be discovered.

Other materials

Following the completion of rockwork, walling and other structural elements, comes the process of filling, followed by surfacing and finishing; for these the components of soil mixtures and the materials for the final stages are required.

Gravels are obtained from natural deposits and also from the crushing of stone. The naturally occurring forms are rounded in shape, whereas those produced by crushing are sharply angular.

Both types are available in several grades, each of which is identified by the mesh size of the sieve through which it has passed; as a result the size is uniform within each grade. For gardening purposes the grades most likely to be used are from 4 mm (⅙ in) to 10 mm (⅜ in).

Flint gravel is usually readily available, either in crushed form or the "pea" type from pits and shingle banks. Different types include crushed quartzite, granite, sandstone and limestone.

Grits are in most cases by-products of gravel processing, with others deriving from sand and silt workings. In general the particles comprising the grit are angular in shape and variable in size, ranging from about that of an apple pip to a coarse sugar granule. Some horticultural suppliers offer two grades; the coarser of these has a higher proportion of larger particles. Most builders' supply merchants carry bulk stocks of grits and gravels and will often deliver locally. Those available at many garden centres are almost invariably packed in conveniently sized 25 kg (55 lb) bags. Only a little more expensive are poultry grits; similarly packed but carefully cleaned and accurately graded. They are worth consideration for small-scale work.

BUILDERS' MERCHANTS

Suppliers of pre-packed materials are not very consistent in their description of the products. What one may offer as "gravel" may be labelled "coarse grit" by another, and there are similar confusions afflicting coarse or sharp sands and grits. Never order such materials without having made sure that they are satisfactory.

Soil is a word that covers all too many substances: clays that are sticky and cold in winter, then baked hard in summer; sandy earth that holds little nourishment or moisture; peaty loam and chalky marl. Not one of them in its raw state is fully satisfactory for the requirements of rock garden plants. The heavy soils are too dense; they lack air spaces in their structure and so resist the spread of fine roots and hold too much water in the wetter months. Light soils usually drain well (often too well), they are quickly parched and lose organic matter

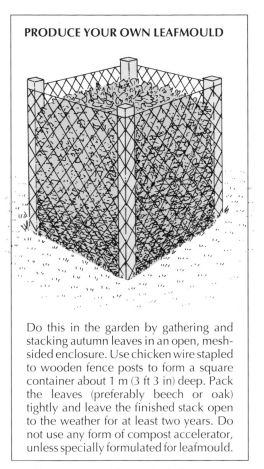

PRODUCE YOUR OWN LEAFMOULD

Do this in the garden by gathering and stacking autumn leaves in an open, mesh-sided enclosure. Use chicken wire stapled to wooden fence posts to form a square container about 1 m (3 ft 3 in) deep. Pack the leaves (preferably beech or oak) tightly and leave the finished stack open to the weather for at least two years. Do not use any form of compost accelerator, unless specially formulated for leafmould.

rapidly. Even good loams lack the necessary aeration and can be too rich in nutrients for plants that are accustomed to spartan conditions in nature.

Peat There are two distinct types of peat: moss peat is the fibrous, rich-brown type with a fairly high level of acidity and sedge peat is darker in colour, almost black, somewhat less fibrous and lower in acidity. Both provide organic, moisture-retentive material for the improvement of the soil structure. A few commercial brands of peat are blends of the two types. Neither has any nutrient value.

Peat continues to be used in large quantities by commercial growers, and even as a fuel where it is abundant. However, for conservation reasons, it is not recommended.

Preparing the site

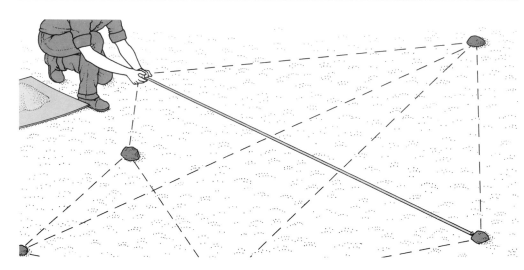

1 For informal shapes, transfer the main dimensions of the rock garden from the plan to the site using a measuring tape. Mark the points with sand or paint.

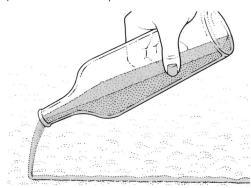

2 For marking out, fill a bottle with dry sand and pour this out to produce a line. Alternatively, use whitewash or emulsion paint and a brush.

Clearing

If the site you have selected is on an established, well-kept lawn your preparation work is very easy. Perennial weeds should be few and the surface already even and uncluttered. Just strip off the turf and stack it grass-side down. Once rotted this becomes a valuable source of loam for the garden. Alternatively, a herbicide can be used. Now you are ready for the next stage.

On sites infested with tough, perennial weeds such as dandelions and docks, or the virulent couch grasses, your clearing work will be much more thorough and lasting if you eradicate the weeds with a herbicide instead of laboriously digging out each individual plant. The hand removal method inevitably leaves behind living fragments of root from which the weeds will regenerate, probably after you have completed the rock garden. You can also smother weeds with a mulch; although this takes time it is effective.

Grassed banks are very difficult to strip and it is far easier and more effective to use a herbicide, following the manufacturer's instructions.

If trees or large shrubs need to be removed it is best to try to dig out as much of the stump and roots as possible. An alternative to this often gruelling task is to saw the stumps off at ground level and treat the cut surface with ammonium sulphamate. This will effectively kill the living tissue and ensure no suckers arise. If the stump is then covered with soil the root system will slowly rot away with little risk of honey fungus (*Armillaria mellea*) moving in. In any case, this disease will not trouble rock plants.

If an existing path crosses or intrudes on the area designated for the rock garden and has to be re-routed you can usually limit the removal work to taking off the surface covering of the path, whether paving, asphalt or brickwork, and leaving the hardcore base in place. This will be covered later by the rock garden and on heavy land can be linked with pipes to the drainage system, so increasing the latter's effectiveness.

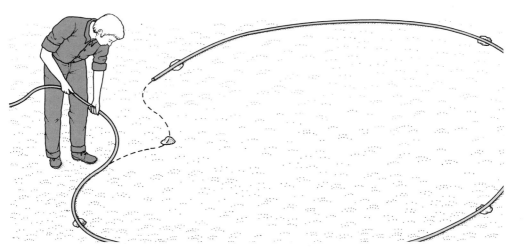

3 Copy the shape from the plan as near as possible using soft, flexible rope or garden hose, working round the dimension marks. Make adjustments until the curves are smooth. Finally, follow the rope or hose outline with sand or paint, as in 2.

HERBICIDE

For killing off grass and weeds use a type based on the chemical glyphosate, which is generally accepted as leaving no harmful deposits and is also neutralized immediately by contact with the ground. Areas treated can be worked upon as soon as the vegetation has died. Always read the maker's directions and follow them exactly.

Working space

On the site give yourself "elbow room" by, if possible, clearing a patch somewhat larger all round than the actual area to be occupied by the rock garden. This creates useful space for working, moving materials and piling or stacking them conveniently close by.

Marking out

The main purpose of marking out is to define the outer edge of the rock garden and the routes of any pathways round or through it. First transfer the principal measurements from the scale

drawing to the surface of the cleared site.

Formal outlines involving only straight lines are easy to establish using lengths of unwarped wood to guide the marker. Irregular shapes are produced with the aid of soft rope or flexible garden hose.

When you are satisfied with the shape mark it on the site by following the line of the rope or hose with a trail of sand or paint. Do not use pegs and twine as the twine is easy to trip over and can also be an obstacle to the essential wheelbarrow. The lines of sand or paint present no such hazards and are surprisingly long-lasting.

Where a drainage system is to be incorporated, mark it out using the same method but a different coloured marker to prevent subsequent confusion.

Levelling and contouring

Where a horizontal surface is required, hammer flat-topped, wooden pegs a little way into the ground at spacings of 1.5 m (5 ft) over the site. Choose a peg at the lowest part of the site as the datum, then hammer it further in until it is obviously lower than the rest. Using a straight piece of timber, 2 m (6 ft 6in) long, and a spirit level, bring the other peg tops one by one level with that of the datum, driving them in deeper and checking frequently with the spirit level. Fill in or take off earth as necessary to level the site.

Contouring can be done by simply piling up earth until it forms an acceptable shape over the area concerned.

Drainage 1

A drainage system collects and disposes of excess water and the need for drainage in a rock garden cannot be overstressed. This is particularly true of level sites with heavy soils or clays which, by their nature, retain high levels of moisture and impede the escape of surplus water. Airless, soggy soil inhibits the growth and function of rock plant roots and is a major cause of plant death. This is not usually a problem on naturally porous, sandy or gravel-rich soils, however, which only become saturated for brief periods during heavy rain or snow-melt.

The first step in planning a drainage system is to establish a place for the water to drain into. A rubble-filled, shallow pit beneath the rock garden is not the answer, especially on heavy soil or clay where it actually holds water creating a "sump". This sustains the wet conditions in the root runs, the very opposite of what is intended. If you are fortunate enough you may be able to arrange an outlet to a path or driveway at a lower level than the base of the planned rock garden, otherwise the best solution is to provide a soakaway.

Soakaway

This is simply a pit filled with broken bricks, stones or large gravel or, alternatively, lined with geotextile (a woven plastic construction fabric), into which the drainage system delivers its water. During dry periods this collected run-off seeps away into the surrounding earth.

A soakaway should be located at some discreet spot in the garden but at the same time be as near to the rock garden site as possible, to keep down the labour and cost of installing the drainage system. Make sure that the soakaway location is not at a higher level than the rock garden site. If in doubt check this by stretching a length of cord or heavy twine between the two places and judge the fall by eye, or use a straight piece of board aligned with the taut cord and a spirit level.

To make a soakaway, excavate an area approximately 1 m (3 ft 3 in) square and the same in depth. The hole created is then filled with rubble, stones or gravel, or lined with geotextile held in place with stakes. Before this is done, however, the delivery pipe from the drainage system must be in place. To complete

1 Check the levels between the site and the soakaway or outlet by lining up a straight-edged board and spirit level along a taut line. The line must be the same height above ground at each end.

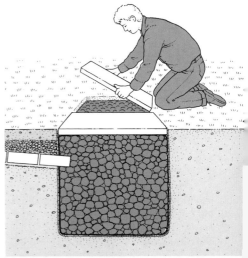

2 For a typical soakaway dig the pit but only fill it with gravel or rubble once the drains and delivery pipe have been laid. Cap the soakaway with paving slabs once it is full.

the work, cap the hole with standard paving slabs, or use natural stone if the soakaway is in a conspicuous position.

CAUTION

Do not attempt to achieve an outlet for the run-off by tapping into the domestic drainage systems. These are installed to precise building and safety regulations and any interference or modification can be a serious breach of these or a possible safety hazard.

The drainage system

Once you have established a soakaway or outlet, it is time to turn your attention to the routes for the drainage channels. It is best to avoid running them beneath a bed or border wherever possible.

A herringbone pattern positioned and spread to serve the area to be occupied by the rock garden is the most conventional layout for a drainage system.

First mark out the pattern with sand or paint (see page 18), making sure that the angle at each junction where a side channel meets the main channel does not exceed 45°. Dig out the central trench, beginning at its source on the site and working towards the outlet. The trench should be no wider than the blade of a spade and as cleanly formed as you can make it. At the start point dig to a depth of 15–20 cm (6–8 in), but at the outlet end the depth will depend on the length and fall of the trench.

The base of the trench must have a fall (that is to say a downhill slope towards the outlet) of at least 1:100. To check this, lay a straight board 2 m (6 ft 6in) in length along the base of the trench, with a spirit level on its top edge. Raise the downhill end of the board until the spirit level registers level, then measure the lift made; it should be a minimum of 2 cm (¾ in).

Once you have dug the main trench check that its bottom is flat by stretching a length of cord or twine along the length and pulling it taut. Any humps or hollows will show up and must be levelled off, otherwise they will form obstacles to the drain laying and subsequent water flow. If you encounter substantial roots when digging, re-route the trench.

The problems of clay

Clay is virtually impermeable to water and so does not allow it to seep away at an adequate rate. There is therefore no point in making a soakaway on clay sites but a good alternative is to dig a pit to collect the run-off. Make this about the same size as the soakaway excavation and, to prevent erosion of its sides, line the pit with strong polythene sheeting held in place by a stake driven upright into each of the corners. The resulting well can be periodically bailed out with buckets or, more easily, with the small gear-type pump that is used with a DIY power drill. Obviously the presence of a water-filled pit is a danger to children and pets, so to prevent accidents, cap the hole securely with robust paving slabs at least 5 cm (2 in) thick and no less than 60 cm (24 in) square. These must be supported by timber or concrete beams crossing the top of the pit. The timber needs to be a minimum of 10 x 5 cm (4 x 2 in) in section and treated against rot. Concrete beams of the same size are superior in both strength and life.

On clay ground dig a collection pit, but do not fill it with rubble or gravel. Line the sides with plastic sheet secured by corner posts. To cover the pit, set a pair of cross-beams flush to the surface to support the capping slabs.

Drainage 2

1 First use sand or paint to mark out the drainage pattern. The number of side branches is mainly determined by the size of the proposed rock garden.

2 Dig the main trench and check its fall using a 2 m (6 ft 6 in) long board and spirit level. Make sure that the base of the trench is free of debris before doing this.

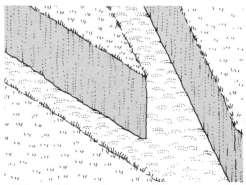

3 Where side trenches meet the main trench the bases must be at the same level.

Next dig out the side trenches using the same technique, and where each side trench meets the main trench make certain that its base is level with that of the main trench. Check also that each side trench has a slight fall towards the main channel.

Installing the drains

There is a choice of hardware both in type and material. The simplest method is to use large gravel laid to within 6–8 cm (2½–3 in) of the trench top. More effective and longer-lasting, however, are land drains, either in the form of short terracotta pipes (often called tiles) or perforated plastic pipe of continuous length, sold by the metre.

If using terracotta tiles, lay them end-to-end along the base of the trench with a gap of no more than 6 mm (¼ in) between their ends. A shallow layer of coarse sand or small gravel on the base of the trench can make it easier to set and align the tiles. Where side branches meet the central run the end-to-end gap needs to be larger, approximately 5 cm (2 in).

4 At the junctions of terracotta tiles use a large piece or two of plant pot shard, or plastic mesh, to cover the gaps.

At the junctions of side branches, the large gap in the main run and the triangular gap made by the meeting up of the side branch must be covered, either with large plant pot shards or a piece of plastic mesh.

The method of laying plastic drains is similar, except that each channel has only a single length of pipe cut to suit. To make the junctions, cut a large hole in the wall of the central pipe and trim the end of the branch pipe at an angle, to roughly fit up to the central pipe. Roof this joint with a piece of plastic mesh or geotextile.

In both systems the next step is to fill the trenches with gravel or shingle in the manner described for the simple unpiped version.

CAUTION

Do not be tempted to fill the trenches merely by returning the excavated earth. Many soils will enter the pipes and slowly block them with sediment.

Finishing off

There are various ways of finishing off drainage systems, depending on the nature of the ground they are laid in. If crossing a lawn, the ideal finishing method is to cover the surface of the gravel in the trench with a length of tough, woven plastic (mesh). This material allows water to pass through, but holds back the soil. An alternative is to use onion or potato sacks made of similar but lighter fabric or geotextile. When this has been done, fill in the remaining 6–8 cm (2½–3 in) of the trench with soil to provide a base for seeding or turfing.

Where the drain lies under a driveway or path then it is simply a matter of topping off the trench with matching material, be it gravel, paving, asphalt or other surfacing. If you have had to run a drain under a flower bed, cap the trench with bricks or strong, flat tiles and disguise them with a covering of soil. This will prevent you from damaging the system with a spade or fork in future digging.

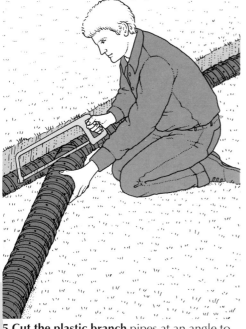

5 Cut the plastic branch pipes at an angle to roughly fit against the main pipe.

6 Finally, fill in the trench with gravel then cover with a layer of plastic mesh. Top off with matching surface material.

Handling materials 1

Limitations

In much rock garden building there is, inevitably, an involvement with heavy objects and substances. The methods described here are aimed at reducing physical effort as far as is reasonably possible, even though this may lengthen the time and preparation needed to achieve the end result. The young and muscular are free to adapt and ignore where they wish – except, that is, in matters of safety.

SAFETY

Any lump of stone exceeding 25 kg (55 lb) in weight should be regarded as too heavy for physical lifting without some aid. For a good proportion of us the limit is considerably lower. Gloves of leather or stout fabric should always be worn when handling rock and footwear needs to be strong enough to give protection to the toes and feet. Rubber boots are inadequate; far safer are the heavier types of hiking or working boots.

Moving rocks and troughs

It is possible to trundle quite heavy rocks and slabs along the ground without having to lift them, but there comes a point when mechanical aids are called for.

Trucking is an effective method of moving on sites which are reasonably firm and even. For this the sack truck, especially if fitted with broad, tyred wheels, is very efficient. Avoid models with small, solid wheels as these are hard to push and tend to sink into the ground. Where the site is on soft ground, or in wet conditions, you will need first to lay down a temporary "roadway", using old doors, planks, scrap building board or similar material between the load and its destination.

Larger, heavier loads which are too much for the trucking method respond to the ancient system of rollers. Unless the route for the load lies along established paths or a driveway, you will find that a temporary "road" is almost always necessary. The system is suitable for any large trough, rock or boulder if it has one good flat side or base. The load is moved with its flat face resting on a row of rollers. Make these from strong steel tubing or hard wood with a diameter

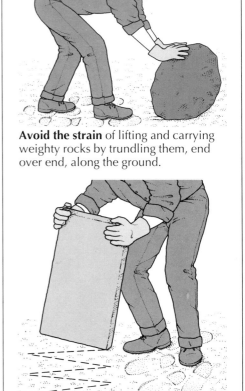

Moving rocks and slabs

Avoid the strain of lifting and carrying weighty rocks by trundling them, end over end, along the ground.

Use similar handling for slabs, "walking" them on their edges

of about 5 cm (2 in) and long enough to protrude a little beyond the width of the load. You will need at least six of these (all the same diameter). The load is made mobile by levering up the leading end and inserting a roller between the track and the base of the load. By then pushing or levering at the back of the load you can roll it forward until you can insert a second roller. To make progress lay additional rollers along the route, about 20 cm (8 in) apart. Continue to push the load over these; extend the route by taking forward and laying down

Trucking large rocks

For trucking first create a gap for the truck plate, using a lever and chocks.

Push the plate of the sack truck into the gap and tilt the truck backwards to take up the load.

Maintain the balance of the truck while pushing forwards.

Moving troughs

Use a system of rollers on a plank track (or similar arrangement of boards) to move larger troughs, or boulders with a face flat enough to run on the rollers. Push or lever the load forwards.

Handling materials 2

each used roller as it emerges from the rear of the advancing load. To steer the load use the back edge of the trough or rock like handlebars and to follow a curving track angle the rollers ahead of the load. In a similar manner to roller recycling, the track can be extended by moving the used sections to new positions in front of the load.

Oddly-shaped, heavy loads require a development of the above method. For this make a wooden cradle to form a "sled" which will travel along the rollers. Lay two lengths of timber on the ground to act as "runners" and roll or lever the load to rest on them. Then build the cradle round the load. Use timber of about 8 x 5 cm (3 x 2 in) in section, firmly nailed for adequate strength. A somewhat simpler alternative is to use a strong flat board as the base, with a few wooden blocks nailed on to hold the load in place, after it has been positioned.

On slopes the problems of handling and moving heavy objects are more severe and there are no easy solutions. Where practical *lower* the load downhill instead of hauling it upwards. Where it has to be taken uphill a helper will be needed to haul on a rope from the top of the slope, taking half of the weight off the pusher.

The manoeuvring of rocks during construction is a recurring task; it is essential to satisfactory positioning and firming in.

To make these movements with less effort, use a crowbar of 1 m (3 ft 3 in) or more in length. Drive it into the earth about 10 cm (4 in) close to the face of the rock needing to be pushed and press forward at the top of the crowbar. The leverage gained multiplies your strength several times. Use the same tool with a fulcrum, such as a house brick or block of wood, for the many small lifts associated with adjusting positions to achieve evenness in the lie of the rockwork.

The need to place one rock on top of another is encountered in a variety of constructions and, unless the blocks are of only moderate weight, you should avoid manual lifting. Try the technique of building a temporary ramp from small stones. Alternatively, prop a short plank against the lower rock to form a similar incline, and roll or drag the upper rock to its resting place, with assistance.

Construct a timber cradle for awkwardly shaped loads, to use as a "sled" on the roller system.

Halve the effort of pushing a load up a slope by having an assistant to haul on a rope attached to the leading end.

Manoeuvre heavy rocks by driving in a crowbar, hard against a face, and pushing forwards on the crowbar to slew the rock on its base, or to push it and firm it into place when constructing the rock garden.

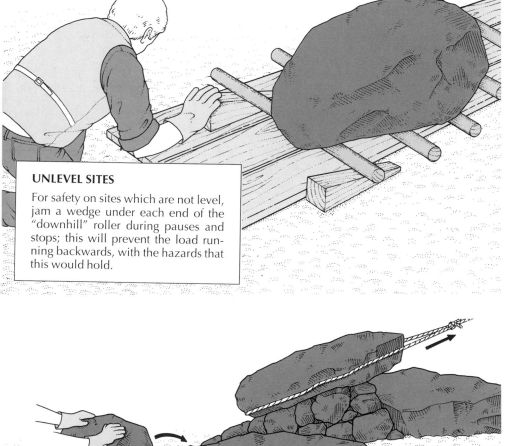

UNLEVEL SITES

For safety on sites which are not level, jam a wedge under each end of the "downhill" roller during pauses and stops; this will prevent the load running backwards, with the hazards that this would hold.

Build a temporary ramp of stones, or use a short, inclined plank to aid the hauling or rolling of one rock onto the top of another.

Cutting and shaping 1

What needs to be cut or shaped?
The blocks or boulders used in rock gardening cannot always be fitted and related as desired without some modification. They may have awkward angles or lumps preventing satisfactory arrangement, or have blemishes spoiling the effect wanted. It is sometimes possible to correct or reduce faults like these by the judicious use of tools.

When laying paving it is frequently necessary to trim and cut the slabs to achieve the required fit or pattern, and the adjusting of individual stones is a regular part of wall building.

Rocks and stones vary in their response to cutting, due chiefly to their type, and to a lesser extent to the condition that they are in. Here it is only possible to generalize very broadly on the behaviour of various stones and to confine guidance to a few working techniques which are relevant, useful and within the capabilities of the gardener. It will be noted where several of the methods apply equally to cement-based synthetic stones and concretes.

Sandstone varies from being hard, close-grained and difficult to cut, to a soft granular composition that behaves like a biscuit under tools. In the slab form its reaction to edge shaping can be erratic, with a tendency to shatter or fracture anywhere other than where was intended. In general, dividing slabs is not difficult if the right technique is employed. Some sandstones have bedded lines which make them easy to cleave; look for darker lines in the stone, running parallel to the surface.

Limestone is much less easy to cut than the majority of sandstones. Stone masons work on this rock in its freshly quarried state, knowing that in a matter of weeks the exposure to air will alter its chemical composition, making it far harder to work. Hence old limestone is extremely resistant to shaping with hand tools. The coarser-grained types, such as Cotswold stone and the local oolitic limestones are somewhat softer and more responsive.

Granite requires the skill, experience and equipment of the professional mason to be

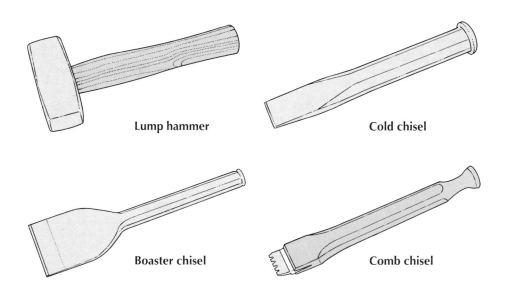

Lump hammer

Cold chisel

Boaster chisel

Comb chisel

successfully worked. It is possible to do some rough shaping of blocks by knocking off chips with a hammer, but on the whole it is a very trying material for the amateur, resisting the chisel and fracturing randomly.

Slate in some of its forms has excellent cleaving properties, as countless roofs will testify. Yet others are contorted in their bedding and split in all directions when worked upon. The use of a chisel almost invariably results in extensive shattering of the slab or block. Commercial cutting is done with diamond saws operating in running water.

The tools and their use

The lump hammer should be not more than 1 kg (2¼ lb) to avoid strain and fatigue for the user. It is used with all the chisel types described and for roughly shaping walling stones.

The cold chisel is a general-purpose cutting tool and also useful in splitting, with its wedge-like shape.

The boaster chisel is used for the edging of walling stone, cutting across slabs and in cleaving. A suitable size is one with a blade width of 60–80 mm (2½–3 in).

The electrician's chisel is a lighter and quite effective alternative of similar shape.

Multi-point or comb chisels can have integral teeth or replaceable types. This is a very useful tool for removing lumps, dressing faces and chipping off material where other chisels skid away from the cut.

SAFETY

For personal protection in the use of these tools and techniques you should wear: goggles, heavy-duty gloves, strong footwear and, if significant dust is generated, a "nuisance" grade dust mask. When using chisels always cut away from your body (see page 30 fig. 1) and never work where flying chips are dangerous.

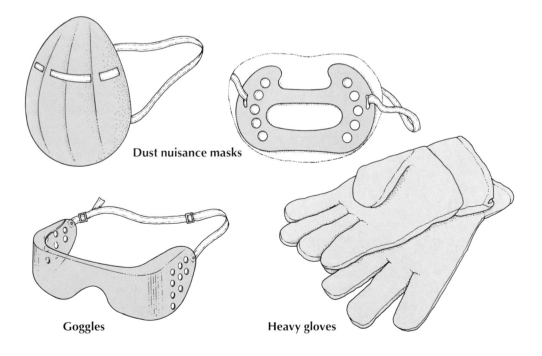

Dust nuisance masks

Goggles

Heavy gloves

Cutting and shaping 2

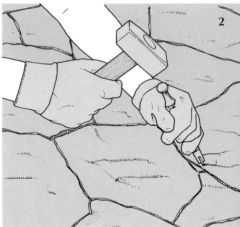

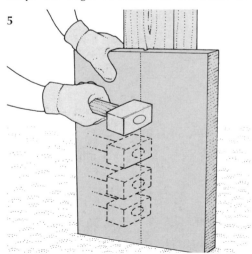

Cutting techniques

1 Remove unwanted protrusions from rocks and stones with a cold chisel, placing the blade at the base of the lump and using firm, heavy blows with the hammer. If the cold chisel skids off the work, remove the material a little at a time with the comb chisel.

2 Clean off raised patches from paving slabs with the comb chisel, working repeatedly over the blemish with a series of short, chipping cuts, in the manner of a sculptor or wood carver. Use a chisel angle of about 45°.

Shape the edges of slabs, whether stone or synthetic, using a boaster chisel. Ensure that the slab is uniformly supported on a firm, flat surface such as concrete or packed earth. Mark the line of the edge required and work towards it from the existing edge, cutting off a series of finger-thick bites. Any attempt to cut immediately along the marked line usually results in the slab cracking.

3–5 Divide slabs, whether stone or synthetic, by first marking the required cutting line on both the upper and the lower faces of the slab, making certain that they coincide. Then with the slab resting on firm, even ground create a shallow groove along the line marked on the upper surface. Use a

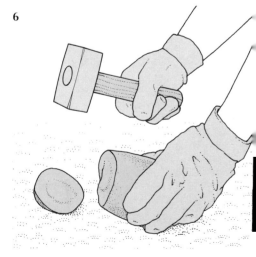

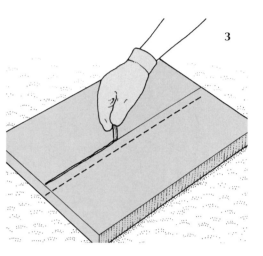

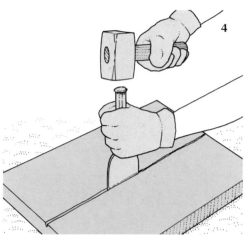

boaster chisel vertically in a series of progressive cuts, each made with a single, moderate blow. Work back along the line in the same manner and repeat until the groove is approximately 3 mm (⅛ in) deep.

Now pull the slab upright to rest fully against a stout wooden post or box and deliver repeated smart hammer blows up and down the marked line on the opposite side to the one which you have grooved. The slab should then fracture cleanly. Do not let the parted slab fall onto a hard surface, or it is likely to crack with the impact.

6 Square off or otherwise shape rounded walling stones by "knapping". Hold the stone firmly on the ground with one hand, or trapped under the foot, and deliver smart vertical hammer blows to one end of the stone. This may take off the excess in one piece or require several "knaps" to achieve the shape required.

7 Cleave slabs of sandstone or slate by following a bedding line with the boaster chisel. Use moderate blows; slowly open a split, then carefully enlarge this until the slab parts.

8 Produce a neat edge on dressed walling blocks, whether stone or synthetic, by working along a line drawn a little distance back from the existing uneven edge, using the boaster chisel angled at about 20° from vertical.

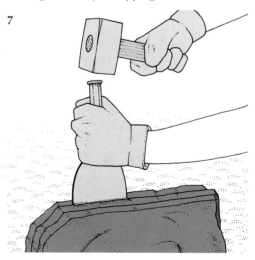

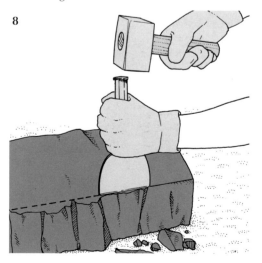

DIY rocks and stones

If you have difficulties in obtaining natural rock and stone it is worth considering the artificial substitutes. Commercial products available are of good quality and realistic appearance; there are walling blocks and paving slabs with attractively figured surfaces and in a range of quite natural colourings simulating various types of different stone.

Unfortunately for the rock gardener these products are formal in shape as both slabs and stones are rectangular or square. The "rockery stones" marketed are very limited in variety of shape and often hollow. These cavities are potential homes for mice, slugs and other pests and need to be packed with sand or earth before the "rocks" are set in place. Where artificial stones are used alongside the real thing their synthetic nature becomes accentuated and the two do not mix visually at all well.

Home-made rocks and stones are not difficult to produce and you have the opportunity to create informal shapes, modelling each piece individually. Just accept that some trial and error will be involved before the end result lives up to your expectations.

A cement-based substance which does not look too much like concrete can be made using a mixture of coarse sand, peat, or peat substitute such as coconut coir, and cement. This compound has become known to gardeners as "hypertufa" and is the raw material for the amateur's synthetic stone. By varying the proportions of the ingredients the texture and colour can be adjusted to some degree. For a resemblance to sandstone, blend two parts coarse brown sand, two parts peat or peat substitute (passed through a 6 mm or ¼ in sieve) and one part cement, all measured by volume. For a finish nearer to limestone use two parts silver sand and only one part peat or peat substitute. You can improve the colour by using concrete colourants, obtainable from builders' merchants and some DIY centres. Most of these dyes are in powder form for adding at the dry

To make artificial paving and walling stones

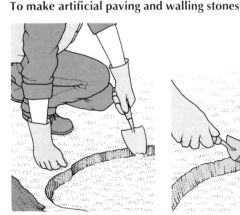

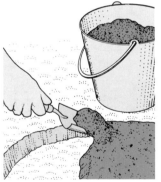

1 Begin by cutting out the required shapes in a level bed of firm, moist sand or earth; make their depth equal to the wanted thickness of the slab or block. Take care not to have a depth of less than 5 cm (2 in) to ensure that the finished piece will have adequate strength.

2 Prepare the hypertufa mixture and trowel this into each of the moulds; make sure that the base of each is flat and clean before filling. Allow the hypertufa to set until it is strong but can still be carved. Cover the moulds with damp cloths during the setting.

3 Use scraping tools such as old knives and spoon handles to create figuring and texture on the surface of each cast. Leave them in their moulds for a further two or three days to complete the curing process, after which they can be levered out with a spade and are ready for use.

mixing stage, but there are now liquid forms for painting onto the finished surface after setting.

To prepare hypertufa, first mix the ingredients (sand, peat or peat substitute and cement, plus any colouring additive) in the dry state until thoroughly blended. Then add water, a little at a time, turning the mixture with a trowel or spade until the consistency resembles that of porridge. It is then ready for use, which should not be delayed more than half an hour.

To make artificial rocks

1 For the moulds, dig out rough shapes of the size required in a bed of moist sand or not-too-dry earth that is free from large stones or roots. Do not be too neat or tidy in shaping the hole.

2 Shovel in the prepared hypertufa mixture, filling the moulds made in the sand or earth. Tamp periodically to prevent cavities using a piece of wood. These "casts" should then be left, covered in wet sacking or newspaper (kept moist) for two or three days.

3 Test the state of setting by scraping with a knife or screwdriver tip. When it can just be carved, the "rock" can be moved.

4 Carefully excavate the cast, first clearing the sides with a trowel, then use a spade or garden fork to lever it out.

5 Clean up the surface with a stiff brush. Use scrapers to remove any blemishes and to create a natural-looking surface.

The outcrop 1

Basic shape

In constructing an outcrop your aim is to produce a realistic effect of bedrock rising clear out of the soil. In nature it does so usually at an angle due to the tilt of the strata and so the rock mass has a front face, sides and a top which slopes back into the ground. The top may have a further slope to one side or the other. The overall shape is similar to that of a wedge. Time and weather erode the rock, crumbling its edges, notching and stepping its faces, but the fundamental form remains. It is very important to bear this basic shape in mind when deciding how your outcrop is to lie on the site.

Building rules

If the site is small, a single mass of the wedge-like form will probably look best. For larger areas you can repeat the form several times to create a group. For this group effect copy a naturally occurring outcrop: all the fronts should face the same way and in parallel lines, all the sides follow the same line roughly at right angles to the front face. The backwards tilt should be consistent throughout the group.

The divisions by cracks and fissures into blocks and slabs in true outcrops is a result of fracturing in the original solid rock. To achieve a similar appearance put together lumps of stone to look as though they were once a single massive piece. There are firm natural rules to the fracture patterns and these apply equally to the garden outcrop. Vertical joints should be in line and not staggered as in brickwork, and horizontal joints parallel although they can occur at differing levels. If you keep to these rules the resulting rockwork will look much more natural.

Construction

Begin construction work by establishing the degree of tilt for the outcrop. This angle is usually between 5° and 10°; anything greater creates building problems and can look excessive. Make a test build of stones on the site to try out various angles and, when you are satisfied, make a simple gauge to work against throughout construction.

For the gauge you will need two wooden stakes approximately 60 cm (24 in) long by 5 cm (2 in) square and a straight wooden batten long enough to reach from front to back of the planned outcrop. Firmly hammer in the stakes at opposite points across the outcrop area. The next step requires an assistant to hold the batten against the stakes and adjust its position. With your eye near ground level, look across the test build of stones and bring the batten into line with the slope of the stones. Fix the batten in this position by nailing it to the stakes. Leave the gauge in place throughout the building phase and use it to set the tilt of each rock to the batten, using your eye to match the angles, as you did in the test build.

Key rocks

From the stockpile of rocks, select the largest and most attractively featured of them for use in the prominent positions at the front of the outcrop. These chosen rocks are the "key" pieces, around which the rest of the rockwork will be built. Before setting them in place, however, you should clear up the site by removing any piles of surplus soil and clutter, then even up the surface, scraping off any humps and filling hollows.

To position the key rocks, first refer to the plan for the locations of the main rock masses and mark the front edges of these on the site. The key rocks will be set to these lines. Working with one rock at a time, first dig out a shallow seating for its base. It is not necessary to bury a large proportion of the rock below ground; this merely hides a great deal of handsome stone, with no benefit to the function of the rockwork. An average location depth of 10 cm (4 in) for the larger rocks and 5 cm (2 in) for the small pieces is quite adequate.

Manoeuvre the key rock to sit in the prepared location and check the tilt of its top edge against the sighting gauge. Adjust this, if necessary, by scraping away or packing in soil beneath the base of the rock. When you are happy with the position, test the rock's stability by standing on it to detect any wobble; eliminate such movement by improving the soil packing. Remember to keep a check on the tilt angle during this correction work.

Bear in mind that in nature the "nose" of an outcrop is usually the most weathered and eroded part, so avoid being too neat and uniform in building up the key rocks; set some of them back from the marked line and make a few steps on the face (see fig. 1).

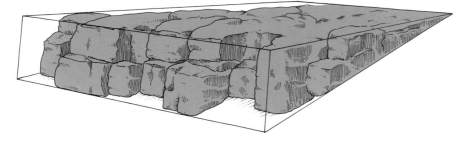

1 The outcrop forms a basic wedge shape, the foremost blocks are the "key" rocks. By repeating the wedge shape, a group of rock masses can be set up to form larger outcrop effects.

2 Natural rules govern the formation of outcrops; vertical fissures occur one above the other, horizontal fissures are parallel and the angle of tilt is constant.

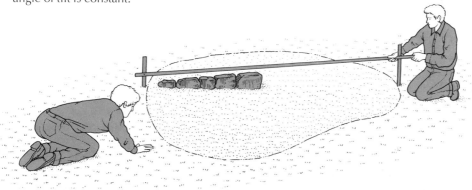

3 Build a test piece of stones to establish the desired tilt for the outcrop; then make a sighting gauge to match this.

The outcrop 2

Completing the feature

Once the key rocks have been firmly positioned the body of the outcrop can be built up around them. Begin by making a second selection of the larger, better-shaped rocks to use alongside the key pieces already in place to extend the "blunt end" of the wedge shape. In the larger constructions, further "noses" can be introduced some way back from the key rocks (see fig. 4),

matching in form and tilt. Bear in mind throughout the work that you are imitating the natural gaps and steps left by erosion and ice-loosened chunks toppling away over the centuries.

Finally, complete the wedge shape, working back from the front face and using progressively smaller rocks. Cut and trim adjoining pieces (see page 30) where necessary to achieve improved fitting of rock to rock. You can often

4 Use the gauge to set up the rockwork during construction

5 During the filling process tread the soil mixture down frequently. Use a blunt-edged stake to pack gaps and pockets between rocks with the mixture.

utilize awkward, badly shaped rocks to bulk up the rockwork by setting them behind those forming the front face. The top face of the outcrop should be reasonably flat, so it is often necessary to raise the shallower pieces of rock up to the required height. It is wasteful to use good rocks as packing pieces for this purpose; old bricks or concrete walling blocks do the job just as well. Firm these packings to make a platform on which the visible rock will sit, then cover them with a layer of soil to form a bed.

Finish the construction by filling with soil mixture. Firm this repeatedly during the process by treading down and ramming into place.

Surfacing and finishing

When the outcrop has settled, following soaking and a rest period of at least a week, add more of the soil mixture to restore the level in any areas that have sunk significantly. Using a gravel which harmonizes with the rock, complete the finishing work by spreading the gravel to a depth of no less than 4 cm (1½ in) over the whole of the soil surface. The gravel should not be too fine; an average of 6–10 mm (¼–⅜ in) is the most suitable size range. Use a fine rake followed by a stiff brush to even up the gravel surface, ensuring that all the bays and pockets in the rockwork are properly covered. This process is known as "top-dressing" and is essential to the welfare of the outcrop and its plants. It discourages the growth of mosses and weeds, acts as a moisture conserver in dry weather and, most importantly, provides the fast-draining, fast-drying surface required by rock plants.

Clint and grykes

As a variation to the outcrop effect you can imitate the clints and grykes of natural limestone pavement by setting out rough stone slabs. These slabs are not easily obtained, but you can make your own from hypertufa, using the casting method described on page 33. Set them on edge in roughly parallel arrangements, and pack the gaps with soil mixture.

SOIL

For simplicity in describing outcrop construction the word "soil" has been used loosely throughout, but for filling the outcrop plain garden soil is most likely to be unsuitable. It is in the filling material that the rock plants will root. Heavy soil is too dense and sticky and light soil too fine and arid. Even good loam has an insufficiently open structure to satisfy rock plants.

The ideal filling material should have a coarse, granular texture making it open and well drained, but it should also contain enough moisture-retentive material to prevent it from drying out too quickly. Its nutrient levels must be only moderate, as many rock plants can be "poisoned" by over-rich soil. At the other extreme, impoverished soils usually produce weak, sickly growth and poor flowering.

Soil improvement

If your soil is light and quick to dry out enrich it with moisture-retaining organic material such as composted bark, very good and well-rotted garden compost or leafmould. Add at least one part of organic material to every three parts of soil, measuring by bulk. Finely-grained sandy soil may also benefit from the addition of grit to let air into its structure. Heavy soil needs even more aeration; a mixture of one part grit to one and a half parts soil is not excessive. Organic material also helps to open up heavy soil structures. A well-balanced garden soil will benefit from the addition of one measure of grit to every two measures of soil.

For the larger rock garden you will find the use of a cement-mixer invaluable in reducing the labour of preparing soil mixtures such as those described. The blending of grit or organic material with large quantities of garden soil is accomplished in a fraction of the time required for manual mixing. Make sure that the ingredients for mixing are barely moist, however they are to be worked on, otherwise the blending will be incomplete and lumpy.

The island bed

In character and purpose the island bed stands between the outcrop and the rock feature. It cannot be said to simulate or even suggest a natural occurrence of rock, but it does function as a home for rock plants to a much greater degree than the rock feature.

Preconstruction work

This is identical to that for the outcrop (see pages 34–7). The quality of the rock used, in terms of form and weathering, is not as important as for the outcrop; in fact the more regular the rock forms, the easier it is to arrange them. The bed can be free or semi-formal in shape and is usually of a two-tier construction. Its rocks are set up squarely, with no tilting, to form enclosures holding prepared soil mixtures.

Construction

The aim is to produce a rugged wall of rock which is fairly even along its top. Use blocks of stone set with their sides in contact and match them as closely as possible to reduce the number of large gaps between joints. This close fitting prevents the contained soil from escaping and helps to retain its moisture in dry

Constructing an island bed

1 Select the largest of the rocks for the first tier. If they have noticeable bedding or strata lines be sure that the rocks are set with these horizontal in every case.

weather. The height of the wall should be between 20–30 cm (8–12 in) but is often dictated by the size of the available rock.

First tier Clearly mark the outline of the bed on the site and follow it with the rocks, placing each with its best face outwards. Make trial matchings with different rocks to achieve the best possible fit between sides, and where it helps in this respect chisel off awkward edges or lumps (see page 30).

Dig a shallow hole of about 5 cm (2 in) to form a seating for each rock. This depth can be increased where necessary to bring the top of a taller rock level with that of its neighbour.

When the rock wall is complete, look for poor and gaping joints (there are always some) and, working on the inside of the wall, close these gaps by inserting slivers of stone. To complete the treatment of the joints lay a drift of gravel along the inside of the wall, up to two-thirds of its height. The purpose of this drift is to prevent the soil washing out through any remaining gaps: it also acts as a secondary drainage system allowing water, but not soil, to escape through the joints. Watch for trickles of gravel appearing on the outside of the wall, indicating where you have missed some gaps, and plug the hole with a stone fragment.

Second tier Construction now moves to the building of a second walled enclosure which is smaller and higher than the first one. To install a foundation for this wall, build up a plinth of old bricks or concrete blocks roughly to the shape of the second tier, making its height approximately 10 cm (4 in) less than the rocks of the first tier. Knock in a few temporary stakes which will mark the shape and extent of the plinth, so that after the first soil filling the second tier can be built accurately over the prepared foundation.

Before you begin the rockwork fill the first tier enclosure with soil up to its top and cover the prepared plinth. After firming the filling by treading and packing (see page 36) and removing the marker stakes, build the second rock wall in the same manner as the first. Fill and firm again to complete the construction, then add top-dressing gravel after a soak and settlement period, as for the outcrop. For details of suitable soil mixtures for filling see page 37.

2 Mark out the shapes of the first and second tiers on the site.

3 Follow the marked outline with close-fitted rocks, adjusting the depth of each seating hole to bring the tops roughly level.

4 Plug any large gaps with stone fragments on the inside face of the wall, then lay a drift of gravel against it.

5 Build a foundation plinth with bricks or blocks to the shape of the second tier.

The shapes in which island beds can be made are numerous; they can be abstract, formal, angular or curved and have various second tiers.

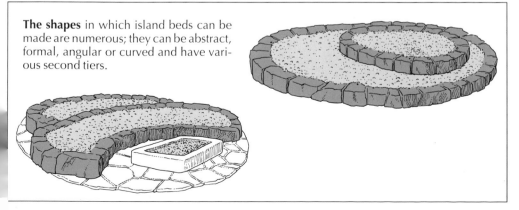

Boulder/pebble beds

The inspiration for these beds comes from natural landscapes dominated by deposits of rounded boulders and stones left by extinct rivers and ice sheets. In these places a surprising number of rock plants are to be found thriving in the mineral-rich shingles and pockets of accumulated humus.

The boulder and pebble bed can stand alone as a garden feature surrounded by lawn or flanked by gravel paths and driveways. It is also well suited to association with a water feature, with its pebbles becoming a "beach" at the edge of a pond.

The type described here is best made with an informal outline, but the same basic effect can be adapted to a more formal setting (see Raised Beds, pages 76–85). To be effective the garden version needs a few large boulders, no smaller than a football for a relatively small bed, and the bigger the better for more extensive constructions. You will also need a collection of variously sized cobbles. Neither these nor the boulders have to be of the same type of stone; the importance is for their shapes to be well rounded, so that they resemble the stones of the sea shore and river bed.

QUANTITY OF GRAVEL

To estimate the quantity of gravel needed, the following rough reckoning will be helpful. A standard 25 kg bag of gravel covers 1 square metre to a depth of approximately 2 cm. Measure the area of the bed in square metres and multiply this number by the depth required in centimetres divided by two and you will have the number of bags needed.

This method of estimation works also for imperial measures. Measure the area of the bed in square yards and multiply this by the depth of the bed required in inches in order to estimate the number of bags needed.

Preconstruction work

On heavy soils or clays it is necessary to open up their structures to improve aeration and drainage. To do this dig off the top 10 cm (4 in) over the area designated for the bed and replace the material removed with grit or fine gravel. Incorporate this by forking over the site

1 Set the boulders in small groups on the bed.

2 Place cobbles in clutches near the boulders.

repeatedly to a depth of 20 cm (8 in). It is much easier to use a powered cultivator for the larger sized beds. On soils which are better drained, thoroughly work in about 5 cm (2 in) of grit. For very sandy soils, use an organic, moisture-retentive material instead of grit.

When the grit or gravel has been thoroughly incorporated level off the mixture with a rake and then firm it by treading over the whole area. After this has been done dig out the trenches and install the hardware of any drainage system required (see pages 20–3).

Construction
You can normally roll rounded boulders into their locations unless they are huge, in which case use the sled and roller system (see page 24). To achieve a realistic appearance for the bed, group the boulders rather than dot them here and there. Dig a shallow seating for each one, sufficient only to make it stable or to hide any disfigurement.

Start with the largest of the cobbles and set some of these close to the boulders and some in clutches at random. There is no need to make seatings for them; they simply lie on the surface.

Surfacing and finishing
To finish you will need rounded gravel that matches the boulders and cobbles. It should be made up of pebbles varying from about pea- to egg-size. If this is not possible use a mixture of two or three grades, utilizing the ornamental types sold in bags for pools and patios.

Spread and rake the gravel evenly over the site, packing it around the larger stones and boulders to a depth of 5–7 cm (2–2¾ in). Some of the cobbles will almost be buried in this process, which is as intended. Complete the work by using a soft brush to even out finely the surface of the gravel and to sweep stray pebbles off the larger stones.

Pathways
It is best to create any pathways through or around the bed by either excluding the cobbles and larger pebbles from the route, to make what is essentially a gravel path, or by setting roundly contoured slabs flush with the surface in the manner of stepping stones. Avoid the use of angular paving pieces or uniform edgings as these are quite out of character in this type of bed.

3 Use a rake to smooth out the gravel covering the bed.

4 Set flat stones into the gravel to create pathways or working access.

Stylized rock features

Visual impact is usually the primary aim in creating a rock feature. Its character may be rugged, dramatic, curious or restful and its plant life can range from being an important inclusion to non-existent. In almost all cases the rock used is massive in comparison with that of a moderately-sized rock garden. There is certainly an artistic side to the rock feature, nowhere more so than in the style perfected by the Japanese.

There are no specific guidelines for building these features; their variety is endless. Instead, here are some examples of various stylized rock features and how they are built.

The slab feature
For this, set up horizontally a number of roughly hewn rock slabs so they provide a sharp contrast with any surrounding prominent vertical forms, such as columnar trees or high walls. The site needs little preconstruction work beyond clearing and levelling and no foundations are necessary due to the inherent stability of the slabs. Reserve the largest of the slabs for topmost positions where they will be fully

displayed. Use the lesser sizes to form plinths or pedestals upon which the large slabs will rest; you can insert slivers of the same stone or hidden pieces of slate to pack any gaps that are causing instability.

Plantings in this style are normally restrained and confined to the low levels. Fill gaps between base slabs with gritty soil and grow carpeting plants such as thymes (*Thymus*), houseleeks (*Sempervivum*) and saxifrages (*Saxifraga*).

The vertical feature
This is the opposite of the slab feature and uses either slabs or blocks to achieve a bold, upright grouping. The base of each slab must be very secure to ensure stability and safety; they should be buried to at least a quarter of their height. Dig a hole to the necessary depth, then lever the slab into it. After it has been positioned upright secure it temporarily by guy ropes or timbers anchored to stout pegs driven into the ground. Firm the slabs by filling the hole with earth and, using a heavy fence post or similar weighty ram, compact the filling. However, if you are using blocks with a broad flat base they

Slab features

Use rough-hewn slabs of stone to create a feature emphasizing horizontals.

Vertical features

Secure tall rocks temporarily with guy ropes until earth has been packed around the base by ramming with a heavy post.

only need a shallow hole to sit in and temporary supports may not be necessary.

It is only feasible to add plants around the base of such features. Pockets and crevices in the elevated rockwork are too quick to dry out and liable to have any soil filling washed out by rain.

The solitary rock

This style features just one huge boulder, carefully chosen for its form and texture. To have the desired impact the weight of this monolith should not be less than 1 tonne (2200 lb) and will require special equipment to transport and manoeuvre it into place. Its shape may allow it simply to rest on the ground, or it may be necessary to excavate a seating hole for its base. To emphasize the solitary grandeur of the rock its base can be surrounded by a bed prepared for low-growing rock plants along with a scattering of much smaller but matching stones.

The Japanese effect

Japanese gardeners go to great lengths to obtain and place a few beautifully formed and weathered rocks to create a tranquil miniature landscape. In its purest form the garden has no flowering plants but relies entirely on form and foliage provided by sparingly planted mosses, ferns, shrubs and perhaps a tree or two. Some include exquisite water elements while others rely on immaculate "pools" of raked gravel.

JAPANESE-STYLE GRAVEL FEATURE

Remove the soil of the site to a depth of about 30 cm (12 in) and replace it with gravel. Sink clay pots containing plants and shrubs in the gravel to just above their rims so the pots are completely hidden. This makes it easy to replace plants and to maintain a weed-free, unsullied gravel surface.

Stepping stones are another common inclusion, giving access to the whole layout for the gardener or visitor, yet leaving undisturbed the carefully tended display.

Japanese-style gravel features

The Japanese effect

Use pot-grown plants and shrubs in deep gravel beds, sinking the pot to just below its rim to hide it completely.

Create pathways of stepping stones through gravel "pools" in Japanese-style features.

Scree beds

The scree bed is an attempt to simulate ground conditions existing on the great debris piles in mountain regions that have built up over countless centuries by the crumbling away of cliffs and ridges. Plants from these natural waste heaps are accustomed to a root run that is extremely stony, riddled with air spaces, low in soil content and superbly free-draining. But these screes are not arid, for beneath their surfaces lie sources of moisture which are by no means generous, but consistent and reliable. These are the conditions that you are simulating in this type of bed.

When making a scree bed you will have to disturb the ground of the site to a considerable depth early on, so any laying of drains should be postponed until later in the work.

Although the scree may be temporarily saturated during very wet weather its surface should never be waterlogged. You can ensure this by raising the bed just a little above the site ground level. The construction method now described incorporates this important elevation. It is only practicable where gravel can be obtained in bulk at a fairly low cost.

Construction

Mark out the bed and, using a spade, take off the top 10 cm (4 in) of soil over the whole area.

For the next stage you will need enough gravel to replace the soil removed; that is to say a layer 10 cm (4 in) deep. See page 41 for the method of estimating the amount of gravel needed. A suitable size of gravel is 4–6 mm (⅙–¼ in). Spread this over the area and level it off using a garden rake.

The gravel must then be thoroughly dug into and mixed with the underlying soil. On smaller beds not exceeding 5 sq m (50 sq ft) in area you can do this with a garden fork, digging to a depth of approximately 20 cm (8 in), which is easily judged against the length of the tines on the fork. Dig over the whole area repeatedly, bringing soil to the surface, then use a hand cultivator or hoe to fully mix the gravel and soil. For beds of larger area a day's hire of a powered cultivator will repay you with a vast reduction of the labour and time involved and produce first-class mixing. Check that the machine is capable of working down to 20 cm (8 in) and set it for this depth.

1 Replace the excavated earth with gravel over the whole of the bed.

2 Mix the gravel with the underlying soil using a garden fork or a powered cultivator.

At this stage you can install the drainage system, if required (see pages 22–23).

In preparation for the surfacing and finishing of the bed, rake the gravel-and-soil mixture reasonably smooth. The level of the bed should be somewhat higher than that of the site. To add interest to the rather uniform appearance of the scree set a few shapely rocks into its surface to give the effect of small boulders embedded in rubble. These rocks should stand above the soil and gravel surface by 5–10 cm (2–4 in). Adjust the depth to which the rocks are sunk in the scree to achieve this upstand. If you use rocks with a reasonably flat top, they will serve as stepping stones for access to the finished bed. With the rockwork in place give the bed a final raking to smooth out its surface.

The bed surround

To contain the slightly elevated body of the bed lay edging stones around its perimeter; use fairly flat pieces and fit their mating edges as neatly as you can. This surround forms a retaining wall and holds in the scree mixture which would otherwise spread out from the bed. In colour and texture these surround stones should be well-matched to those in the scree.

Finishing

To give the bed a neat, clean and fast-draining finish, apply a final layer of gravel, matching that mixed with the soil, over the whole of the bed to a depth of 5 cm (2 in). Use a stiff hand brush to tidy up the edges where the gravel meets the surround and to clear scattered pebbles off the rocks.

SANDY SITES

If the garden soil is light and sandy it may well be unable to hold sufficient moisture reserves for the plants in the scree. To rectify this deficiency follow the procedure given for preparing the soil, but enrich the gravel with composted bark, in the proportions of two gravel to one bark. Mix this blend with the soil as described. The finishing work is unchanged, employing pure gravel for the final surfacing.

3 Use fairly flat rocks sunk into the scree to give more interest to the surface and also to edge the bed.

4 With a soft brush give a final smoothing and tidying to the surface of the finished scree.

Terracing

1 First measure the gradient of the slope.

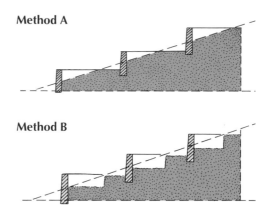

Method A

Method B

2 Method A of construction is adequate for light soil. **Method B** is for heavy soil or clay.

The main reasons for agricultural terracing are purely practical, for terracing makes an otherwise difficult piece of ground easy to work on and also halts the downhill slide of soil and plants. The appearance created is to a large extent incidental.

In the ornamental garden, however, appearance is a priority. For the rock gardener the dressed stone and precisely mortared jointing of the classical terrace are out of place, as they are too formal and restrictive for plants that delight in creeping over and nestling among stonework. Walls of random stone which are mortared only enough to give strength and stability, however, offer a host of residential nooks and crannies to rock plants. Alternatively, the "walls" can be formed from a line of substantial blocks in order to produce the effect of a stepped cliff, again incorporating plenty of good planting places.

There are two ways of constructing a terrace depending on your soil type. Method A is for sandy soils, while you should follow method B if you have heavy, clay soil.

Preconstruction

First it is necessary to measure the gradient of your slope or bank, for which you will need two pieces of straight timber about 4 cm (1½ in) square, of lengths 70 cm (2 ft 3 in) and 1.2 m

CONSTRUCTION PLANNING

A slope or bank with a rise of less than one in five is really too shallow to warrant terracing, whereas anything in excess of one in two is not only difficult to work on but needs very deep steps and hence tall walls, which can be far too dominant. An initial sizing up of the slope, together with a little planning, can save you unnecessary and abortive work.

(4 ft). Take the shorter of these and drive it vertically into the ground at the foot of the slope to a depth of 10 cm (4 in). Next, rest one end of the longer piece (the batten) on the slope, with its other end against the upright piece. Adjust the batten until it lies level (checking with a spirit level), then measure its height from the base of the upright. This dimension set against the length of the batten is the gradient.

Once you have measured the slope, make a simple scale drawing and work out the number of steps needed, the height of the walls and the width of each terrace. The terrace must be wide enough for a plant bed plus access path. Keep the width of the plant bed to a maximum of 1 m (3 ft 3in) for easy working on the finished terrace.

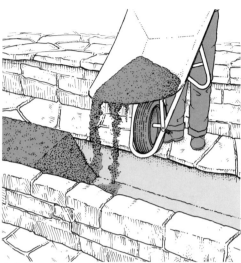

3 Add gravel (method A) or a prepared soil mixture (**method B**) to fill the terraces.

4 Use close-fitting rocks as an alternative to walling.

On heavy, poor-draining soils the walls should be set deeper into the slope to allow for the removal of some 20–30 cm (8–12 in) of soil from each terrace (method B). This excavated amount will later be replaced with a suitable soil mixture.

Construction

It is very unlikely that you will need to install drainage on the slope even if the soil is heavy, but water may collect at the foot of the incline and so you will need to dig a simple channel to take away the surplus. However, if a path runs along the bottom of the slope it will often act as an adequate escape route.

Mark out the lines of the terracing walls along the face of the slope and, depending on which method you are following, cut out the steps (method A) or make more extensive excavations (method B).

For the construction of stone walls refer to Using Walls (see pages 56–9). If you are using large blocks the building method is easier: simply set each block firmly in the earth, in much the same way as for the island bed (see page 39), adjusting the depth of its seating to bring its top roughly level with those of its neighbours. If the required wall height cannot be achieved with single blocks put a second layer on top of the first, making sure you minimize any gaps.

A slight backward tilt to all the blocks will produce a stronger and more stable structure.

Path laying

Access pathways should be laid on the undisturbed earth at the foot of each wall. Normally these require only a shallow layer of grit to form a bed for paving, or they can be composed entirely of gravel retained by edging stones. Hardcore is not usually necessary on such well-drained ground.

Filling and finishing

Once the paths have been completed and any steps included the plant beds can be prepared. In method A terracing you should first incorporate grit or fine gravel with the exposed soil, at the same time levelling it out. Then top up the bed with a gravel and soil mixture (see page 36); tread it down during the process but the resulting bed should be slightly overfilled. The excess will be taken up in the subsequent settlement of the filling. To complete the work lay a top-dressing of clean gravel, adding decorative rocks if desired.

The filling for method B terracing uses a separately prepared soil and gravel mixture throughout, loaded in by means of the wheelbarrow. Surfacing and finishing are the same as for method A.

Facing with rock

In principle, the facing of a slope with slabs of rock is like laying crazy paving on a steep hill. However, the main difference is that the slabs used in facing are thicker and preferably rougher than those of paving. Facing is an excellent solution to the problem presented by a slope which is too steep for terracing or other rock garden forms, such as screes and outcrops.

It is extremely difficult and risky to work the soil of a sheer incline, so much so that it is best to avoid it altogether. Instead, add a layer of ready-prepared soil and gravel mixture as the work progresses.

The size of the slabs should be in proportion to the height and extent of the slope; small slabs look too much like irregular tiling when used over a large area and large ones produce an overwhelming effect if laid on a small bank, as well as being deficient in offering potential planting places.

A rough guide to attaining a good balance is that the facing should be completed in no more than three to four stages of slab laying, the stages being the "rows" of slabs running across the slope. Choose the thickest of the slabs for those at the bottom of the slope and grade the remainder so that you position the thinnest at the top.

Construction
Begin work by coating the lowest part of the slope with a mixture of good soil and fine gravel to a depth of 10 cm (4 in), blending two parts soil with one part gravel, by bulk. This layer should reach far enough up the incline to take the tallest of the slabs in the bottom row.

First stage
Take the first slab for the bottom row and examine its lower edge. Dig a shallow trench at the foot of the slope sufficient to hide this edge and to provide a firm, stable seating. Stand the slab in this trench and lower it onto the coated slope. It is very important that you pack any cavities or loose spots beneath the positioned slab with soil and gravel mixture. Use a short length of timber as a ram and repeat this procedure for all the bottom slabs.

Second stage
Spread more of the coating mixture up the slope and lay the second stage slabs on it. These should rest with their lower edges in contact with the upper edges of the bottom slabs. While it is not necessary to achieve a close match at this interface the gaps should not be excessive, otherwise the resulting planting places will be vulnerable to being washed out by heavy rain. You should repeat this procedure for the third and possibly fourth stage slabs until the whole slope is covered.

Facing with rock

1 Spread a coating of soil and gravel mixture on the slope before laying the slabs.

4 Lay second stage slabs with their bases resting on the top edges of the bottom slabs.

Filling and finishing

Work over the completed facing, firmly filling the gaps with soil and gravel mixture to about 2.5 cm (1 in) below the slab surface. Finish by topping off with a layer of gravel; this will prevent the filling eroding and also provide a well-drained seating for the plants when they are establishing their root systems. Make sure that this filling is thorough and firm by using a wooden hammer.

THE "SKYLINE"

At the crest of the slope it is often necessary to add fillers using pieces of rock to reduce jaggedness and blend with the upper ground level. For a dramatic effect leave the uppermost slabs to project beyond the top of the incline, although this is usually more successful in large rather than small constructions.

2 Stand bottom row slabs in the prepared trench, then lower them into place.

3 Pack any cavities beneath the slab with soil and gravel mixture.

5 Fill the gaps with soil and gravel mixture, packing it thoroughly.

6 Even out jaggedness on the crest of the slope using suitable filler pieces of rock.

The bluff effect

1 Dig out a generous recess for each of the foundation blocks.

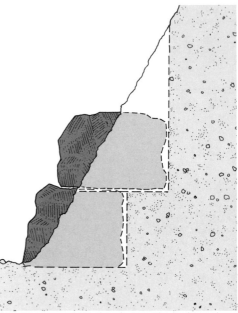

2 Cut a recess into the slope to hide the tail end of the second stage block(s).

This form of rockwork is best used in the larger landscape scheme because, when reduced in scale, it becomes just a few stones protruding from a bank of earth, which is exactly what it will look like. It is also only possible to produce the bluff effect on very steep slopes.

You may be able to establish crevice plants in some of the joints of this feature, although it is essentially an architectural structure. One of its most effective positions is on the approaches to a true rock garden or to form an impressive background to outcrop and scree beds.

Construction
Large blocks of rock with reasonably flat tops and bases are essential for both construction purposes and aesthetic reasons. These are set into the slope in order to create the illusion of an exposed mass of rock with a broad and sheer face and with its flanks running back into the hillside.

First stage
Use the largest of the blocks at the base of the bluff to form the foundation stones. Working on each block individually prepare a bed for it by

digging into the slope to create a recess big enough to hold the entire block plus extra room for handling the block. Shape the floor of the recess to follow approximately the profile of the block's base so that you will only need to make minor adjustments when it is being set in place.

Select a second block to lie alongside the first with a good match between the mating sides. As before, dig out a recess and move this second block into position. Repeat the working procedure for however many blocks are required to produce the desired width for the face of the bluff. When these foundation stones have been set up complete the seating and firming of each one by packing stones and earth into any base cavities.

Second stage
The second stage involves moving and placing the blocks to sit on the foundation layer, but before this work begins the slope must be cut back to take the tail ends of the second-stage blocks. The base of the excavation must be level with the top of the foundation block. To provide an adjustable seating for the second stage, spread a 5 cm (2 in) layer of two parts soil

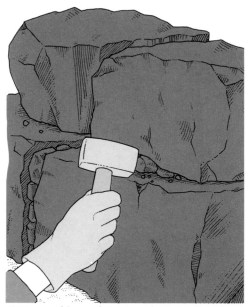

3 Cover the tops of the foundation blocks and the recess with a layer of soil and gravel mix.

4 Use packings of stone and rammed earth to achieve a firm, stable joint between blocks.

to one part gravel mixture over the top of the foundation block and on the floor of the excavation. The second block can then be installed either by lowering it down the slope or lifting it into place. Whichever of these methods you employ careful and safety-conscious working is an absolute priority for the stone blocks are very heavy. If you lack the mechanical aids needed or are doubtful about the handling methods bring in professional expertise.

Filling and finishing

To complete the bluff restore the earth taken from the slope around the blocks, packing it down firmly so that the tail ends of the blocks are completely buried. This will make the bluff look like a natural feature rather than a purpose-built stack of rocks.

The final touch is the clothing of the slope surrounding the bluff. Turfing or seeding will give an authentic appearance, if the grass is kept well trimmed to suggest grazed ground. Alternatively, plant the slope with ground cover such as heathers and mat-forming species. Where possible, insert crevice plants in the face of the bluff.

5 Restore the slope around the bluff, packing it down firmly with soil filling.

The cliff effect

Cliff construction is only viable for very steep slopes and requires large, well-shaped rocks both for appearances and structural stability. It is similar to making a bluff, the main differences being the greater extent of the cliff feature and its capacity for supporting plants.

Although the height of a cliff is constrained by the practicalities of construction, its length is virtually unlimited. Whereas the bluff is principally architectural in function the cliff can be contrived to incorporate plenty of planting accommodation ideal for the needs and display of rock plants. In this respect the cliff is independent of the type of earth against which it is built, as the planting features are designed to hold specially prepared soil mixtures.

Construction

To aid the incorporation of planting places similar to those found on natural cliffs, the face must be built to include ledges and crevice-type root runs. These soil-holding pockets and cavities are created by adding supports behind some of the rocks made up from surplus chunks of rock, bricks or blocks in the form of dwarf walls. These are built behind the rock and with a gap of not less than 10 cm (4 in) between the two. These supports have the dual purpose of bearing the overlying rock and forming the back of a cavity which will be later filled with soil mixture.

First stage

First dig out recesses at the base of the slope to house the foundation rocks and the support dwarf walls behind them, after which the supports can be installed. Next, position the rocks

1 **Build support walls** before putting the rocks in place.

2 **A prepared soil mixture** is used to pack behind crevice planting places and to fill the ledges created.

3 **In some cases** rocks will be entirely supported by the wall. This will create a wide planting ledge.

and secure them in the same manner as for the bluff (see page 50), but with some of them set back to form bays in the face of the cliff.

Second stage

When all the foundation rocks have been placed, proceed with the work in a series of tiers. Carefully plan the position of each rock: each tier should, in general, be set back a little from the one below to produce ledges and horizontal crevices. In some cases the ledges should extend all the way back to a support wall, creating an open shelf which can be subsequently filled with soil mixture. Where this occurs, the overlying rock will sit entirely on the support wall. The illustration shows how horizontal crevices are backed by a cavity filled with soil mixture. The vertical crevices, intended for planting, should always narrow toward the bottom and ideally form a slim "V" shape. This should really be arranged when mating neighbouring rocks during the build, as it is vital for retaining the filling mixture in the crevice.

Filling and finishing

As you complete each tier of the rockwork it is essential that you fill and pack all the spaces behind and beneath the rocks with earth. Fill

---

CLIFF ASPECTS

In most cases you have no choice in the aspect of the cliff as it is usually built against an existing slope, but the way it faces can influence construction to some degree. Sunny cliffs can become very arid in summer, so you will need to enrich the soil mixture with moisture-retentive material. If possible shield exposed cliffs with a windbreak to temper the icy, drying blasts that cold weather can bring. Avoid a shady aspect; it will be cold and damp for most of the time and offer little hospitality to all but a very few rock plants. Cliffs that receive sun for part of the day are warmer, wetter and on the whole the most successful.

---

the planting cavities and ledges with appropriate soil mixture. Only when you are sure that these tasks have been done should you proceed with the next tier.

Where soil mixture is visible on the ledges of the finished cliff it should be top-dressed with a layer of fine gravel, 5 cm (2 in) thick. This will discourage weeds, prevent erosion and provide an acceptable surface for the rock plant occupants.

4 Step some rocks back to produce bays and avoid making the face of the cliff too straight and even.

The scree slope

1 Prepare the soil surface by lightly forking over the area to be covered by the scree.

2 Edge the scree with rocks set horizontally and of a thickness equal to the depth of the gravel before laying the gravel.

There is a limit to the gradient upon which this type of bed can be made due to the "creeping" effect of a large mass of gravel on a slope. For inclines up to one in three the method is viable. Because a slope automatically sheds surplus water there is no need to work on improving the drainage capability of the soil on the site, even if this is heavy. The preparation is less than that required for a level scree bed.

The bulk of the scree is made up of pure gravel. The type you choose is a matter of personal choice, but the size should be in the grade range of 4–8 mm (⅙–⅓ in). The ideal is a mixture of these sizes. Obtain sufficient gravel to cover the area of the scree to a depth of 15 cm (6 in). Use the estimating method given on page 41 to determine the amount required. Heap the gravel close to the site for ease of working when laying down the scree.

Once the site has been thoroughly cleared of all perennial weeds mark out the area intended for the scree. Lightly fork over the ground to a depth of 5 cm (2 in) or so to produce a loose layer of crumbled soil. For this work choose a day when the earth is moist, but not wet, to get the best results. Fork carefully and methodically over the whole area until the entire surface has been uniformly broken up, leaving no humps or hollows. Never stand or walk on the soil after it has been forked. If all parts are

within reach finish with a light raking to improve the evenness of the surface.

The next stage of the work should follow immediately, or at least before rainfall spoils the prepared soil. Starting at the bottom of the slope, lay down a band of gravel across it to a depth of 15 cm (6 in). Treading only on the gravel laid, put a second band across the slope immediately above the first. Move progressively uphill, spreading successive bands until the whole area has been covered. You need not be too precise about achieving the depth stated; this is an average measurement, so err on the generous side.

The addition of the gravel will significantly raise the level of the scree area above the surrounding earth, requiring it to be edged by suitably thick stones. Use flattish pieces, set just a little into the earth and following the outline of the scree. Try to keep them horizontal rather than parallel with the slope so that they form a stepped edge, which looks more natural.

Although the layer of pure gravel might seem to be inadequate to sustain plants, do not add soil or other enrichment; the plants will make their own particular use of the root run provided. Some will push straight down through the gravel into the underlying soil (which you have prepared to aid root penetration), whilst others, especially those native to scree habitats

3 Lay down the gravel in bands across the slope, starting at the bottom and working uphill.

4 Smooth out the completed gravel laying with a rake.

VARIATIONS

The method described applies to the great majority of soil types, but if your site is on light, sandy soil you can improve its moisture reserves by adding organic material such as bark, spent hops or compost during the forking operation.

Where the garden is in an area of high rainfall, the scree may produce better results if the depth of gravel is increased to 25 or even 30 cm (10–12 in). This ensures that the root run is free from excessive water at all times.

5 Set rocks into the scree to improve the appearance and stability.

may prefer to confine their spreading roots to the gravel, doing little more than touch the soil surface to take up moisture and nutrients.

Finishing touches

While the work so far described completes the scree as a growing place, the uniform expanse of gravel can present a drab, featureless appearance. You can give more character to the slope by first adding a scattering of larger gravel (matching that which is already laid), then setting rocks into the surface here and there. The latter will aid the future stability of the scree and can also serve as stepping stones for planting and maintenance. Remember that the whole area will settle in time, so you should always over-fill to some extent with the gravel to compensate for this. A stiff brush is useful for final levelling.

It is a prudent precaution to store an extra quantity of matching gravel for future repairs and renovation when replantings and modifications are needed.

Using walls 1

1 Take out a few stones, making a note of their relative positions.

2 On double walls, clean out the cavity as far as you can reach.

3 Replace the stones and introduce plants, packing behind and around them with soil mixture.

4 Finish off the raked-out the joints by pointing them with mortar.

For rock gardeners and rock garden plants alike, a wall can be an acceptable substitute for a natural rock face. Informally laid and open-jointed walling presents an expanse of stone with a network of nooks and crevices, offering planting places that are invulnerable to water-logging, even in the wettest weather. It is fruitless simply to tease the roots of a plant into the gap between two stones in the hope that it will somehow settle in; it will more than likely die. Walls, like other forms of rock garden, have to be prepared for planting.

Retaining walls

This type of wall is built against a vertical bank of earth. Retaining walls which are already in existence and part of the garden landscape need only some modification. To prepare planting places begin by making an exploratory extraction of a few stones in one location. If possible choose a spot where the stonework is already loose and easy to remove. Before starting the extractions make a note of the order in which the stones are removed so that you can return them to their original positions in the wall. Unless the wall is already in a dangerous state there should be little risk of it collapsing by localized dismantling.

When the selected stones have been eased out of the wall use the cavity created to make an inspection of the wall's construction. If there is earth visible at the back of the cavity the preparation for planting is fairly simple. You may, however, discover that you have penetrated only the outer part of a double wall, with probably some rubble filling between the two. In such cases planting places can still be contrived but require a different approach.

SAFETY

To avoid excessive weakening of the wall work only on one planting location at any time and complete this before moving on to another. Also, leave a distance of not less than 1 m (3 ft 3 in) between the edge of one cavity and the next. Avoid having locations close to ground level as these can be damaged by garden traffic.

The single wall

After you have removed the stones, clear out the cavity as far as you can reach, to extract mortar rubble, weeds and any penetrating roots. With the clean-up completed you can then replace the walling stones in the reverse order of dismantling, one by one. As each stone is returned, bed it and pack it round with a mixture of soil and grit in equal proportions incorporating plants as you do so. Make certain that there is no gap left between the rear end of the stone and the earth backing the cavity. The packing of the final stone can present difficulties and is therefore limited to what is possible within the working constraints.

In certain situations the work can end at this stage, but for more durability it is better to finish off by adding mortar to the joints. Mix five parts of building sand with one part of cement (by volume) and add water until the consistency resembles stiff porridge. Leave the mix to stand for a few minutes and meanwhile rake out the joints between the stones to a depth of approximately 5 cm (2 in), using the handle of an old toothbrush or something similar. Clean up the work with a stiff hand brush, then trowel the mortar into the joints in the manner used for pointing brickwork.

For planting techniques see pages 130–133.

The double wall

As far as creating the cavity, the preparation of planting places follows the same pattern and process as used for the single wall. Then the method changes because the earth is still concealed by the inner wall. Instead of using the soil mixture packing as a link to the earth behind the wall, create a substantial pocket of rooting material in the cavity.

Remove any mortar, small stones and rubble within comfortable reach inside the cavity. The rooting material needs to be very fibrous in order to stay in place within the wall. Spent mushroom compost is ideal; alternatively you can use rotted turves. Both possess fibrous and moisture-retentive properties which are sufficient for the purpose. Pack the cavity with whichever material you choose, replacing the stones as work progresses, and finish by mortaring the joints as already explained for the single wall (see above).

For planting techniques see pages 130–133.

Retaining wall showing cantilever piece

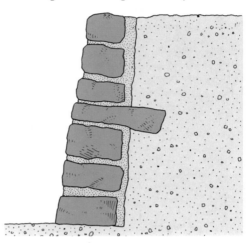

Building new retaining walls

Retaining walls are normally built to support the face of earth caused by a significant change in level. They can be constructed as dry-stone walls or the stones can be bonded with mortar. The general building method is the same for both types.

Although the face of the earth may be vertical the wall should have a slight backwards lean to its front surface (known as "batter") to increase its stability and strength. To this end, use the largest stones in the lower courses and work with progressively smaller sizes as the height of the wall increases.

Several of the longest stones should be reserved for cantilever pieces to be set end-on in the wall with their rear ends penetrating the earth face. These pieces give further strength to the wall. In the lowest course make every fourth or fifth vertical joint between stones about 4 cm (1½ in) wide and omit mortaring in order to create water outlets.

When two or three courses of stone have been laid and any mortar used allowed to set, pack the space between the wall and the earth face with a mixture of soil, bark and grit in equal proportions. This same mixture is also used in joints where plants are to be inserted (as described under Plants and Planting, see pages 130–133).

The top course of stone should be fully mortared for stability.

Using walls 2

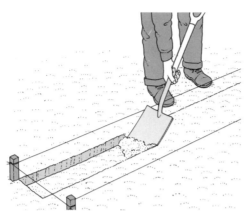

1 Dig out shallow trench foundations.

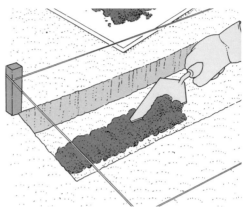

2 Fill the trench with concrete up to the surface level.

Hollow walls

The majority of walls made in this style are of modest height, quite formal in appearance and used in the creation of floral edgings for driveways and patios. They are in fact double walls built parallel to one another, with a gap between them which is filled with soil. To prevent water from lodging in the soil-filled gap, open joints are left at intervals along the bottom course. Structures of this type provide ideal growing conditions for many species of rock plant as they are elevated and well-drained. They are also separated from the rest of the garden plantings.

Hollow walls can be built straight onto finished surfaces such as paving or gravel, or on simple foundations laid in the earth. The quality of the building material is particularly important as ill-fitting or badly matched walling is more conspicuous in this type of structure. Natural or synthetic stone, brick and even broken paving slabs can be used, provided that their thickness does not exceed 8 cm (3 in). Larger sizes spoil the appearance of what is in effect a dwarf wall. Typical proportions for a balanced look to the finished work are a height of 30 cm (12 in) maximum and a width of not more than 50 cm (20 in). These dimensions assume that the width of each of the two walls does not exceed 15 cm (6 in). Due to their small stature the walls are vulnerable to damage unless fully mortared. Frost and garden traffic can easily dislodge or distort unmortared walling of this type.

Preparation

Where the wall is to stand on an already surfaced area, the only preparation you need to do prior to walling is clearing the ground of weeds and moss. On a base of bare earth a foundation will be necessary; dig out a trench 7–10 cm (about 3–4 in) deep, following the line of each wall, with a width a little greater than that of the walling material. Fill this trench with concrete of one part cement, two parts sand and three parts gravel to within approximately 2 cm (¾ in) of the trench top. If you have used concrete, leave that to set for a couple of days before doing further work. Mark out the position of the wall using a length of string pulled taut around pegs, or stakes set in the ground.

Building the wall

The following method describes both pre-surfaced areas and prepared foundations.

Mix a manageable quantity of mortar in the following manner: take five parts of building sand and one part of cement. If the sand is anything more than just moist, dry it out before using it. Mix the two together until they are well blended. Add water, a little at a time, until the mortar is suitable for use. To assess this fill a container such as a small bucket or an old wash bowl to its brim with the mixture, invert the container and examine the result. If the mixture slumps a little but still holds some of the container's shape it is satisfactory; if it sags to a low mound it is too wet. An insufficiently

3 Check and adjust carefully each piece laid, until it is level.

4 Stagger the vertical joints when laying the next course.

wet mixture will stay in the precise shape of the container, like a sand pie.

Using a cementing trowel and starting at one end of the wall put down a ribbon of mortar to a depth of about 5 cm (2 in) and a width of roughly two-thirds that of the walling material. Make the ribbon approximately 1 m (3 ft 3 in) long. Take a piece of walling material and with its outer edge parallel to the line of the wall lay it on the mortar. Tap it smartly at each end with the butt of the trowel handle to settle it in and check it both lengthways and across with a spirit level. Make any adjustments needed by further taps until it lies level. Leaving an end-to-end gap of about 12 mm (½ in) lay and level up a second piece, and so on, until you reach the end of the mortar ribbon. Then put down a further ribbon and continue in the same way to the end of the wall. As you build each level, check the vertical using a builder's level. Before the mortar stiffens, clear out joints at intervals of roughly 60–80 cm (2–2 ft 9 in) to create drainage outlets.

Using the same procedure, lay the first course of the opposite wall and ends.

Lay the second and subsequent courses in the same manner, but take care to avoid coincidence of vertical joints. This technique is known as bonding and can be clearly seen in the alternate pattern of brickwork.

Always clean off surplus mortar in one course before progressing to the next. The scraping out of joints for drainage only applies to the first course.

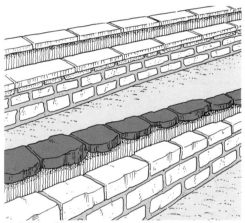

5 Finish off with neat mortaring, or cap the walls with slabs.

To complete the walling either neatly mortar the joints of the final course or cap it with slabs set in mortar.

Filling and finishing
The nature of the soil mixture used to fill the interior of the wall depends on the type of plants that you plan to grow there. As a general rule use mixtures which are rather more fibrous and moisture-retentive than those prescribed for beds, otherwise they tend to dry out rapidly as they only occupy a small volume within the wall. Leave the filling to settle for two or three weeks, then top up with gravel to provide the finished surface.

The rock pool

You should decide on the position and extent of the pool at the design stage when planning the rock garden. For an effective siting, arrange the pool to occupy a bay at the base of the rockwork, giving it a back and sides. To avoid errors and unnecessary work first position the surrounding rocks temporarily and adjust them until you are satisfied with the pool setting that they form. It is most important that these rocks rest on ground that has been made truly level beforehand, using a straightedge and spirit level to check the work. With the rocks in their true but temporary positions dig out the pool shape working right up to them. Make a careful note of each rock's position, if necessary draw a rough sketch, or even take a photograph, then move them to one side to allow further work on the pool.

Trimming the shape

Take out a little more earth where the pool sides meet the rocks, so that when these are repositioned they will overhang the water by about 5 cm (2 in). Remove any protruding stones or root ends from the sides and bottom of the pool excavation and eliminate any sharp bumps or hollows in the surface.

Liners

Modern pond liners made of plastic or butyl rubber are long-lasting and offer the easiest means for achieving a watertight pool. Once the excavation has been completed the preparation for installing a liner is quite simple. Cover the sides and bottom with either a proprietary liner underlay or a 2 cm (¾ in) layer of moist sand which should be trowelled on and smoothed like plaster. Old carpet has been used successfully for the same purpose.

Lining the pool

Obtain sufficient liner material to line the pool and also to extend over the surrounding earth far enough to lie beneath the surrounding rocks. Lining material suppliers will normally help you to work out the amount required. Following the manufacturer's instructions, install the liner, filling the pool gradually with water as the work progresses and the liner moulds itself to the pool's shape. When the pool is full, you can return the surround rocks to their positions so that they sit on the lining material and slightly overhang the water. Fold the surplus liner up behind the rocks, holding it in place with stones or earth, and trim off the excess to leave an upturn of some 5–7 cm (2–2¾ in). This upturn will be hidden as the remainder of the rockwork is added, but its purpose is to raise the level of the pool just

1 With the surround rocks temporarily in place, dig out the pool shape, working right up to the rocks.

2 After installing the liner return the rocks to their permanent positions.

enough to meet the overhanging rocks and hide the liner. Make sure that the bases of the rocks used have no sharp protrusions which could cut the liner. At the open end of the pool you can lay stone slabs or flakes of rock directly onto the liner to form the outer edge of the pool. Overflow water will escape between these slabs and seep away into the surrounding ground. An alternative is to make a "beach" of pebbles, which requires a gentle slope to take the pebble layer from ground level to beneath the water surface.

Adding interest

A rock or two, placed in the pool to form "islands", can add to its attraction. Choose rocks with a smooth base and put them in place before filling the pond. For additional protection of the liner insert a mat made from a doubled piece of spare liner beneath each rock.

PRE-FORMED POOLS

Similar rock pools can be made using moulded plastic or glass fibre shells. The latter are the more expensive, but easier to install, and harder-wearing.

Installing the shell Prepare the site in the same way as for the liner, ensuring that the surface is absolutely level. Dig out a hole that is 15 cm (6 in) bigger all round and 2–3 cm (about 1 in) deeper than the shell. Compact the floor of the hole by treading and tamping. Sit the shell in the hole, on a layer of sand spread over the floor, adjusting this until the rim of the shell is exactly level with the surrounding earth.

Firming in For glass fibre shells the firming in is simply a matter of packing sand into the space between the shell and the hole and keeping a watchful eye on the alignment of the rim and the earth surface. The less rigid plastic shell is packed in the same way, but it needs to be filled progressively with water as the packing proceeds to prevent distortion of the shell sides.

The rock surround Place rocks around the rim of the shell, overhanging the water a little to give realism and hide the lip of the shell.

3 Bring the liner a little way up at the back of the rocks to raise the pool level slightly.

4 Use stone slabs or make a pebble "beach" along the edge of the pool, which is not bounded by rockwork.

The pool and bog garden

A bog garden is a permanently wet, but not completely waterlogged, area of ground. It associates very well with a water feature and in fact can be an extension to it. The conditions created suit the marginal plants of ponds and streams and other species favouring saturated ground. The overflow from a pool can be used as the feeder to maintain wet conditions in an adjacent bog.

Linking pool and bog garden

Like the pool, the bog garden requires an absolutely level site, and this is best prepared at the same time as the pool. Mark out the combined area of pool and bog, level off the surface and check its accuracy using a straightedge and spirit level.

Excavations

Dig out the pool in relation to the rock surround (see page 60). Then make a similar excavation for the bog, to a depth of 30 cm (12 in), but leave a "bridge" of earth about 30 cm (12 in) wide between the pool and bog. Select a few slabs of stone, roughly 8 cm (3 in) thick, to lie along the top of the "bridge". Then take off a matching thickness of earth from the top of the "bridge".

Liner installation

If the quantity of liner required to cover both pool and bog garden is manageable, lay this in place, leaving a generous surplus around the edges. For larger areas use separate liners, overlapping them at the "bridge", with the pool liner uppermost. Fill both liners to reach almost the top of the "bridge", letting the water mould the liners to the shapes excavated, then put the "bridge" capping stones in place.

Making the bog

Remove the water from the bog liner by bailing, pumping or syphoning. With a garden fork, puncture the floor of the liner at roughly 60 cm (24 in) spacing, to create drainage outlets. Fill the bog liner with prepared soil, adding plenty of fibrous, organic material to clayey or sandy types. To prevent soil seepage back into the pool insert a strip of fine plastic mesh between the "bridge" capping stones and the bog filling.

1 Dig out pool and bog at the same time, leaving a "bridge".

2 After installing the liner, cap the "bridge" with stone slabs.

Finishing off
Complete the filling of the pool and saturate the bog using a fine hose. You will probably find it necessary to top up both areas several times, before achieving a balance of water content between pool and bog. Also, you may have to add further soil filling to the bog, as it settles due to saturation.

Around the edge of the bog area use substantial pieces of stone or paving laid on top of the liner and finish by trimming off surplus liner material. An alternative method is to bury the liner edge under surrounding turf. However, this leads to problems of maintenance in the longer term, especially if the surround is a lawn edge requiring regular trimming.

READY-MADE CONTAINMENT

It is quite feasible to use pre-formed pond shells to contain the bog garden, as an alternative to the liner system.

Set the shell in place, as described for the rock pool (see page 61), using the same "bridge" system in relation to the pool. Drill 12 mm (½ in) holes in the base of the shell, about 30 cm (12 in) apart, to provide the necessary leakage. Then fill the shell with suitable soil and proceed as for the liner system, ensuring that the shell is not over-stressed

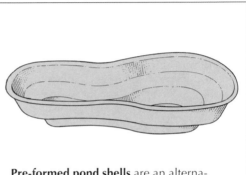

Pre-formed pond shells are an alternative to the liner method.

3 Put fine plastic mesh between the capping stones and bog filling.

4 Edging stones can be laid on the liner to border the bog garden.

Streams and waterfalls

Running water adds sound and movement to the rock garden, whether gently, as a rivulet, or boisterously, as a splashing cascade. To a great extent the expanse and height of the rock garden govern the character of any water feature introduced. Low-lying rockwork provides an appropriate setting for a wandering rill, but waterfalls require the height offered by cliffs or terraced rockwork.

The water supply

Unless you are extremely fortunate in having a natural source of running water in your garden, its introduction will involve an electrically pumped re-circulating system, which requires a reservoir to feed it. Although it is possible to hide this reservoir by using a buried tank, it is more usual to incorporate it in the form of a pool. A range of submersible pumps is available, designed to sit on the bottom of the pool. The alternative type is the surface pump, which requires a special "land-based" installation.

Whichever type is used, the operating principle of the re-circulating system is the same. The pump draws water from the reservoir, or pool, and delivers it in a steady flow via a pipe to the top of the watercourse, from where it runs freely back to the reservoir. Unless it is very small indeed, the rock pool will provide an adequate reservoir for the scale of water feature associated with it.

Streams

In a re-circulating system the pool, acting as a reservoir, is at the lowest point of the watercourse. Having decided on the route that the stream will take, be sure that its "source" is higher than the surface of the pool. If in doubt, check the fall using a straightedge and spirit level (see page 20).

The stream bed

Mark out the course of the stream from its source to the reservoir pool. Following this route, dig out a broad trench with a rounded channel in its base, varying the width randomly to prevent the end result from looking like a canal. The channel forms the actual bed of the stream and the shelves at each side will hold the rocks forming the banks of the stream.

After removing any protrusions, sharp stones and root ends from the excavated surfaces coat the channel and shelves with a 2 cm (¾ in) layer of damp sand, using a trowel to obtain a smooth finish. Before the sand begins to dry, cover it with pond liner material, moulding this by hand to the contours of the channel and shelves.

The banks

Edge the stream with rocks set on the shelves, then trim off the surplus liner with a knife or scissors, leaving a small upturn at the back of the rocks. Pebbles heavy enough not to be washed away, together with larger stones, can be laid here and there in the bottom of the channel to produce swirls and tiny falls in the flow. Complete the banks by filling in with earth behind the edging rocks.

Waterfalls

Cut out the watercourse in the same way as for the stream, but make a vertical face where you wish the waterfall to be. Cover the whole of the course with pond liner material, including the vertical face. Select an appropriately sized slab of stone for the lip of the fall, with its outer edge overhanging the vertical face. Set this firmly in place, anchoring it with flanking rocks. Select a further slab to lie against the vertical face, with its bottom edge resting on a base rock. Add flanking rocks to hold this slab tightly against the liner-covered face, and also to anchor the base slab at the bottom of the fall. Check the construction for strength and rigidity, then trim off any surplus liner material. You can then add the remainder of the surrounding rockwork, including the banks of the stream, which are finished off as already described.

ALTERNATIVE BUILDING METHODS

Ready-made cascades are commercially available, usually as glass fibre sections moulded to set forms. Their installation follows, basically, the method described earlier for pre-formed pools. The surrounding rock-work has to be tailored to the fixed shape of the moulding and should hide as much of the material as possible.

Concrete construction requires a far higher level of skill, involving techniques best left to professionals.

1 Dig out a broad trench with a deeper channel in its base, following the marked out course.

2 Cover the excavation with a layer of damp sand.

3 Lay pond liner material over the sand, moulding it to fit.

4 Set rocks on the side shelves to form the banks of the stream.

5 Place pebbles and larger stones in the bed of the stream.

6 Cut a vertical face where a waterfall is to occur.

7 Set the lip, back and base slabs firmly in place.

8 Add flanking rocks to anchor the waterfall construction.

Tufa

What is tufa?

Tufa is a natural substance that is found in limestone regions. It has a sponge-like structure with a consistency similar to chalk and it is easily cut with a coarse saw or carved with a knife. Where mossy vegetation and leaf litter are saturated with lime-rich water they become encased in a chalky deposit and over the years this process leads to the formation of a soft "rock". When this is quarried out in irregular chunks it becomes the source of tufa for rock gardeners. Weight for weight tufa is much more expensive than true rock; on the other hand, it has unique properties. Its highly porous structure causes it to store moisture, much like the sponge that it resembles. The soft, granular make-up with its countless cavities allows fine roots to penetrate deeply.

How is tufa used?

Certain types of rock plants, particularly those that naturally inhabit rock fissures, revel in this substance which provides sufficient nutrients for their needs. A carefully selected group of rock plants can be grown to perfection on a block of tufa and for some it is the best possible method of successful cultivation. Of course the tufa is limy and hence unsuitable for species requiring acid conditions.

Avoiding problems

The two drawbacks to the use of tufa are its tendency to become overgrown with moss and its disintegration due to frost; both arise because it is permanently too wet. To counter these defects the tufa must be correctly set up initially.

Setting up

Tufa can be employed in just the same way as rock for building outcrops, island beds and terraced slopes, but its cost usually discourages such large-scale usage. More often tufa is limited to special features, or even isolated as a single boulder. However it is used, tufa must have its contact with the ground carefully limited as its porosity acts like a wick to draw up moisture; the more of its bulk that is buried, the wetter the tufa will be, encouraging the growth of moss and increasing the risk of rupture when the excess water freezes.

Where annual rainfall is no more than 600 mm (24 in), it is safe to bury up to one third of the tufa's bulk, but in wetter areas with up to 1000 mm (40 in), only about one fifth should be submerged. If the rainfall is even greater then blocks and boulders should virtually sit on the surface of the ground.

In addition to limiting ground contact you

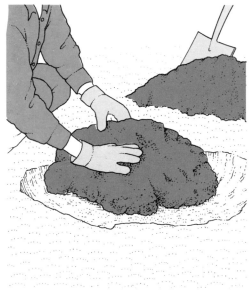

1 Set tufa blocks in a scree bed, to minimize moss and frost damage problems.

2 Cover a prepared bed with close-fitting pieces.

should choose sunny, well-aired places for tufa. This will help to keep the surface as dry as possible, further discouraging mossy growth and frost damage.

Tufa in beds

A reasonably safe way to use tufa in the garden is to set blocks of the material in a limestone scree. There the ground moisture level is low and in addition the capillary action is interrupted by the many stones in which the blocks sit.

To make effective use of moderately sized lumps set them like paving to cover the surface of a bed. The ease with which tufa can be shaped allows the achievement of close fits between the lumps. The bed should already be prepared for rock plants, with a 50 per cent gravel content in the soil mixture. Plants can be grown both through and in the tufa; some will root down into the underlying soil mixture. Weeds are greatly discouraged by the "armour plating" that the covering presents.

A tufa feature

To feature a single free-standing boulder of tufa choose a spot which has no tendency to wetness and dig out a 15 cm- (6 in-) deep hole wide enough to take the base of the boulder. Put in a layer of gravel, approximately 8 cm (3 in) deep and position the boulder, using wedging stones where needed to obtain stability. Complete the work by packing gravel round the boulder's base, adding more until the hole is totally full.

PREPARING TUFA

Tufa is usually coated in sticky waste from the quarrying process. Use a hose with a strong jet to wash away this encrustation, otherwise it will quickly attract algae and mosses. This washing treatment will also reveal and lift off any fractured pieces. Allow the blocks or boulders to drain and dry off for three or four days before putting them to use.

Previously used tufa is almost certain to be infested with unwanted growths and plant pests. Eliminate these by disinfecting with boiling water, simply poured over the surfaces. For a sure result repeat the operation the following day, then leave the tufa to dry out for two or three days. Use a stiff hand brush to scrub off the dead remains and clean up the surface generally.

3 Use an old log saw and axe to carve the tufa pieces for a close fit.

4 Set up a feature boulder in a shallow hole and pack round its base with gravel.

Making a gorge 1

1 Having marked out the area, dig out the route of the sunken gorge, with extra width at each side for the rock walls.

2 Make each additional tier of rocks longer than the last, to meet the rise of the path at each end.

Sunken pathways and natural depressions in the garden can be utilized to form small-scale gorges by introducing rockwork. It is also possible to make the feature by locally altering the lie of the land, where the garden conditions are favourable. In both cases the most important consideration is drainage, as any existing depression, or particularly one which has been newly excavated, is a potential catchment for water. On very free-draining land it is unlikely that hollows will flood, but elsewhere you should allow for the installation of drains. This means, of course, that the outlet for the drain will have to lie at a point lower than the base of the excavation.

As a preliminary to commencing work, check the behaviour of the intended location during wet weather, adding a trial trench if excavation is involved. Any noticeable gathering and lingering of water signals a need for drainage. See pages 20–23 for details of drainage installation.

A quite different approach is to create a mound with a gorge running through it. In many cases this will involve the importation of soil, but the advantage is that, by working from site ground level, the need for special drainage is avoided.

The sunken gorge

Unless you are utilizing an existing gully you will need to excavate the basic shape on the proposed site. Where this is on relatively level ground it will require digging out earth to a depth which is equal to the planned height of the gorge walls.

First mark out the intended route of the pathway that will lie along the floor of the gorge. In doing this you should take into account the lighting that the walls will receive. The gorge

3 Build the rockwork up to the site ground level, packing with soil mixture as each tier is completed.

should receive both sunlight and shadow during the day. Curving the route produces a useful variety of lighting.

Following the marked route dig out to the required depth, making a slope at each end to take the path from ground level to the floor of the gorge. Next, to accommodate the rock walls, take out more earth from each side of the excavation to the same depth as the path and of a width sufficient to take the largest of the rocks used in the wall.

Starting at the lowest level, and using the largest of the walling rocks, build a close-fitting tier along the full extent of the level section of the floor. Cut a good seating for each rock so that it is positioned firmly. Consolidate this first tier by packing the space between rocks and the excavation wall with a blend of soil, peat substitute and grit, in equal proportions. Use blunt-ended lengths of wood as tamping tools

to aid the packing of pockets and clefts.

Using progressively smaller pieces of rock, build up further tiers until the walls formed are level with the top of the excavation, packing in soil mixture at the completion of each tier. Each additional tier will lengthen in order to follow the upward rise of the path at each of its ends. The final stage of construction is the surfacing of the pathway with an appropriate finish. Its inclined ends can be simply paved as the rest of the path or have steps set in them (see pages 114–117 for how to build paths and steps).

Adaptations

Where the gorge is making use of an existing gully, the construction follows the method described, once the sides and floor have been cleaned up and contoured. The whole area involved must be thoroughly cleared of weeds before work is begun.

Making a gorge 2

The ground-level gorge
This could almost be regarded as an inverted version of the sunken form as there is no excavation required and building progresses from ground level upwards. Begin by laying down the first tier of rockwork directly onto the ground. This tier runs the entire length of the gorge. With the soil mixture already specified, pack behind the rocks to form a ramp. Lay down the next tier, making it a little shorter than the first, and add more packing mixture to the ramp. The number and lengths of the additional tiers will depend on the depth of the gorge that you are planning and the size of the rocks you are using. The aim is to produce a rock wall which will clad each side of a "cutting" through a mound of soil.

After completing the rock walls and their supporting ramps you will need some earth to gently blend the structure into the surrounding garden. Build slopes from the top of the rockwork down to ground level using plain soil, unless you intend to add further rockwork, in which case continue with the soil mixture. During the making of the slopes tread down the soil repeatedly to consolidate the ground and to minimize subsequent settlement.

Final treatment of the slopes will depend on your plans for their use. You can simply sow or turf them for a lawned surface, or you may choose to add outcrops, bluffs or terracing.

The completion of work by installing the pathway is easier than in the excavated version, as there are no changes in its level.

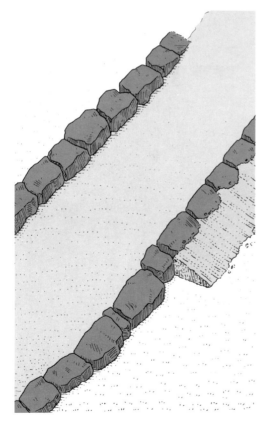

1 Begin the ground-level gorge by laying down the first tier of rocks for the full length.

2 Make a ramp behind the rockwork with the soil mixture, packing it into the crevices.

Reducing the cost

An economical alternative for the larger construction is to build a low wall behind the rockwork and about ¾ of the rockwork height, leaving a gap of roughly 30 cm (12 in) between them. This greatly reduces the amount of prepared soil mixture required to just sufficiently fill the gap. The remainder of the ramp can then be made with earth. Use old bricks or blocks to build the wall as, when the work is complete, it will be buried and completely hidden.

Suitable rock

For sufficient reliability and good finished appearance, individual rocks should be of adequate size, not less than 30 cm (12 in) in length and width, and at least 20 cm (8 in) thick.

A sloping gorge

The techniques described can be applied to making a rocky breach in ground with a considerable slope. The differences are confined to the initial excavation, which involves the cutting of an inclined passage through the earth of the slope. It is very unlikely that the floor of such a gorge would be satisfactory in any other form than a flight of steps.

To integrate the steps with the rocky walls, build the steps first, making them rather wider than required. When the mortaring has fully set, sit the first rocks on the ends of the steps as though the steps were foundations. If necessary use mortar to fix the rocks firmly in place. Following this, build up the rock-work as for the sunken-gorge construction (see pages 68–69).

3 Blend the structure into the garden with gently sloping banks of earth.

A sloping gorge will need to have steps built into the floor.

Rock gardens in shade 1

In planning for shade it is important to understand its meaning in gardening terms. There are degrees of shade.

Light shade describes the level of lighting that you would find, for example, in a greenhouse with muslin sun blinds, or on the ground beneath delicate foliage.

Moderate (or partial) shade occurs where an area is sunlit in the earlier and later part of the day, but is shadowed for the remainder.

Full shade is produced in dense woodland, where the sky is obscured by the leafy canopy, or in a place open to the sky, but permanently in the shadow of nearby buildings or trees.

Dappled shade is rather different, in that it allows direct sunlight to reach the ground in a shifting pattern so that plants there receive some full sun, but in a succession of short periods. This is "rationed" light.

Certain groups of rock plants benefit from light shade and a number will accept moderate shade levels, but only a few will thrive in full shade. Most of the woodland plants grown by rock gardeners come from the fringes and glades and so enjoy dappled shade.

The worst possible condition, from a planting point of view, is a combination of dryness and full shade. Those plants tolerant of full shading are almost all needful of a reasonably moist root run; a typical example being ferns.

Lessening the shade

You may be able to improve matters somewhat by arranging some reflected light. Where walls cause shadows coat them with white masonry paint to bring light from the sky into the area. In

1 Paint shade-casting walls white to bring in reflected light.

2 Fix the damp-resistant membrane to the wall with masonry nails.

very small and confined town gardens, large second-hand mirrors can be used to considerable effect. Set against a wall a mirror will not only bring in extra light but also give the illusion of increased space by producing a reflection of the garden itself, making it appear to extend beyond the wall. Coat the backs of mirrors with weatherproof paint to protect the silvering from damage by moisture.

Making the best of shade

The secret of successful gardening in shade is to use the condition to advantage, rather than battle against it. Many shade plants come to us from deep gorges, cave entrances and shady cliffs, so tailor the rock garden to accommodate such species, building rockwork with plenty of clefts and ledges. Use the walls creating the shade as supports for the rockwork. If they are the walls of buildings avoid causing problems of dampness by introducing a waterproof membrane between garden and wall.

Practicalities

This section focuses on conditions of full shade, leaving the other categories to be more appropriately covered where beds requiring a certain amount of shading are addressed.

Rock gardens on shadowed sites

Because of nearby tall buildings or neighbouring trees you may find that you have no options for the siting of your rock garden, other than a place which is in shadow for most, or all of the day. While this will limit the range and types of plants you can grow, it puts little constraint on the style of rock garden that can be built there. Outcrops, terraced rockwork and cliffs are all viable, provided you take precautions in the construction, positioning and materials used.

3 Set a large mirror on the wall to reflect both light and space.

Rock gardens in shade 2

Avoid soft, granular rock, such as the coarser sandstones and tufa; the lack of direct sunlight will encourage lichens, liverworts and mosses to clothe the porous surfaces of these materials. Granites, slates and fine-grained sandstones offer much more resistance to these green invaders. Many limestones are unsuitable as they are also vulnerable to mossy growths.

Ensure that the site is faultlessly drained and quite clear of overhanging branches or any other feature that constitutes a source of drips.

Be generous with top-dressing, and follow the above exclusions of unsuitable stone in selecting the gravel used.

Keep nearby shrubs well pruned in order to maximize the amount of incidental light reaching the site.

Choose plants with special regard to their light requirements, but include some classified as moderate shade types – they may produce a pleasant surprise.

Do not aggravate the shade situation by introducing tall features or densely-leaved plants into the vicinity of the rock garden.

Be prepared to put winter covers over some of the choice plants to combat the lingering wetness that afflicts shaded sites more than those areas in sun.

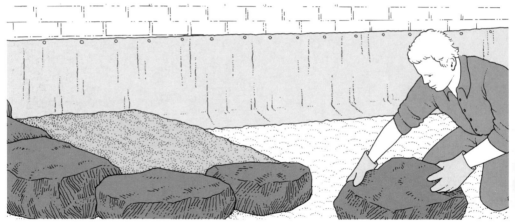

4 Lay down the base of the rockwork, packing with soil mixture.

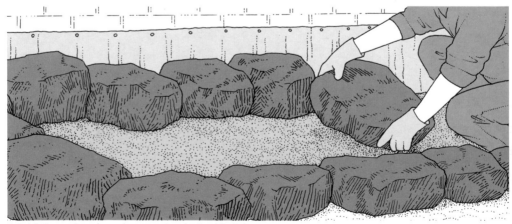

5 Add tiers of rockwork up to the desired height.

A rock garden for a shaded wall

Pond liner material makes an excellent membrane to protect a wall from moisture. Use a piece big enough to cover the wall up to a level just higher than the planned rockwork and to lie along the ground for a distance of 30 cm (12 in) out from the base of the wall. You must, of course, avoid covering and building over any ventilators present in the wall. Use masonry nails (or carpet tacks, if the wall is cement-rendered) to hold the membrane temporarily against the wall.

Lay down the base of the rockwork, packing behind and between the rocks with a fibrous soil mixture such as one made up from equal quantities of good soil, bark or leafmould and sharp sand. Add a further one or more tiers of rockwork, supported on rough plinths of bricks or concrete blocks, as in outcrop construction (see page 34). Make sure some of the rocks in the top tier are in contact with the wall; this will help to hold the membrane securely in place.

After completing the filling with soil mixture, trim off the surplus membrane material with a knife or scissors. Put a layer of gravel over all the soil surfaces to a depth of 5 cm (2 in) to discourage the growth of moss, which is more prevalent in shaded situations.

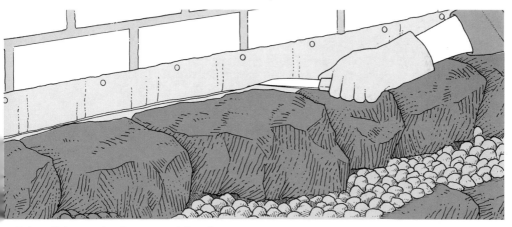

6 Trim off the surplus liner material and remove.

7 Prune nearby shrubs well back to maximize light levels.

Raised beds 1

The raised bed is simply a walled enclosure holding a prepared soil mixture; its primary function is to lift an entire growing area above the general level of the garden. It can be quite formal in style and construction or of a relaxed and rustic character. Any normal walling material may be used, including timber. There are no rules dictating the size of the raised bed, although working practicalities do impose their own limits on certain dimensions.

Dimensions

The length of a raised bed is essentially unlimited, but its width and height are constrained by practical considerations. A width exceeding 1.3 m (4¼ ft) will prevent you from comfortably reaching the centre of the bed for planting and maintenance, so regard this dimension as an absolute maximum. Height has other limitations, for while taller beds make working on them easier they also increase the task and cost, of building and filling. Another penalty of height is settlement; this is when the filling material sinks over a period of time to take the surface below the level of the bed walls. You can expect a settlement of 2–3 cm (about 1 in) for every 30 cm (12 in) of height. There are ways of compensating for settlement, to some extent, which will be explained in the section dealing with filling (see page 85).

Formal styles

Around a main entrance or flanking neat paths and driveways raised beds of a formal character provide a pleasing link between house and garden; they echo the hard lines of the building but are softened by the plants that they hold. A reasonable match between the materials of the house and bed walls helps this effect.

Free styles

Less formal walling can be made using random stone which is as-quarried and of irregular shape. Drystone walls are built with this type of stone. By its nature random walling is suited to the open garden and associates in a very natural way with rockwork. The skill required in its use is different, but no more difficult than that applied to formal wall building.

Alternative materials

Broken concrete paving slabs are a low-cost substitute for stone. Their uniform thickness makes for easy building but produces an unavoidable formality which is not eased by the unrelieved, drab texture. Weatherproof dyes are now widely available for use on concrete; when applied with some variation these can improve the looks of the finished wall.

Synthetic, or so-called "reconstituted", stone is available in several textures and tints, but only simulates the more formal walling styles.

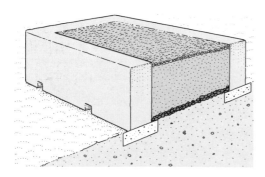

The basics of a typical raised bed, showing the main features.

Broken paving slabs provide an alternative walling material.

Nevertheless, they offer a close resemblance to true dressed-stone in some cases, and weathering improves the likeness.

Timber, in the form of large boughs and trunks stripped of their branches but retaining their bark, responds to artful arrangement for rustic beds suited to woodland and ericaceous plantings. They will eventually rot away, but if of oak, yew or elm the deterioration takes many years and actually improves their appearance in the process.

Redundant railway sleepers are becoming scarce and increasingly expensive, but their size and consistent dimensions do make wall building a quick and straightforward operation. As they are deeply impregnated with rot-proofing compounds their garden life can be counted in tens of years.

Pre-construction work

Begin by cleaning the site and clearing the ground of persistent weeds, including buried roots which might sprout new shoots. Unless the chosen place is apt to flood in wet weather there is no need for you to lay drains as the raised bed sheds its surplus water at ground level. Do not disturb the ground by digging more than is strictly necessary during clearance, otherwise the preparation of any foundations may be made more difficult. Remember to include sufficient space for access pathways adjacent to the bed when cleaning and clearing the site. These should not be less than 60 cm (24 in) wide.

Preparation

To avoid a lot of wasted effort, collect all the bed-building materials close to the site. Stack the walling stone or blocks neatly and heap the sand, gravel and soil on boards, or strong plastic sheet, not directly on the ground. Protect all these from rain; wet materials are impossible to handle and mix properly, and walling must be dry when it is being laid in order to obtain a satisfactory result.

Keep cement in closed bags or containers in dry conditions, otherwise it may solidify due to moisture in the atmosphere.

Make sure that trowels to be used for laying and pointing are clean and free from rust; this is necessary to facilitate smooth working and a neat finish.

1 Make the foundation trench a little wider than the walling material.

2 Tamp the gravel or sand base to firm it up.

3 Fill the trench to its brim with the concrete mixture and smooth the surface off with the back of the spade.

Raised beds 2

Foundations

With the exception of timber-built raised beds foundations are needed for the strength and long-term stability of the walling. First excavate the area. Follow the marked-out shape of the bed, digging a neat trench to a depth of 15 cm (6 in) and a breadth exceeding the width of the walling material by approximately 10 cm (4 in). The outer edge of the trench should be some 5 cm (2 in) beyond the marked line. Where any ground has been loosened during site clearance, you may have to increase the depth of the trench until undisturbed earth is reached.

Provide a base for the concrete filling by spreading a 7–8 cm (about 3 in) layer of gravel or coarse sand evenly over the bottom of the trench. Tamp it down firmly using a stout length of timber. Prepare the foundation concrete by first mixing thoroughly together one part of cement, two parts of sand and three parts of gravel, in the dry state. Continue mixing, adding water gradually, until the concrete achieves a consistency of stiff porridge. Fill up the trench with the mixture to its brim and leave it to set for at least two days, protecting it, if necessary, from rain or frost by a covering of plastic sheeting. The surface of the concrete need not be precisely flat but a final smoothing with the back of the spade or shovel will give you a good working base for the walling.

Estimating walling material

To prepare for building the walls of the bed you will need to quantify the amount of walling material required. To obtain a reliable estimate, use either a scale drawing of the shape, or mark it out on the site and measure the total length of the wall that forms the bed. The other dimension required is the height of the wall. With these figures determined the method used to complete the estimation depends upon the material to be used.

Choosing walling material

Random stone (also known as freestone) is the traditional drystone walling material. Some suppliers still sell by the "running yard", which is the amount of stone required to produce a single wall one yard long and one yard high, which makes estimating an easy task. Others

---

WALLING WITH RANDOM STONE

Whether the wall is to be made of stone, brick, or a synthetic substitute, the actual process of building it is essentially the same. In the case of random walling some preparatory work will greatly assist in the construction.

Preparation

Lay the first course of stone in the "dry" state, that is, without using mortar. This will allow you to swap and change pieces to achieve the best fit and to find places for awkward shapes. Remove four or five stones, lay them to one side in exactly the order that they were removed, then introduce mortar before returning and laying the stones, one by one, to their previous positions. Repeat the technique until the whole of the first course has been laid in mortar. Do the same for each successive course and you will have a well-fitting wall with a minimum of non-fitting pieces left over.

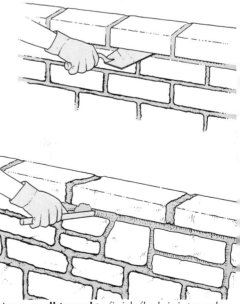

Use a small trowel to finish flush joints and a round-ended stick or spoon to rake out.

sell by weight, in which case you can avoid mistakes by first obtaining a sample amount of, say, 100 kg (2 cwt) and determining how far this will go by building a trial wall. A little multiplication will then give you the total needed. When building with random stone you are constantly searching for pieces that will fit together, rather like crazy paving, and it is never possible to find a place for every bit in the stockpile, so you should order about 20 per cent more than the calculated requirement.

Dressed stone is symmetrical in shape and therefore easier to assess. Usually the supplier will help you to work out the quantity needed,

if you provide the dimensions; otherwise you can resort to the trial build method described above.

Synthetic stones and concrete walling blocks are made to precise dimensions and often imitate dressed stone, hence the method used for the latter will suffice.

Bricks are normally sold loose, by the hundred, or in pallets holding a set number. As the brick is a standard size and shape estimating is simplified, and just a matter of dividing the total length of walling by the length of a brick, and the wall height by the thickness of a brick. The two numbers multiplied together give the required total. You should then reduce the total by 10 percent to compensate for the space taken up by the mortar between the bricks.

Capping

Although walling can be completed by neatly mortaring the final course, capping pieces set in mortar give a more finished look to the wall and a clean edging to the top of the bed. Use slabs which are slightly wider than the wall and set them with a slight overhang on the outer face.

Capping pieces provide a finishing touch to walling.

Work to a taut line when laying straight runs. Use a builder's level to frequently check the work.

Raised beds 3

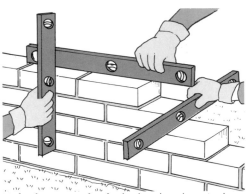

Make frequent checks for level and vertical during the build.

Leave a few joints unmortared in the first course, for drainage.

Stack old railway sleepers to form a stout wall.

Laying the wall

The method and procedure are the same as those explained for hollow walling (see page 58) as far as the setting and mortaring are concerned, but as raised beds can require larger structures there are certain points to be noted and some variations in finishing.

Joint finishing

Joints can either be finished flush or raked out. Flush joints are commonly seen in general brickwork and are produced by first slicing away any mortar left protruding, then smoothing along the joint to make the mortar flush with the bricks. Use a small builder's trowel for this work and carry it out as part of the laying process.

Raked joints are more often seen in stone walling but can be applied to brickwork for a bold effect. You should delay raking until the mortar is partially

MORTAR

This is used in the laying of all the materials discussed so far. It consists of building sand and cement, in the proportions of five to one, measured by volume.

The sand used should never be any more than just damp, to ensure thorough amalgamation with the cement. Avoid preparing more than two bucketfuls of mortar in one operation if you can, otherwise, not only will the physical work entailed be heavy, but the mixture may stiffen up before it has all been used, making it unworkable. Mix the sand and cement in the "dry" state, repeatedly turning the combined heap with a shovel or an old spade. When blending is complete (shown by evenness of colour throughout the heap) add water gradually and continue to turn the mixture until the resultant mortar is fairly firm, but easily spread. See pages 58–59 for testing the mixture.

Plasticizers are additives which are put into the water used for mixing; they make the handling properties of mortar significantly better and are well worth using where an appreciable amount of walling is involved.

set (after eight to ten hours). Use a round-ended stick or an old spoon to scrape out the joints to a depth of 1–2 cm (⅜–¾ in), finishing off with a moderately stiff brush to smooth and clean up the work.

Corners
At the corners of the bed brickwork should be bonded by laying alternate courses end on. If using stone, reserve large pieces for the corners to give strength and stability.

Drainage
Leave vertical joints unmortared at intervals of approximately 60 cm (24 in) in the first course of the walling, to provide the all-important drainage outlets for the bed. Check that these do not become blocked with mortar during the laying of the second course.

Building with timber
Old railway sleepers are heavy but otherwise easy to use; they quickly form a solid wall. However, their size and shape constrains their use to rectangular layouts and level sites. Foundations are not needed and preparation is limited to levelling and smoothing the ground on which they will lie. Leave a gap of 2.5 cm (1 in) between the ends of the sleepers in the first layer, to form drainage outlets, and stagger the joints of successive layers. To combat the dislodging effect of hard frosts use a long joiner's auger to bore a 12 mm (½ in) hole through the upper and lower sleeper where joints occur, and at the corners. Obtain metal rods to fit these holes, of a length 2.5 cm (1 in) less than the thickness of two sleepers. Hammer these rods fully into the bored holes.

Sections of tree trunk, preferably of oak, elm or yew can be set vertically, side by side, to form a rugged bed that is suited to woodland or ericaceous plantings. The sections should be approximately 60 cm (24 in) long and be well treated beforehand with a timber preservative that is not harmful to plants. Set each section of tree trunk in place, fitting them together close, in a trench 30 cm (12 in) deep, dug round the profile of the bed. Return the excavated earth, packing it tightly round each section. The many small gaps that will exist between neighbouring timbers will provide sufficient drainage outlets. There are few limits to the bed shapes that can be made using this method.

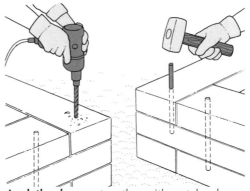

Lock the sleepers together with metal rods inserted into bored holes.

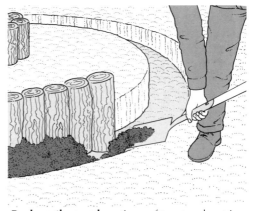

Pack earth round sections of tree trunk set in a prepared trench.

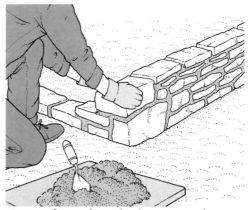

Reserve large pieces for the corners of stone walling.

81

Raised beds 4

Mixing and filling

Use a plastic sheet for the "rollover" method of mixing.

A powered mixer can usually empty directly into the bed.

Filling and finishing
Materials

In deciding upon the make-up of the soil mixture filling material for the bed it is important to take into account the types of plants that you wish to grow, and the climate in your area.

If the bed is to be devoted to plants of a particular type, then you can prepare a soil mixture specially for them, but if the planting is less specialized it is a matter of compromising with a mixture that is ideal for some plants and acceptable to the rest.

Climatic variations call for adjustments to the make-up of soil mixtures. It would be impractical to prescribe mixtures to meet all conditions, but the examples given are from widely different regions and can be used as a guide to finding mixtures suited to your local environment.

Adding nutrients

For each of the mixtures given in the examples, an initial amount of nutrient is incorporated by adding 100 gm (4 oz) of balanced, low nitrogen

---

SOIL MIXTURES

For rock plants in regions with cool, wet summers and wet, fairly mild winters, with an average annual rainfall of 1000 mm (40 in), use this general mixture (by volume):

2 parts gravel or grit, 1 part good soil, 1 part peat substitute

The scree mixture should comprise (by volume):

3 parts gravel and one part fibrous soil.

For rock plants in regions with warm, dry summers and cold, fairly dry winters with harsh winds, with an average annual rainfall of 600 mm (24 in), use this general mixture (by volume):

1 part gravel or grit, 1 part good soil and 1 part peat substitute.

The scree mixture should comprise (by volume):

3 parts gravel and 2 parts fibrous soil.

Fix a stout plank to form a ramp for the wheelbarrow.

fertilizer to each barrow-load. Suitable fertilizers are blood, fish and bone, or rose fertilizer. Take a barrow-load as being approximately 50 litres (10 gallons).

Mixing

For small quantities of up to two or three barrow-loads you can mix the materials by piling them together and turning the heap with a spade or shovel. The "rollover" method will, however, greatly reduce the effort required. For this you require a strong plastic sheet 2.7–3.6 m (9–12 ft) long and 1.5–2 m (5–6 ft 6 in) wide. Lay the sheet on an even surface and pile the mixture constituents on it at one end. Then, with an assistant, take hold of the two corners near the heap and walk towards the other end. The materials will be rolled forward, mixing as they go. Reverse the movement to return the materials to the start position, repeat the same moves again and the mixing should be adequate. A barrow-load is about the right quantity for this energy-saving process, which can be used

numerous times to process large quantities.

A power-driven cement mixer will blend the materials in less than a minute, but requires manual labour for shovelling them into its rotating drum. Nevertheless, for large beds you will at least halve the work involved by hiring one of these machines.

AIDS TO FILLING

If you use a powered mixer you may be able to arrange for it to empty straight into the bed by wheeling it to several positions. Otherwise the filling must be shovelled directly into the bed or barrowed to where it is required. Stout planks, securely positioned between ground level and the top of the bed wall, will provide ramps for the wheelbarrow. The longer the plank the gentler the slope and the easier it is to push a loaded barrow up it.

Raised beds 5

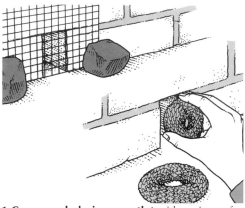

1 Cover each drainage outlet with a piece of plastic mesh, or insert a plastic panscrub.

2 Spread a layer of coarse gravel over the bottom of the bed.

3 Put a layer of plastic mesh over the drainage gravel.

Preparing to fill

Before starting to fill the bed, fix a piece of strong plastic mesh to cover each of the drainage outlets, on the inside of the walls. Two fist-sized stones will usually suffice to hold the mesh in place. Alternatively, stuff one of the "doughnut" type panscrubs into each hole. These precautions are needed to prevent leakage of soil mixture without hindering the flow of water.

Filling procedure

Filling begins with the drainage layer. Cover the bottom of the bed with a 5 cm (2 in) deep layer of 10–15 mm (⅜–½ in) gravel. Lay a covering of plastic mesh, old onion sacks or geotextile over this to protect the drainage layer from blockage by soil. The bed is then ready to receive the soil mixture.

As the soil mixture is deposited into the bed, scrape it roughly level with the edge of a spade or a rake, and when a depth of 15 cm (6 in) has been built up tread down the mixture. If the inner faces of the walls are uneven make sure that all the irregularities are fully packed, particularly under any shelves formed by inwardly jutting stones. Repeat the treading and packing after each layer of mixture has been added, until the bed is full to within 2.5 cm (1 in) of the tops of the walls.

Finishing

When the bed has been completely filled with soil mixture, top-dress its surface with gravel, preferably using a mixture of sizes ranging from 5–10 mm (¼–⅜ in). The depth of the top-dressing should be between 2.5–4 cm (1–1½ in) to bring the finished surface level with the tops of the bed's walls. Remember to include compensation for future settlement, as explained.

Rocks set into the surface will both add interest and provide special planting places. Put in a few pieces with their raised ends facing north to give small patches of shade and create crevices with partnering rocks. For a bed which will house crevice plants, introduce more rocks to provide a host of clefts and fissures.

An assortment of rounded pebbles makes an attractive alternative to the more often used stone chippings in top dressing, especially if you include a few larger cobbles of the same stone here and there.

Beds for ericaceous and woodland plantings are more appropriately finished with a layer of chipped bark, cocoa shell, or the product of the garden shredder. Settlement in this type of bed is likely to be more pronounced, so compensate for this with generous amounts of filling and top-dressing. There is no need to tread down the soil mixture to the extent recommended for other types of filling. A light firming is sufficient in this case.

Allowing for settlement

No matter how well you have trodden and packed the filling it will sink a little after a year or so; about 2.5 cm (1 in) for every 30 cm (12 in) of bed height. In taller beds this settlement is quite noticeable, marring the appearance. It can be compensated for by either overfilling, or by adding a temporary, unmortared top course to the walling. The humped overfilling will level out with settlement. The temporary top course is removed after the filling has sunk sufficiently.

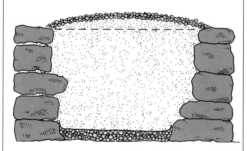

Overfill the bed slightly, as it will level out with settlement.

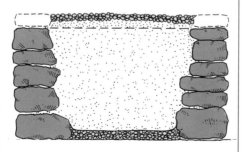

Alternatively, use a temporary top course, removed after settlement.

Finishing

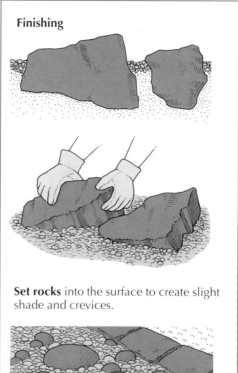

Set rocks into the surface to create slight shade and crevices.

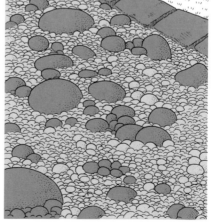

Use rounded pebbles and cobbles for an alternative surface finish.

Ericaceous plantings

The soil

In building special beds for ericaceous species your first consideration must be the pH value of the soil in your garden. The pH is a measure of the quantity of lime in the soil, with pH 6.5 being neutral. Lower values show increasing acidity and higher ones indicate the presence of significant lime content. Almost without exception ericaceous plants will be distressed by pH values above 7, and actually killed by higher levels. At the other extreme, values below pH 4 can be too acidic, causing even species from peaty environments to become stunted and poor in health.

Assumptions based on local geology are not always reliable guides; soils overlying limestone can in fact be acidic and some sandstones have quite a high calcium content, taking them up to as much as pH 8.

To be reasonably sure of your own soil's pH value, check it using one of the proprietary devices available from garden suppliers. The cheapest of these employs a chemical which is diluted with distilled water and poured into a glass phial containing a small measured sample of soil. When the sediment has settled the colour of the liquid is checked against the chart supplied to obtain the pH value. A more expensive but extremely simple device which lasts indefinitely is the pH meter, which consists of a read-out dial mounted on a metal rod. By pushing the rod into the soil it is possible to obtain an immediate reading.

Soil improvement

Ericaceous plants, on the whole, have fine root systems which do not penetrate deeply into the ground. They are accustomed to fairly light but fibrous soils which retain plenty of water, yet at the same time are free-draining.

Clays and heavy soils resist the spreading of fine roots and need to be opened up by the addition of lime-free grit and organic matter. This also has the effect of improving the drainage properties of the soil.

Sandy soils are usually deficient in plant nutrients and almost devoid of moisture-holding organic substances. Large amounts of fibrous material are needed to make them acceptable for ericaceous plants.

On chalky and other naturally limy sites the ericaceous bed must be isolated from the lime-rich ground. One of the most effective means of achieving this is to enclose the bed filling within a porous membrane.

Lowering the pH

If your soil is only marginally above the limiting pH value you may be able to reduce it by

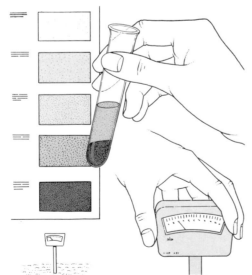

Use a testing kit or pH meter to check the quantity of lime in your soil.

Lay rockwork to form a containment on naturally limy soils.

adding a substance to counteract the lime to some extent. Sulphur and sulphate of iron are moderately effective in this. Spread 250 gm (10 oz) of powdered sulphur over each square metre (1¼ sq yd) of soil, raking it lightly afterwards, or use 150 gm (6 oz) of iron sulphate in the same manner. After a few days of rain have washed in these dressings, check the result with a pH test. It will probably prove necessary to repeat the dressing every year or two to maintain the lowered pH. Sequestrene is a more expensive neutralizer which can be applied to the establishing planting. Repeated applications or excessive use of any neutralizer can, in time, be harmful to the plants.

Siting the bed

Although quite a few ericaceous species are native to moorland, in general they are vulnerable to harsh, drying winds. These take moisture out of the foliage more rapidly than the plant can replace it, resulting in the crippling and loss of leaves, and in some instances the death of the plant. If possible choose a site which is not exposed in this way, but if strong winds are prevalent arrange shelter on the windward side with a dense hedge or shrubbery.

Some shade is needed by some ericaceous plants. If the bed can receive the dappled

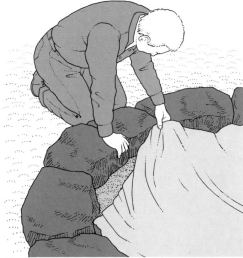

Line the rock containment with a porous membrane.

SUITABLE SOIL MIXTURES

There is no need for precision in making up a soil mixture for ericaceous subjects; it is the physical properties of the mixture that matter, rather than the ingredients. Your soil may already be free-draining and lime-free, in which case you need only add fibrous matter such as shredded prunings, chipped bark, leafmould or composted bark. Less open soils will require the addition of non-limy grit to increase their porosity. However, if you have the problem of a naturally limy location with a pH above 6.5, the specially prepared mixture becomes a necessity. A typical make-up consists of the following. Equal parts by volume of: fairly light, lime-free loam; leafmould; lime-free coarse sand; composted bark or high-quality garden compost.

shadow, but not the drips, from a nearby tree then the light level will be satisfactory. Be aware, however, that other species require plenty of light to flower well, so allow only part of the bed to be shaded if you wish to grow a varied collection of plants.

Building the bed

In style, preparation and construction ericaceous beds are essentially the same as those made for outcrops and island beds (see pages 34–37 and 38–39). The exception is the bed sited on limy ground.

On limy sites the contents of the bed must be isolated from the lime-rich earth. This can be done by lining the bed with a porous membrane. The material of this membrane can be the woven plastic matting now so common in garden centre display areas, geotextile or finely perforated plastic sheet sold off the roll by the metre. These should not be confused with the products made for shading and forming windbreaks, which are too coarse for the purpose. The function of the porous lining is to allow water to pass through, but to prevent contact between the acid mixture in the bed and the limy earth of the garden. It will also act as a barrier to worms, stopping them from bringing limy soil into the bed.

A place for woodlanders 1

To edge the bed use large boughs
secured to stakes driven into the ground.

Soil

The preparation of soil for woodland species is more or less the same as for ericaceous plantings, but without the necessity for excluding lime; there are many woodlanders from regions with calcareous soils. It is quite feasible to have a mixed planting of both ericaceous and woodland types if you avoid the inclusion of woodlanders needing lime.

Materials

There is a natural relationship between timber and stone which allows the two to be combined in the garden, giving the same pleasing results that we see in old buildings. Old tree stumps do not look out of place alongside mossy boulders and they offer excellent planting pockets in their hollows. The best forms are those which have been grubbed out with the upper parts of their roots retained. Look for them where new roads are under construction, or on building sites where trees have been removed.

If you wish to raise a bed slightly and at the same time keep a woodland character use large, trimmed boughs of a timber which is slow to rot, such as elm or oak. Secure them in place with stakes driven into the ground and nailed to the timber. An alternative edging can be made with rounded stones laid in the form of a low wall.

Shading

If your site lacks shade you can remedy this by planting slow-growing trees, such as Japanese maples (*Acer japonicum* and *A. palmatum*), to cast dappled shadow. As they mature prune away their lower branches so eventually they form a delicate canopy over the growing area.

Blending with the rock garden

If the garden is large enough the woodland planting can be situated at the outskirts of the rock garden proper, or as a background to it giving a natural transition from open space to a cooler, softer environment. Avoid the use of peat blocks as an edging to the bed, for not only does this conflict with conservation aims, but the wall formed will be unstable and prone to shrinking in dry weather.

Alternatively make an edging with a low
wall of rounded stones.

Prune small trees to encourage them to form a
shading canopy over the site.

A place for woodlanders 2

Surfacing
These plants look out of place if surrounded by a top-dressing of gravel; in their natural homes the ground is more often covered in leaf litter or low plantlife, such as mosses. For a more appropriate finish spread chipped bark, cocoa shell, shredded prunings over the soil surface to a depth of not less than 5 cm (2 in) as an initial finish. Hold a quantity in reserve for later use.

Unfortunately, these materials are attractive to birds as they harbour worms and insects and the amount of disturbance and scattering they cause can be surprising. However, cats can be an even greater problem as they use the covering on a daily basis and leave unpleasant deposits partially buried. To discourage these visitors without causing them harm lay plastic netting of the type used for protecting fruit bushes over the top-dressing. Peg the netting down with skewers or small tent pegs and hide it with a thin additional layer of top-dressing material. Birds may still scratch around, but

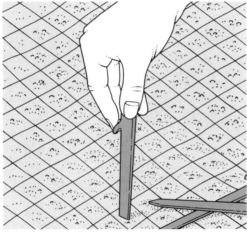

1 Protect the top-dressing with plastic netting held down with pegs.

2 To make artificial boulders carve cores from polystyrene foam blocks.

3 Cover the core with handfuls of the hypertufa mixture, after coating with adhesive.

4 Wrap the finished "boulder" in the polythene sheet on which it has been prepared.

only shallowly, and cats, finding they are unable to dig, will usually be put off. The netting is easily snipped away locally for the introduction of plants.

Adding character to the bed

If you are able to obtain small rounded boulders of sandstone or limestone these will enhance the look of the bed if grouped here and there. To encourage and speed up the mellowing of these stones paint their surfaces with milk or liquid manure after positioning them. This will initiate the growth of lichens and mosses.

Substitutes for natural boulders are not difficult to make using the hypertufa compound already described for artificial rock making (see page 32). For these simulated boulders you will need some large blocks of rigid polystyrene foam as used for packing delicate equipment. Carve the blocks into rounded forms using an old but sharp knife. The finish does not need to be smooth. Working on a sheet of polythene and wearing tough, waterproof gloves, cover the block surface with suitable adhesive, then take handfuls of the hypertufa mixture and coat the roughly-shaped core to a thickness of not less than 5 cm (2 in) all over the surface. Using your gloved hands and a soft brush smooth up the finished surface, then clear away all loose material from the sheet. Pull the sheet up round the "boulder" and tie it up like a pudding cloth. Leave this package out of the sun for a week to ensure the hypertufa is fully set before moving it to its place in the bed. Hypertufa mellows quite quickly, you will find when it is used in this way, especially if it is treated with an encouraging liquid, in the same way as for stone.

The tree stump feature already mentioned should be set in the soil of the bed with the junctions between the roots and the trunk still visible. If the stump is in-situ scrape away soil, if necessary, to produce the same effect. The hollows and crannies between the root tops form excellent planting places. It is common for the centre of a stump to decay first, giving you the opportunity to add another planting dimension by digging out the decayed wood and replacing it with a suitable soil mixture.

On sloping ground the bed may be terraced using either logs or slices from a large tree trunk. Lay logs across the slope, securing them with stout stakes driven 30 cm (12 in) deep into the earth. If you choose to use slices set these with half of their height buried in the bed and in close contact with one another. In finishing, allow the surface material to cover most of the top surfaces of logs or slices.

Creating features using tree stumps

Set tree stumps with the junctions of roots and trunk exposed, or scrape soil away for the same effect on existing stumps.

Use long horizontal logs or slices of tree trunk to terrace sloping sites.

91

Pavement beds

Pavement beds may be made with stone or concrete slabs, bricks, blocks or crazy paving. Within limits you can convert an established area of paving by improving the growing conditions at chosen spots, but existing paving is not really suitable; if it has been properly laid it will rest on a layer of sand overlying a hardcore base of rubble. Such foundations usually have excellent drainage but offer little by way of nutrients, so only coarse weeds are likely to gain a foothold. This is not to say that pathways and other paved areas are unsuitable; they can be converted to the purpose with some modification.

Existing pavement

On the more formal types, where rectangular slabs have been used, lift a few of them here and there and dig out the base material until you reach the earth beneath. Refill the holes with a half-and-half mixture of soil and fine gravel, tamping it down to prevent later settlement. Return the slabs to their original positions but do not use mortar, either beneath or between the slabs. Brush fine gravel or coarse sand into the joints to finish the work.

Alternatively, instead of replacing the slabs cover the refilled holes with a top-dressing of gravel to produce large planting pockets that will accommodate groups of plants or larger-growing specimens.

These methods are equally applicable to areas surfaced with crazy paving and where bricks or blocks have been used. The only variation is that at each chosen spot several bricks or slabs should be lifted to create an adequately sized hole.

For conversions with greater scope and variety the most successful treatment is to modify the whole area, or a large part of it, by taking up and then re-laying the paving over an improved base. Before beginning the work

drive in wooden pegs at intervals along the edges of the existing paving, until their tops are level with the paving surface. These will be the reference points for the re-laying work. Lift off the paving and dig out the original base material down to the soil. If the depth of this excavation is less than 20 cm (8 in) continue digging out until this depth is achieved. Fill the

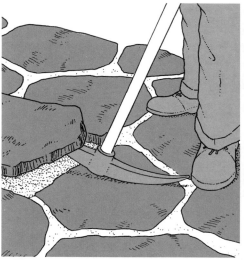

1 Lift paving with the aid of a pickaxe or an old spade.

2 Dig out the old base material down to the underlying earth.

> ### CAUTION
> Large-scale conversion of existing paving is not valid for driveways in regular use or busy paths, as the soil and gravel base has insufficient strength to take frequent and heavy loads. In addition, plantings would suffer to the point of extinction from in such a situation.

excavation with a half-and-half mixture of good-quality soil and 4–6 mm (⅙–¼ in) gravel, treading and tamping this down firmly. Surface the filling with a 2–4 cm (¾–1½ in) layer of coarse sand. On this re-lay the paving using the marker pegs as reference together with a long, straight edge to achieve an even finish. Scrape away or add a little of the surfacing sand to make the necessary laying adjustments. In the laying leave plenty of generous gaps between the pavings for subsequent planting, or omit pavings to create larger pockets. A gap of 2.5 cm (1 in) is sufficient for the introduction of young plants. To complete the work brush fine gravel or grit into all the joints and surface pockets with a top-dressing of gravel.

3 Drive in wooden pegs to fix the level for re-paving.

4 Set re-laid paving to the marker pegs, checking with a straightedge.

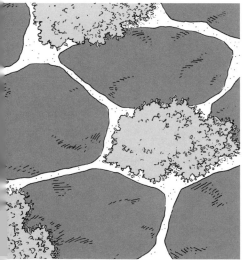

Leave out slabs in random positions to provide planting pockets.

6 Brush fine gravel into the open joints of the finished paving.

93

Making new pavement beds

On the whole the types of plants most suited to pavement beds are sun-loving species accustomed to rather poor sandy or stony soils. In this respect a new construction has advantages over one which has been converted for the purpose: doubtful drainage can be remedied by adding a piped system; the siting can take account of the need for sunlight; and materials can be chosen with a view to contriving the best planting arrangements possible

Preparation

If your garden is on sandy, free-draining soil the amount of preparation may be limited to a levelling of the site (see page 19); the paving is then laid directly onto the soil. On heavier soils it is necessary to dig out the area to a depth of 20 cm (8 in) to accommodate a more suitable rooting medium. Where this excavation has been carried out further work should be delayed until rainfall has revealed whether or not a catchment for water has been created. If the site quickly sheds any collected water then you can proceed to the next stage of the work – the filling. If water lingers it will be wise to install a drainage system (see pages 20–23).

Filling

Using good-quality "imported" soil or your own improved by the addition of organic material and grit, mix it with an equal quantity of 4–6 mm (⅙–¼ in) gravel. Fill the excavation with this mixture, treading it down repeatedly during the process until the surface of the filling is within 4 cm (1½ in) of the site ground level. Remove any humps and hollows in the surface, checking the result with a straightedge.

Adjustment

The dimensions that are given above apply to the majority of paving slabs. If bricks, blocks or irregular pieces of stone are used, however, then adjustments have to be made. The thickness of natural stone slabs is not consistent and the variations have to be accommodated by scraping away or adding to the filling mixture on which they are bedded. In the laying of normal paths and driveways it is common practice to set paving slabs on small heaps of mortar. This is, however, undesirable for paving beds as it can leave air space beneath the paving which may prove detrimental to the plants.

If you use bricks or blocks note that these are

On rectangular beds (1) position a setting piece at each corner. For informal shapes **(2)** position pieces at three or four widely spaced points around the edge.

Make regular checks with a straightedge across the setting pieces as laying work proceeds.

of a greater thickness than most paving slabs and you should therefore finish off the filling to a lower level to allow for this extra thickness.

Laying the pavement

Whatever the type of paving you use, start laying at one corner of the site, placing a slab, brick, or block in position to establish a setting piece. On rectangular-shaped beds do the same at the other three corners, and on asymmetrical shapes put these setting pieces at three or four locations around the edge and as far apart as possible.

Proceed with the laying from one of the setting pieces, checking repeatedly by laying a straightedge across different setting pieces. These checks are essential in order to achieve an even surface.

Style

The pattern of laying depends to a large extent upon personal preference. Rectangular slabs can be arranged with their joints in line or staggered. They may be all of one size or an assortment. Crazy paving relies on the artful arrangement and interlocking of random shapes, with care taken to attain an even mixture of sizes over the whole area of paving. Bricks and blocks may be set in a variety of symmetrical patterns.

Allowance for planting

When laying slabs avoid the tendency to fit one piece hard against the next; even those plants which are natural crevice-dwellers need a little space in which to root down. Crazy paving offers plenty of planting places in the irregular joints and gaps which are characteristic of the style. The more uniform, symmetrical types of paving need generous joint widths; 2–3 cm (about 1 in) is the minimum for successful planting.

Open pockets in the bed are most easily introduced during the laying. Do this by omitting pieces at random points or to a regular pattern. In brick- or block-type paving, such pockets are the only satisfactory planting arrangement.

Finishing

The filling of joints and surfacing of pockets follow exactly the same procedure described for converted pavement (see page 93).

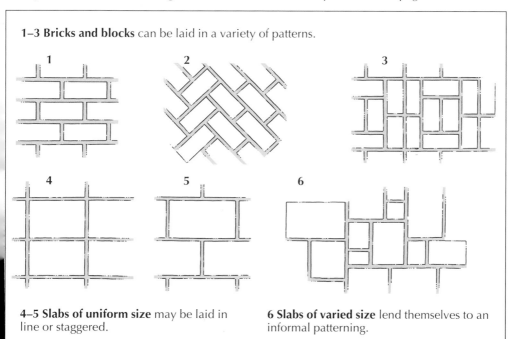

1–3 Bricks and blocks can be laid in a variety of patterns.

1

2

3

4

5

6

4–5 Slabs of uniform size may be laid in line or staggered.

6 Slabs of varied size lend themselves to an informal patterning.

Table beds 1

Types and constructions

The table bed is a very special form of rock garden. In size it lies between the trough and the raised bed but it is taller: the height is literally that of a normal table, approximately 75 cm (30 in). This is a pleasing height to both work at and enjoy the feature. Strength is the principal concern in the construction of the table, as the great weight of the table section and its contents must be firmly and safely borne by the supports.

Materials

If you are lucky enough to be able to obtain one large slab of slate, for instance from an old billiard table, then you will possess the ideal material for the base of the bed. However, these are hard to come by and it is much more usual to use a number of smaller slabs. There is still a plentiful supply of the pre-metric (3 ft x 2 ft) concrete pavings in the stockpiles of second-hand building materials. These have adequate strength for the purpose provided that their thickness is not less than the normal 2 in. They should be carefully examined for flaws such as incipient cracks before use. Substantial baulks of timber or thick sheets of exterior grade plywood suitably treated against rot are acceptable alternatives for the table base, although they will have a limited life.

The support pillars for the table base may be built from any of the accepted walling materials, although symmetrical blocks or bricks are best. Unless of massive proportions, timber is not recommended.

The containment for the bed is made with an edging of dwarf walls which can be built in a variety of materials (and methods).

Preparation

When looking at where to place your table bed, reject any area where the ground has been recently disturbed by digging or where filling has been added; the loosened earth will have inadequate strength to hold the foundations required for the supports. Significantly sloping ground should also be avoided. Once you have decided on a spot, clear an area to 60 cm (24 in) beyond the intended outline of the bed to produce a firm, level surface.

Design

The positions of the support pillars will be determined by the slabs used for the table base: the joints between the slabs must lie along the

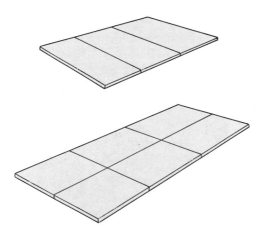

1 Make a small table base with three rectangular paving slabs, or a larger version with six.

2 Position support pillars so that they will lie centrally beneath the joints of the slabs.

centres of the pillars, but at the ends the slabs should overhang the outer pillars by 10 cm (4 in). When building a table, make sure that the pillars are at the correct "pitch" (i.e. distance apart).

For a small bed use three paving slabs of the type described earlier, arranged with their long sides together. You will need four pillars, the centre pair pitched at the width of a slab and the outer two at 10 cm (4 in) less to leave an overhang. For a larger bed, use six slabs and space the central pillars more widely to take the length of a slab; the outer ones will have a lesser pitch. This geometry is adaptable for various slab sizes and layouts.

If you choose to use timber for the table base, it must be adequately protected against rot with a treatment which is not detrimental to plants. The timber should have a minimum thickness of 5 cm (2 in) for planks and 2.5 cm (1 in) for plywood. In both cases supports should not be more than 75 cm (30 in) apart.

For the edges, use bricks on their edges, dwarf stone walling or the long slabs sold as path edgings. Edge wooden tables with suitably treated planks secured by galvanized screws or bolts and angle brackets.

Foundations

After marking out the position and size of each support pillar, add a further 10 cm (4 in) to the outlines to establish the sizes for the foundations. Working to these increased dimensions, dig out a neat trench at each pillar position to a depth of 20 cm (8 in). Fill each of these with concrete up to ground level, and allow three days for setting before proceeding with construction work.

FOUNDATION CONCRETE

Mix the following materials (measured by volume) in the "dry" state:

1 part cement; 2 parts sand;
3 parts 6–12 mm (¼–½ in) gravel.

Add water gradually, while continuing to mix. To check the concrete for correct consistency, fill a bucket with the mixture, then invert it "sand pie" fashion. The resultant "mould" should slump a little, but not flow into a low mound. If it stays rigidly to the form, add a little more water to the mix.

3 Mark out the position and shape of each support pillar, then add 10 cm (4 in) all round for the size of the foundation trench.

4 Dig out the foundation trenches and fill them with concrete.

Table beds 2

Building the pillars

Begin with building the support pillars. If using bricks make the pillars two brick-widths wide and alternate the brick orientation with each course laid. If using stone or walling blocks aim for a similar pillar width and alternate the laying in the same way.

With a piece of chalk, mark out the outline of each pillar on its foundation concrete, double checking that the pillars are parallel to one another and at the correct distance apart to take the base slabs.

Using the marking out as a guide, lay down a 2 cm (¾ in) thickness of mortar within the pillar outline. (For mortar mixing see page 80.) Set the first course of bricks, stones or blocks on the mortar, tapping each one firmly with the shaft of a hammer to settle it in position. With a spirit level, check the course along its length and across its width, tapping again where necessary to make adjustments so the surface is level. Lay the second course in the same way, but with an altered orientation to stagger the joints. Repeat these two procedures, checking regularly with the spirit level, until the pillars attain the required height (see box). With the aid of a straightedge, make a final check for level over the tops of the pillars, placing the straightedge diagonally across the outer corners. Any small errors can be made good when laying the table slabs, but larger mistakes must be rectified before the mortar begins to set. Allow two to three days for the mortar to set before going on to the next stage of construction.

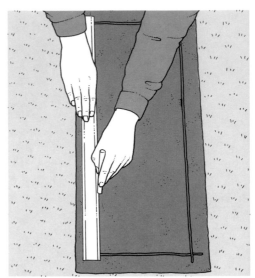

1 Mark out the pillar position on the foundation concrete.

PILLAR HEIGHT

Working to a finished bed surface height of 75 cm (30 in) and allowing 20 cm (8 in) for the depth of the bed, you need to include the thickness of the base slab to establish the required pillar height. For example, if the slab thickness is 5 cm (2 in), then subtracting (20 + 5) from the overall 75 gives a pillar of 50 cm (20 in).

Table slabs

It is essential that the base slabs are truly level when set in their final positions on the pillars. You will not be able to do this on your own, so do make sure that you have some help at hand.

Start with one of the central slabs and lay a 2.5 cm (1 in) thick bed of mortar over the tops of those pillars. Place the slab in position and tap it firmly along the edges in contact with the mortar, using a wooden mallet or the shaft end of a heavy hammer. Check the bedding down of the slab with a spirit level, adjusting with further taps on the high spots until the slab is level in all directions. Also, make sure that the slab is parallel to the support pillars and correctly positioned over them. Lay further slabs, working outwards from the first one, checking their level against it with a straightedge and aligning their edges to it.

Leave the completed slab assembly for a day or two to allow the mortar to set. Do not allow the long edges of the slabs to meet; leave a gap of 6mm (¼ in) to aid drainage.

Breeze blocks are useful for reducing the time and effort involved in building the support pillars since they are large and light in weight. Only a few are required for each support, and the mortaring is consequently much less. Because they are very porous (yet frost-proof), they absorb water from the mortar, so mix this to a thinner consistency than normal to compensate. One or two small trial mixes will make clear what is needed.

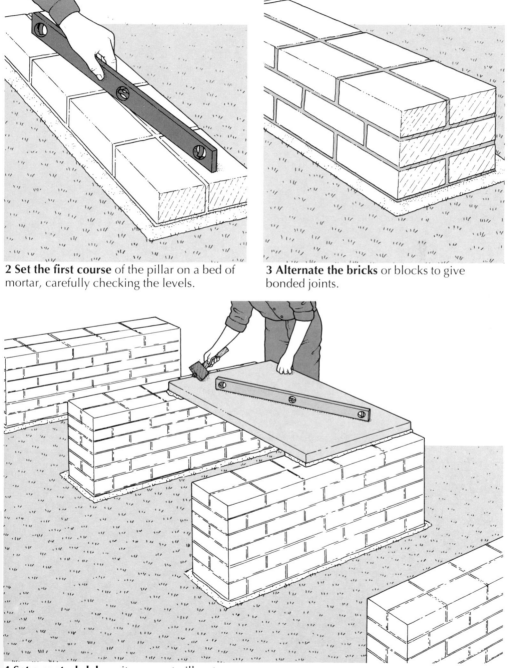

2 Set the first course of the pillar on a bed of mortar, carefully checking the levels.

3 Alternate the bricks or blocks to give bonded joints.

4 Set a central slab on its support pillars to begin the assembly of the table base.

Table beds 3

Edging the bed

The narrower types of walling blocks make strong and permanent edging for the table. Lay them, as for walling, to a height of 20 cm (8 in) round the sides of the table base slabs, making sure that the corners are bonded (see page 80). An alternative, which is quick to build but somewhat weaker than walling, is to use slabs of the type sold for edging paths and driveways. Set these on their edges in mortar, avoiding coincidence of the joints with those of the slabs.

For both walling and slab-type edging you must leave some vertical joints unmortared to provide drainage outlets for the bed. The slab type will need reinforcement in the form of rust-proof brackets and plates, secured with bolts through holes made with a masonry drill.

Drainage

Before filling the bed with soil mixture, cover the insides of drainage gaps with plastic mesh. Then lay gravel to a depth of 2.5 cm (1 in) over the base slabs. See page 84 for the mesh covering of outlets.

Filling and finishing

Soil mixture and filling methods follow closely those described for the raised bed and hollow walls (see pages 59 and 82). Surfacing is also similar, but take account of weights when planning surface features as everything must be

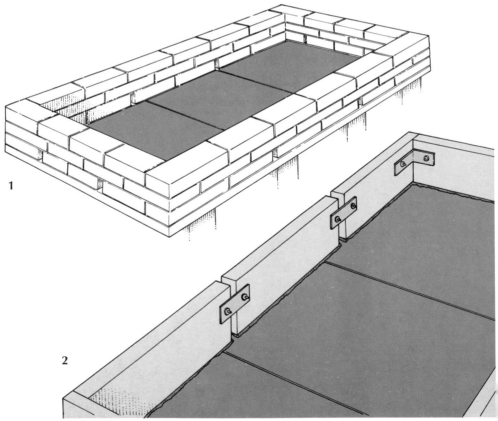

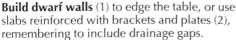

Build dwarf walls (1) to edge the table, or use slabs reinforced with brackets and plates (2), remembering to include drainage gaps.

lifted up onto the table top. For smooth and attractive access to the bed, with particular regard to disabled gardeners, a paved finish to the ground surrounding the bed provides an ideal surface and enhances the appearance of the completed work.

TIMBER VERSIONS

For table beds with a wooden base build the support pillars in just the same way. Then lay the base directly onto the pillars. You do not need any securement as the final weight of the bed will hold them in place. Make necessary adjustments to achieve the essential flat level of the base; use slim packing pieces of slate or tough plastic between the timber and the pillar tops.

The surest means of securing the timber edgings to the base is to drive large galvanized wood screws up through the base and into the underside of them. For an easier and quite effective alternative secure the edgings with strong, rust-proof angle brackets bolted to the timbers. In both cases the corners need strengthening with additional angle brackets.

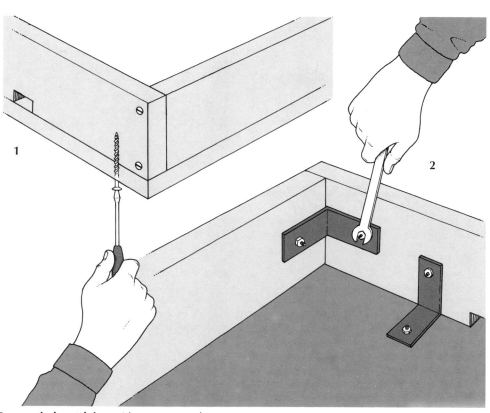

Secure timber edging with strong wood screws (1), or use bolted brackets (2).

Troughs

Hire a power drill and large bit to bore out a drainage hole.

Alternatively, drill a circle of smaller holes and punch out the centre.

Introduction

Troughs are available in a great range of shapes and sizes, made from a variety of materials. There is little doubt that the authentic stone trough is particularly well-suited for the rock garden, but it is becoming increasingly scarce, ranking almost as an antique and priced accordingly. Such is the demand for the "real thing", however, that a small industry has been re-born to produce genuiné stone troughs, which are made with modern, powered-cutting tools to minimize labour. These replicas are a little less costly than the originals, although still expensive, and just as heavy. Other replicas moulded from synthetic stone are quite realistic in appearance, especially after a year or two of weathering, and they are significantly cheaper. They are also a good deal lighter and consequently easier to transport and handle.

Make your own troughs

Making your own troughs using simple materials and techniques is quite an easy task, and the advantages are that you can choose their size and shape and produce them at a very low cost. Some types may be built in-situ, on the very

place that you intend them to stand. No special tools or skills are needed, nor is the work particularly strenuous.

Preparation for use

If you are lucky or determined enough to obtain the genuine article, then unless it is the shallow type, the forerunner of the kitchen sink, it may well have no hole in its base. An outlet is absolutely vital for the drainage of the trough and, if absent, one must be created. Other than for a really large trough, a single, central hole a minimum of 2 cm (¾ in) in diameter is sufficient, although the bigger you make the hole, the less likely it will be to block, but take care not to weaken the trough. 5 cm (2 in) is the upper limit for the diameter. Bearing in mind the value of the trough, it pays to hire a heavy duty power drill and a large masonry bit to bore the hole cleanly and safely. Failing this, drill a ring of small holes and punch out the centre with a slim chisel.

Repairs

In old troughs it is not uncommon to discover cracks which, from their aged appearance,

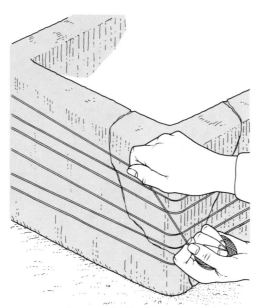

Use a weatherproof adhesive to repair fractured troughs, holding the joint together with tight cord binding during setting.

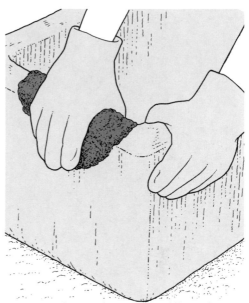

Restore a damaged area with a filling of hypertufa.

have been there for years. These are best left alone and the trough handled gently. If such cracks become fractures, it is possible to make repairs. First clean up the faces of the fracture with a wire brush and then scrub with hot water. After checking that all traces of mould and dirt have been removed leave the stone to dry out. Set the trough on a firm base, with its fracture rejoined, using bricks or cord binding to hold the parts together. Check that the fit is good, then dismantle and coat the fracture faces with a weatherpoof grade of PVA adhesive. Re-assemble, with the bricks or cord holding the joint firmly together, and follow the manufacturer's instructions for cleaning up and setting times.

Where a trough has lost a piece completely the damage can be made good by filling. Clean up the fracture faces as above and leave to dry, then coat them with PVA adhesive. When the latter has become tacky, usually after about 10 to 15 minutes, fill in the damage with hypertufa mixture (see page 32), using your hands to shape and smooth it into place. Always wear strong rubber gloves for this work as cement can cause skin problems. Cover the finished

repair with moist cloths to prevent premature drying and allow at least three days for satisfactory setting.

ADAPTING AND CONVERTING

Apart from troughs, there are other containers suitable for rock plants. Given a drainage hole, post stones (as once were used to hold the base of a gatepost or signpost) make very attractive small troughs, and quern stones, shaped like a conical Chinese hat, may be similarly modified. Pig troughs and domestic sinks made from earthenware and salt glazed to a chestnut brown can be used as they are, or improved with a stone-like coating of hypertufa (see page 108).

Ridge stones or tiles from the roofs of old buildings make attractive "V" or "U" shaped troughs when inverted. Cement a filling piece at each end, leaving a small gap for drainage, and set up the trough on supports. The type masoned from solid stone is the best.

Making troughs 1

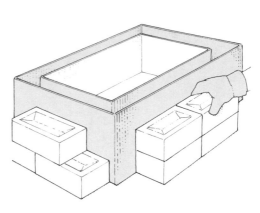

1 Find an inner box which will fit within the outer one, leaving a gap of 5–6 cm (2–2½ in) all round.

The casting method

This is a simple way of producing a stone-like trough of medium size using hypertufa to fill a mould made from cardboard boxes.

Making the mould

Having decided upon the size of trough you want to make, look for a strong cardboard box with the required length and width; its height is less important so long as it is at least equal to that of the trough – any surplus can be trimmed off. You then need a second which will fit inside the first, leaving an all-round gap of 5–6 cm (2–2½ in). The height of this smaller box should be 5 cm (2 in) less than that of the larger one. The only remaining items required for the mould are: enough dry sand to fill the smaller box and 12 to 15 house bricks.

Choose a shaded area with a firm, flat surface as the place to make the trough. The next step is to prepare the hypertufa mixture. To ascertain how much you need first fill the outer box with peat or peat substitute, to a depth of 5 cm (2 in). Sit the inner box on this peat base and use more to fill the gap between the sides of the boxes. Empty out the peat or peat substitute into a bucket. The number of bucketfuls produced by emptying is the *volume* of mixture required to make the trough.

To prepare the hypertufa, mix together the

2 Stack bricks against the ends and sides of the outer box to prevent excessive bulging after filling.

following materials in their "dry" state, measured by bulk and not weight. One part cement; two parts coarse sand; one and a half parts peat or peat substitute such as coconut coir, passed through a 6 mm (¼ in) sieve.

After the ingredients have been thoroughly blended make a low mound, with a crater in its middle. Half fill this crater with water, then continue the mixing, adding further water as necessary until the hypertufa has the character of stiff porridge.

Filling the mould

Stack bricks hard against the sides and ends of the outer box to prevent them from bulging excessively when filled. Lay a 5 cm (2 in) layer of mixture over the bottom of the box, consolidating it by tamping with a blunt-ended stick. Check the depth of this layer using a marked plant label like a dip-stick. Add more filling wherever needed to achieve an even thickness. Sit the inner box on this layer, making sure that the gap between the two boxes is equal all round. Fill the inner box with sand, taking care not to spill any into the gap. This sand filling is needed to prevent collapse of the inner box. Next, fill the gap with mixture a little at a time, tamping it down frequently as the level rises in order to eliminate air pockets.

Once completed, cover the mould with wet

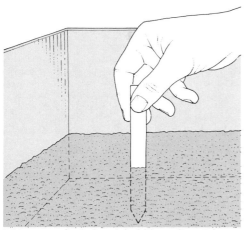

3 Use a marked plant label like a dip-stick to gauge the depth of the base filling.

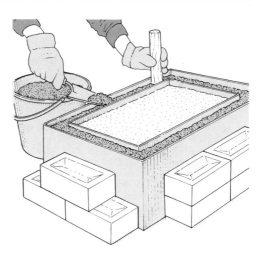

4 Fill the gap between the inner and outer boxes, tamping it down frequently.

hessian or swathe it in polythene sheeting to slow down the drying of the hypertufa.

Finishing

After about 36 hours, lift the covers from the mould and test the state of the hypertufa. If it can be carved by firm pressure from a knife blade or the end of a large screwdriver it is ready for the finishing process. If only gentle scraping is needed to remove material leave the mould for a further six to eight hours and then try again.

For the finishing work, take away the support bricks and peel off the soggy cardboard from the outside of the trough. Then carefully dig out the sand and remove the inner box. At this stage do not try to move the trough. Using an old table knife or wood chisel, round off all sharp edges and corners and scrape away any imprints left by the cardboard. Finish off with a stiff brush to remove loose material and minor blemishes. You will find that some sagging of the cardboard has given the trough a pleasing amount of irregularity to its shape, giving it the look of old, worn stone.

When you are satisfied with the finished appearance of the trough carry out the final task of cutting the drainage hole. Do this by using a knife or chisel as a boring tool, twisting it round like a screwdriver and applying pressure at the

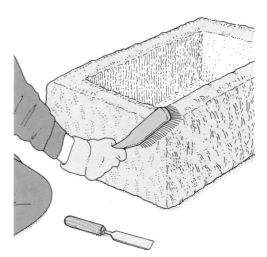

5 Eliminate blemishes and give the partially set trough soft contours using scraping tools and a hand brush.

same time until you have fully penetrated the base of the trough. Enlarge the hole by carving the sides as necessary, but do not waste time in trying to make it circular as the shape is not at all important.

Re-cover the trough with hessian or polythene for a further four days to set thoroughly, after which it can be put to use.

Making troughs 2

Ready-made moulds

Plastic bowls, whether circular, oval or rectangular, can be used as moulds for making moderately sized troughs from hypertufa.

Prepare the bowl by applying a coat of furniture polish over the whole of its outer surface. Lay a plastic sheet over a flat, even surface and invert the bowl onto it. Using the hypertufa mixture specified on page 104 and wearing strong rubber gloves, pack the mixture round the lower part of the bowl to a thickness of approximately 5 cm (2 in). Add further bands of the mixture, working upwards, and continue over the top to fully encase the bowl in an even thickness. You can then scoop out a drainage hole using a spoon and also do some modelling of the surface to imitate worked stone using other tools.

Cover the completed moulding with a plastic bin bag or sheet, then leave the work for four to five days to harden fully. After this stage, roll the moulding over to stand on its base and with-

1 Start the build-up of the hypertufa covering by packing a band of the mixture round the lower part of the bowl mould.

2 Add progressive layers until the entire bowl is evenly covered.

3 Scoop out a drainage hole with a spoon, then finish and clean up the surface using scrapers and a brush.

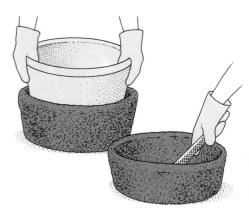

4 After the mould has fully set, prise up and withdraw the bowl. Use an old file to round off sharp edges.

draw the bowl. Use a screwdriver to make the initial leverage, then simply pull the bowl out. Finish the work by removing any sharp edges with an old file, taking particular care round the rim of the trough.

Building a trough

This is a method which allows you to assemble a trough from a collection of scrap pieces, using a single slab as a base. The latter can be a rectangular paving or a large flake of stone with an irregular outline. The walls of the trough are built up from small pieces of stone which can be obtained from rubble piles or construction waste heaps. Even broken roofing tiles will serve the purpose.

Set up the base slab in the place that the trough is to stand so you do not move it later. Sit the base on two stout walling blocks set firm and level on the ground. When in position, use slim packing pieces to correct any slope on the slab's surface, after checking with a spirit level. A level top to the slab is essential for good drainage in the completed trough.

To build the walls, estimate the amount of walling pieces required to produce a dwarf wall 15 cm (6 in) high all round the edge of the slab.

Remember that there will be a layer of mortar some 12 mm (½ in) thick between each layer of the walling pieces. To be sure of having sufficient pieces to select from during the wall building you should obtain roughly twice the amount of pieces estimated.

Using a mortar mixed from one part cement and three parts building sand lay the first course of the wall. At the mid-point along each side and end leave a gap of about 18 mm (¾ in) to provide drainage outlets. Following the laying methods described on page 80, add further courses until the wall is approximately 8 cm (3 in) high. Then stop work and allow the mortar to harden for at least 12 hours. After this period you can complete the wall building to the full height of 15–18 cm (6–7 in). Work carefully in the selection and laying of the final pieces. To give the top course added strength for resisting knocks and frost action coat the underside of each piece with waterproof PVA adhesive just before laying it in place. To ensure thorough setting and hardening of the mortar cover the finished trough with wet hessian or polythene sheeting, then leave it untouched for three days, after which it is ready for filling and planting.

Building the trough walls

1 Set the slab on two support blocks. Lay the first course of walling pieces leaving drainage gaps in the sides and ends.

2 Coat the base of each top course piece with adhesive before laying it in place.

Other containers

The popularity of troughs in the garden has given rise to some innovative uses of other similarly sized and shaped containers. Some are used just as they are, while others are formed with the container as a core.

Tubs

Simple rectangular wooden tubs are not difficult to make. Use rough-cut timber of about 2 cm (¾ in) thickness, and treat it with a preservative which is harmless to plants. Make the base first, then nail or screw the sides to it and use similar fastenings to fix the corners. Galvanized nails or woodscrews will last the life of the tub.

Coating a container

1 Prepare the container for coating by brushing on a suitable adhesive.

Pots and pans

A large, normally proportioned flowerpot is quite satisfactory as a home for a small collection of dwarf rock plants, but the less tall pan, or half-pot, has a more balanced appearance for its low-growing occupants. There are very few plastic versions of sufficient size, but plenty made from terracotta, or "clay" as it is often called. Be sure when selecting such a pan that it is specified as frost-proof, as it will need to withstand everything that the seasons bring. Terracotta is porous and the compost it contains loses moisture far more quickly than it does in plastics, so watering needs regular attention in dry weather. For adequate volume and growing space, choose a pan of not less than 30 cm (12 in) diameter, and preferably larger. Regard a pan depth of half the diameter as a minimum; do not use anything shallower.

Window boxes

The scale and behaviour of rock plants make them very good subjects for the confined space

2 Next cut a drainage hole in the base of the container.

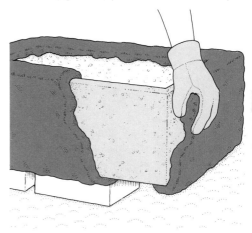

3 Stand the container on a plinth of bricks to apply the coating. Apply the coating by hand (wearing heavy-duty rubber gloves), taking it a little way under the base.

of a window box, yet few are to be seen planted in this way. Today's garden centres offer these containers in many patterns and materials, including plastics with simulated stone finishes, and often provide purpose-made mounting brackets to go with them.

Coated containers

Boxes and formed packaging made from expanded polystyrene (such as fish boxes) combine a good measure of rigidity with a wonderful lightness. These may be coated with a skin of hypertufa mixture (see pages 32–33) to create a very convincing stone-like container. To obtain the essential adhesion, brush on a thin coating of PVA adhesive (waterproof grade) over the container surfaces and allow this to dry until tacky. The hypertufa, which should be ready-mixed and waiting, is then smeared on and built up to a thickness of 1.5–2 cm (½–¾ in). Cover the finished work with polythene sheeting, and leave it in a shady place to set for three to four days.

It is impractical to attempt coating of all the surfaces at once, as the moving involved will damage coating already applied. To overcome this problem stand the container on a plinth of bricks for the coating process, and take the hypertufa a little way under the base. During this phase of the work you can incorporate the drainage hole by cutting a hole in the container base and bringing the coating up to it.

When the coating has hardened you can then invert the moulding and complete the covering. This will require a new batch of hypertufa mixture and an application of adhesive over the base and the edges of the previous coating.

Although the interior will be hidden when the container is filled and planted, it is a benefit to the overall strength, and the life of the coating, to take the hypertufa down the sides and over the bottom. Exactly the same technique is used to coat glazed sinks, toilet cisterns, animal feed troughs, or any other vessel provided that the material is rigid and stable (not prone to swelling when moist).

MAINTAINING HYPERTUFA

The hypertufa coating does not have an unlimited life; frost, hard knocks and general weathering will, after some years, cause flaking and fracturing. While localized damage of this kind can be repaired to some extent, it is more satisfactory to strip and re-coat, or in the case of polystyrene-cored mouldings, make a replacement.

¹ For the strongest result, coat the inside of the container, leaving the drainage hole clear.

5 When the coating has hardened, invert the moulding and coat the base. This completes the covering process.

Making a container garden

Miniature outcrops

Crevice making

Make a miniature outcrop with just a few well chosen stones.

In rock gardening the most popular use of troughs and containers is as objects to hold miniature landscape features, planted with carefully chosen dwarf, slow-growing species. And the choice is not limited to rock plants only – there are trees and shrubs of naturally dwarf form which can be included in the schemes. How these are set up depends to a large extent on each individual plant's habit of growth, and how this will affect the overall arrangement as the planting matures. The scheme may concentrate on a particular type of plant, such as crevice-dwellers, carpeters, or dwarf bulbs, or it may hold a mixture of types.

The miniature outcrop
In troughs up to a size of 60 cm (24 in) long by 45 cm (18 in) wide, just three or four fist-sized stones are sufficient to create a tiny outcrop. For such a small quantity you can afford to be very selective in obtaining some really attractive pieces. There is no need to put in supports; just set the stones in a natural array, bedding them slightly into the soil mixture with which the trough has been filled. For larger troughs you can increase the size and number of stones in the outcrop proportionally.

Set slabs of stone on edge to form a group of crevices.

Rock pools
On such a small scale, pools are invariably a failure; their water capacity is so small that a summer's day can dry them out, and they are quickly disfigured by debris and slime.

Crevice plantings
For a collection of crevice-dwelling plants, try the "edge-on" method, both to provide realistic rooting conditions, and to display the plants in natural settings. Use small slabs of stone with a thickness of 2–5 cm (¾–2 in), set as near vertical as possible in the trough filling. To be sufficiently firm the slabs should reach down to at least two-thirds of the trough's inside depth, and to achieve the required effect should stand proud of the trough's surface by up to 15 cm (6 in). Leave a gap of 1.5–2 cm (½–¾ in) between the faces of the slabs for packing and planting.

Carpet planting
Many mat-forming species of rock plant root down from their ground-hugging stems, and for these a quick-draining, but open, surface is needed. Stone chippings or gravel, in the size

Woodland plantings

Add a piece of driftwood or some mossy stones to embellish a planting of ericaceous or woodland species.

Small schemes

A single stone is often sufficient for a very small scheme, such as one created in a pan.

range 3–4 mm (⅛-⅙ in), covering the surface of the trough to a depth of 2.5–3.5 cm (1–1¼ in), will provide the "ground condition" required. To add interest, set a few pieces of attractively shaped stone in the gravel, around which the plants can spread.

Soft surfacing

Wooden tubs and other containers, including troughs, intended for woodland or ericaceous plantings, benefit in both appearance and growing conditions if they are surfaced with a complementary material such as bark chips or leaf litter. Crumbled leaves and stems of bracken also produce the desired effect. To introduce height and character you can add pieces of driftwood or mossy stones.

Small troughs, pans and window boxes

The approach for the small trough or clay pan and for most window boxes is more or less the same as already described, but in dealing with these small areas there is a danger of spoiling the effect by overdoing things. Often a single stone

is adequate to set the scene for a miniature rock garden and plants must be selected with great care if they are not to outgrow their place in a short time. It is possible to create midget gardens, but it must be done with an acceptance that in three, or at most, four years they will be overgrown and ready for replacement.

OVERLOADING

There is a considerable range of sizes for window boxes, the larger of which need extra attention. The weight of a miniature rock garden set up in a long window box may exceed its load-bearing capability, and the consequence can be dangerous sagging or splitting of its fabric, or at worst, total collapse. If your window box is a commercial product try to obtain the maker's recommendations on this aspect, otherwise fix a few extra brackets to be on the safe side.

111

Setting up troughs

Most of the troughs seen in rock gardens are raised above the ground level on short pillars or plinths. This elevation has little functional benefit, but does help to draw attention to the trough as a garden feature, and also brings its small occupants nearer to the eye. But getting the trough onto its supports requires methodical and careful handling, otherwise trapped fingers and worse injuries are a very real danger.

The jacking method
This method can be applied to most troughs, but is perhaps particularly applicable to the larger, heavier ones which defy manual lifting. It is both unwise and hazardous to attempt this work single-handedly: you need an assistant, although not necessarily one with exceptional strength. The only tool involved is a crowbar or ,failing that, a stout fence post with a pointed end, for use as a lever.

With the trough in the position that it is to occupy permanently, place nearby the pieces with which the supports will be built. These can be stone slabs or other walling material. Using a wooden block or brick as a fulcrum, push the tip of the lever under one end of the trough and raise this sufficiently to allow one of the support pieces to be pushed beneath it. The placing of the support piece is done by the assistant, who – to avoid accident or injury – should never allow his or her hands to go beneath the tilted trough, but instead use a wooden pusher before the hands get too close.

When the first support piece has been positioned, ease the trough down onto it. The same operation is then carried out at the other end of the trough. Further pieces are added in the same manner. Work alternately in this way, end to end, until the supports have reached the desired height.

1 Obtain assistance for the placing of the support pieces when you lever the trough upwards using a fulcrum.

The tipping method

For reasons of safe working it is better to limit the use of this method to small and medium-sized troughs. It requires the use of a strong, low, hand trolley.

Start by building the support to the full height, using a little mortaring if necessary to gain strength and rigidity. Place the trough on the bed of the trolley, resting on one of its long sides, then wheel the trolley alongside the support, as close as possible, and with the cavity of the trough facing away from the support. With an assistant leaning on the outside edge of the trolley, to provide a counterbalance, carefully tip the trough over until it rests upon the support. Having made sure that the trough has fully transferred its weight to the support, remove the trolley, and then make any necessary positional adjustments.

FINAL CHECKS

When the trough is firmly seated on its support there may be a need for some minor adjustments regarding drainage. Test for these by pouring a little water into the trough. If a puddle remains on the base after the bulk of water has escaped through the drainage hole, make adjustments to improve drainage with slim packings of slate or plantpot shards, between the underside of the trough and the support top.

Another impediment to drainage can be the positioning of a support under the outlet hole, so it is advisable to check for this if the outflow is sluggish.

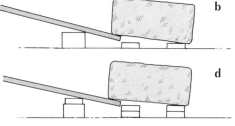
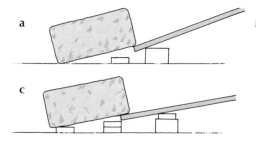

2 (a–d) Build up the supports, levering the trough up at alternate ends.

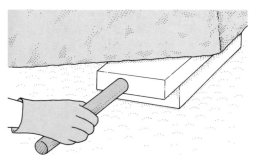

3 Keep hands clear of the raised trough, and use a wooden pusher for the final moves.

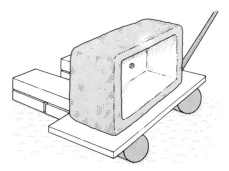

Position the trough alongside the finished support, using a trolley.

Paths

Today there are numerous types of path-making materials in use, but for the rock garden most of them are unsuitable, being too colourful, too formal, and even too neat. In this section, therefore, attention will be focused on materials and constructions which blend with and enhance the rock garden.

Paved paths
Crazy paving, if composed of natural stone, associates well with rockwork, especially if matching in colour and texture. Like other forms of paving it requires a firm, well-drained foundation if it is to remain in good condition for many years.

Working to the full width of the planned path, mark out its route over the site. Normally the surface of the finished path is level with the ground on which the path is laid and requires a foundation beneath it at least 10 cm (4 in) deep. Allowing 5 cm (2 in) for the paving thickness, dig out the pathway to a depth of 15 cm (6 in), leaving a clean finish to the work. If the excavation shows a tendency to hold water you should arrange for this to drain away by providing a trench or soakaway (see page 20).

Cover the surface of the excavation with a 10 cm- (4 in-) thick layer of hardcore, consisting of small rubble or coarse gravel, and consolidate this filling by tamping it down with a baulk of timber. On top of the hardcore spread coarse sand to produce a smooth, even bed over the whole of the pathway. Lay the paving directly onto the sand, scraping away or adding a little sand to compensate for any thickness variations. Stand on each piece of paving, after it has been laid, to check for wobble, correcting any revealed by packing with sand. Do not make the gaps between the paving pieces too narrow, or you will have difficulties later on inserting the grouting; aim for a minimum gap of about 1.5 cm (½ in).

When all the paving has been laid the gaps must be filled with a grout of mortar, made from four parts sand to one part cement. Use a small (pointing) trowel to work the grout into the gaps, and to smooth it off flush with the paving. Start at one end of the path and work backwards, kneeling on a broad board to prevent any dislodging of the paving pieces. Try to prevent use of the finished path for three days, to allow full hardening of the mortar grouting.

1 After putting down the hardcore, consolidate it by tamping.

4 Lay paving stones for a slab path edge to edge, on a shallow bed of coarse sand.

Slab paths
No form of path is more in keeping with rockwork than one built from matching rough-hewn stone slabs. These should be of a length roughly equal to the required width of the path, and laid edge to edge like closely set stepping stones. Little preparation is necessary, as the self-weight of the slabs holds them in place, and in most cases they need only be laid on a token bed of sand, for minor adjustments to be made.

2 Lay paving onto a bed of coarse sand spread over the hardcore.

3 Fill the gaps between the paving with a mortar grout.

5 Finish off by filling the gaps in slab paths with an appropriate gravel.

6 Set bars into gravel or bark surfaced paths on slopes to prevent downhill "creep".

To complete the work brush a suitable gravel, similar in colour to the slabs, into the gaps between them. Use a gravel size of no more than 0.5 cm (¼ in).

Gravel paths

Gravel provides a first-class seed bed for a host of weeds, and suffers disturbance every time it is walked upon, becoming rutted and heaped in a short time. Weeding and raking are regular chores. Prepare the path as for paving, surfacing it with a layer of gravel 5 cm (2 in) deep. The stability of the gravel can be improved by selecting one which is angular in form.

"Soft" paths

In areas with woodland and/or ericaceous plantings, the forest bark products offer path surfacing materials which harmonize extremely well with their surroundings.

Steps

1 Cut steps into the earth of the slope, reducing their height to allow for filling and paving.

2 Build the riser wall of the first step on a light foundation of gravel or coarse sand.

3 Lay the paving (or slab) onto a mortar bed spread over the surface of the tread.

Like paths, steps may be built in many styles and materials, but to maintain the concentration on types best suited to the rock garden, the following are confined to forms which can be combined with the specific path types covered in the previous section.

Paved steps

These can be used in conjunction with any of the path forms described earlier. You have the choice of making paved steps, or building with single slabs. The construction is virtually the same for both types.

Begin by cutting the steps into the earth of the slope, but with their top surfaces (treads) some 10 cm (4 in) lower than the required finished level.

Prepare a light foundation at the base of the first step by digging out a trench 15 cm (6 in) wide by 8 cm (3 in) deep and filling it with compacted gravel or coarse sand. On this foundation build a dwarf wall across the full width of the step. The height of the wall should be 15 cm (6 in), less the thickness of the paving that will cover the tread, and its top must be level. Bring the tread surface level with the wall top by filling with gravel or sand, then spread a layer of mortar over the wall top and tread filling, to form the bedding for the tread paving.

The paving may consist of several pieces or a single slab. In either case lay it in place, tapping it with the shaft of a hammer to settle it into the bedding mortar. Leave this first step to set before proceeding further. The second and subsequent steps are built in the same manner,

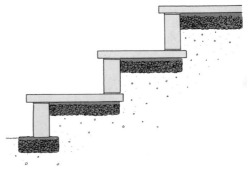

4 Section through a flight of paved steps.

but with the riser wall resting on the paving of the previous step. It is customary for the paving to overhang the riser wall by approximately 2–3 cm (1 in), in order to improve the finished appearance of the steps.

Block steps
For small access paths running through the rock garden it is possible to use blocks of stone to form steps. Start with the bottom step, cutting a snug slot in the earth to hold it. Lay the next block immediately behind the first, adjusting the depth of the slot to give a rise of 15 cm (6 in). Further blocks are laid in the same way to complete the flight.

Timber steps
For the "soft" pathways, and in woodland or ericaceous plantings, steps formed with whole logs (complete with bark) have an appropriately rustic appearance and are comparatively easy to build. Dig out a ramp in the slope that the steps are to climb and lay the logs across it, fixing them in place with preservative-treated hardwood stakes. The stakes are driven into the earth, hard against the front of the log. Fill and level-off the slope between the logs with gravel or coarse sand, tamped down, and finish the surface with a covering of chipped bark.

Steps for gravel paths
Steps surfaced in gravel should be avoided; the gravel shifts underfoot, to create a hazard, and is soon scattered away from where it should be.

Paved steps associate very well with gravel pathways, especially if an effort is made to match its colour with that of the paving.

GENERAL CONSIDERATIONS
The "traffic" in a private garden is nothing like as heavy and frequent as that in public places, hence steps need not be so sturdily constructed. The gardener is concerned mainly with appearance and a quality in the work done that is adequate for what will be relatively light usage.

For all steps there are what might be termed "standard dimensions", making them comfortable and safe to use. The accepted height for a step is 15 cm (6 in) and the tread (distance from front to back) of the step is, ideally, not less than 30 cm (12 in). This limits the incline to one in two, but on steeper slopes it may be necessary to reduce the tread to 22 cm (9 in). Anything steeper than this produces rather precarious steps and should be avoided by taking the flight diagonally across the slope.

A step which is different in height from the others is a potential cause of accidents, so in planning a flight of steps make sure that the overall height can be evenly divided into 15 cm (6 in) levels, if necessary modifying the excavation to achieve this.

5 Use substantial blocks of stone to build steps in rock garden access paths.

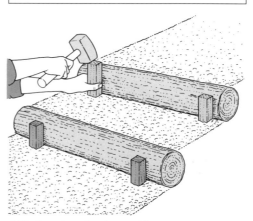

6 Fix log steps in place with preservative-treated stakes, driven into the ground.

Bridges

In the rock garden, bridges are more often used to carry a pathway across a gully or gap than to span a watercourse. In the same way, ornate or severely functional designs are equally out of place among rockwork and so the aim is to produce a structure which will be in harmony and at ease with its surroundings. The forms now to be described are quite different in character, but both of them will enhance the garden landscape.

Building a clapper bridge

1 Build support piers for the clapper bridge using the walling technique (see pages 96–101). The end supports are recessed into the earth.

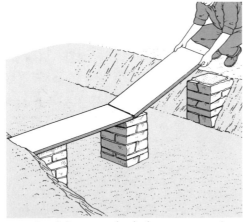

2 Lay the slabs onto a bed of mortar spread over the top of each support pier.

The clapper bridge

This is a bridge in its simplest form, comprising slabs supported on piers. Spans of up to 1 m (3 ft 3 in) are usually made with a single slab, but for greater reaches two or more are laid end to end, with their junctions sharing the support piers. The slabs used must be sound and at least 6 cm (2½ in) thick to have adequate strength, and should be at least 60 cm (2 ft) wide for safe walking.

The supporting piers are built from walling material in the form of rectangular pillars. To provide necessary stability and strength they need to be fully mortared and supported on a firm foundation. Dig out the foundations to a depth of at least 20 cm (8 in), and more if need be, to reach solid, undisturbed earth. The dimensions of the excavation should be approximately 20 per cent larger than those of the pier. Fill the hole made with a concrete mixture and leave this to set for three or four days. Note that the surface of the concrete filling should be just below the surrounding ground level, so that it will be hidden when the work is completed.

Build the piers, using the walling technique (see page 80), to the required height of the bridge, less the thickness of the slabs that they will support. The width of the pier is a little less than that of the slab. Allow three full days for the finished piers to attain full strength, then spread a layer of mortar over the top of each one and lay the slabs in place. All that remains to complete the bridge is to clean off any surplus mortar pushed out by the slabs.

The packhorse bridge

This arched bridge form presents a greater challenge to the garden builder but is not as difficult to construct as it looks.

Start by digging out the locations for the end supports, which are the abutments, and need to be set into recesses. Make these recesses large enough to permit the work of building the abutments. At the base of each recess a foundation is needed, which is formed in the same way as that for the clapper bridge. When the abutments are finished, and the mortar has completely hardened, pack rubble tightly between the rear face of the abutment and the recess, and then fill in the remaining space with consolidated earth.

Building a packhorse bridge

1 Build the abutments for the packhorse bridge in recesses cut into the sides of the gap to be spanned. Note the seating shape for the end of the arch.

2 Fix the timber formers in place and roof them with lengths of board or similar material, nailed in position. This completes the support.

To build the arch you must first cut out a hardboard template to the desired curve for the underside of the arch, checking its size and fit against the abutments. Use the template to mark out the arch on two pieces of plywood or blockboard, which need to be at least 1.5 cm (½ in) thick; these are the formers upon which the arch will be built. Fix some timber strengthening legs to the formers with stout nails, then set them in position. To complete the support, roof it over with lengths of scrap floorboarding, or similar timber, nailed to the formers.

Using walling slabs set on edge, begin the arch building from one of the supports, mortaring between each adjoining piece as you progress, until you reach the middle of the span. Then build from the opposite end to complete the arch. After leaving the work for a week, to strengthen fully, dismantle the timber support, and tidy up the mortaring on the underside of the arch. Do not be too ambitious with your first arch building project; a span of no more than 1 m (3 ft 3 in) is sufficient to test your skill.

3 Use walling stones set on edge to construct the arch, mortaring between them.

119

Alpine house rock gardens

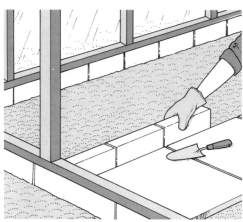

1 Edge the access path with a low wall to contain the rock garden.

2 Introduce low-level ventilators where possible.

Not all alpine houses hold a collection of pot-grown plants; some are used to contain small rock gardens, giving the plants (and their owners) year-round protection from the elements. These rock gardens are built either at floor-level or on raised staging. In terms of cost and ease of construction, the floor-level type has the advantage, but all the work and attention involve squatting or kneeling, whereas the raised version offers much more comfort for the grower, but requires a special structure which costs more to build.

The floor-level approach

In the conventional layout the floor of the alpine house is bisected by a central pathway, giving equal growing areas on either side, but for a rock garden the layout can be quite different. You may choose to have the path along one side of the house, or have it wandering through the rock garden. Having decided on the layout, your priority is then the laying down of a path to establish access for the work to follow. Path types and their construction have already been covered (see pages 114–115, and apply here, with the exception of the gravel-finished forms, which are uncomfortable and unstable to work from and difficult to keep clean and tidy later.

Although it is feasible to build the rock garden at soil level, you will find it more satisfactory to raise it a little above the path by building a low edging wall (see page 100). This

helps to contain the garden and improves the drainage. With the path and edgings completed, you then need to prepare the soil by forking it over, repeatedly, to a depth of 15–20cm (6–8 in), until it is finely broken up. If the soil is light and sandy, spread a 7.5 cm (3 in) layer of peat substitute, such as composted bark, garden compost or spent hops over the whole surface and incorporate it by further forking. Heavy soils require a similar volume of coarse grit or 3 mm ($\frac{1}{8}$ in) gravel, worked in in the same way. At this stage the soil level will have risen appreciably, but this will be reduced when you firm-in by leaning your weight on your clenched fists, working over the whole of the soil area.

The benefit of the edging wall then becomes apparent, as it should allow extra soil mixture to be laid down, bringing the surface almost level with the top of the wall. For this additional soil mixture use a blend of equal quantities of 3 mm ($\frac{1}{8}$ in) gravel or grit and good quality garden topsoil. This extra filling should then be pressed down firmly, in the same manner as the soil.

Before laying down the top-dressing, create any desired landscaping by adding rockwork. The top-dressing should then bring the finished surface to a level slightly higher than the edging wall. You can, of course, slope the bed by building a taller wall or raised rock work at the back of the bed, but do not make the slope too steep for stability.

3 Finish the bed with top-dressing to just above the wall top.

4 Make the raised bed "landscape" with a minimum of heavy rocks to keep down the weight – or use tufa as an alternative.

LIGHT AND AIR

Only alpine houses glazed to the base are suitable for floor-level rock gardens; solid walls or brick or timber exclude too much light and the plants will suffer accordingly. If possible, install opening lights or louvres in the bottom glazing to improve the ventilation at low level.

The raised bed approach

The structure required for the elevated rock garden is essentially the same as that of a raised plunge bed (see page 150), and so confines the layout to a long rectangle. The principal difference from the plunge bed is that the box-like containment is filled with a soil mixture (not sand) and because the volume is relatively small it is worthwhile using John Innes Potting Compost No. 2 for the filling, to benefit from its being free from pests and weeds. To give the bed filling its necessary open and free-draining structure, mix the John Innes Potting Compost No. 2 with half its bulk of coarse grit or 3 mm (⅛ in) gravel.

Take care not to overload the structure of the bed by using too many heavy rocks in the mini-landscape. In this respect tufa or homemade hypertufa as described earlier (see page 32) is an excellent material for rockwork, as it is very light for its mass, and because of the protection

SOIL PROBLEMS

The soil on the floor of an alpine house is quite likely to be in a poor state, particularly if the house has been in use for some time. It may have lain beneath paving or gravel, or been used for growing other plants and it probably contains pests, weeds and sources of disease. You can either dig out the existing soil, to a spade's depth, and replace it with good quality topsoil, or restore it to an acceptable condition.

There are proprietary disinfectants for riding soil of pests and diseases. The structures can be improved by adding organic material and grit, and the fertility may be increased with the use of suitable fertilisers (see page 162).

Nearby shrubs and trees may infiltrate their roots into the soil under the alpine house, in which case you should remove the soil to a spade's depth, cut away all roots discovered and line the excavation with one of the porous membrane materials marketed for such purposes. The soil can then be returned and will be armoured against further intrusions.

provided by the alpine house it does not suffer weather damage or overgrowth by moss caused by overwetting.

Cliffs under glass

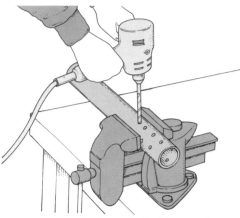

1 Drill holes in the lower half of the supply pipe.

2 Insert supply pipes into the filling mixture.

Alternatively, embed the "seep" hose in the filling. Rout it serpent fashion behind the cliff.

An artificial cliff face, sheltered from the weather, allows the rock gardener to grow choice crevice-dwelling species which would fail if exposed to outdoor conditions. These highly adapted plants resent frequent and prolonged wettings at any time and particularly while they are in the winter dormant state. Protection of a cliff also counters the erosion of soil (and plants) from crevices, which is a major problem on outdoor constructions.

The two vital requirements for a cliff, in any of its variations, are absolute stability and a fully effective watering system. There must be no danger of its component rocks becoming loose and unsafe and water must be supplied evenly throughout the inaccessible root runs without wetting the plants.

Construction

Currently, the most favoured and reliable method is to build the cliff against a strong wall, which may already exist or be built for the purpose. The cliff is broadest at its base and inclined towards the wall – this is achieved by constructing it in a series of step-like terraces, very steeply. A cliff higher than 2 m (6 ft 6 in) can cause serious problems in construction and upkeep, so be conservative when planning it. Its length, however, may be anything you choose, within the bounds of effort, space available and cost.

Use the largest of the rocks for the bottom of the cliff and progressively smaller pieces as the height increases. The root runs for the cliff plants have to be incorporated during building, using a fairly rich soil mixture, such as John Innes Potting Compost No. 2 lightened with one third grit, or good quality sieved soil, peat substitute and grit, in equal proportions. Pack this mixture firmly behind and between the rocks as they are set in place. Most of this filling material should go into the cavity between the back of the cliff and the wall. This space needs to be, on average, 30 cm (12 in) wide behind the bottom layer of rocks, narrowing to 20 cm (8 in) at the top of the cliff.

The watering system

This is installed during construction, in the form of either several "top-up" supply points, or a hidden feeder hose.

For the supply points use plastic drainpipe

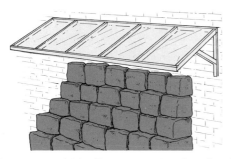

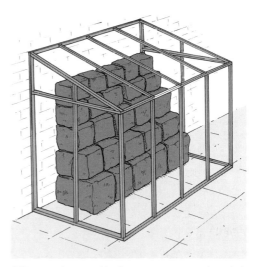

about 5 cm (2 in) in diameter, cut into lengths of 30 cm (12 in) and perforated over half that length with 12–15 holes, made with a 0.5 cm (¼ in) drill bit: they need not be spaced too accurately. Seal the perforated end of the pipe with a plastic or cork bung. As cliff building progresses beyond the lowest layer of the rocks, insert the pipes into the filling mixture wherever the rockwork permits and at spacings of, very roughly, 75 cm (2 ft 6 in), so that the final cliff face is evenly served with supply points. Leave the top of each pipe standing just clear of the

Section through a typical cliff construction.

filling surface and hide its presence with a "lid" made from a small piece of matching rock.

The alternative watering system makes use of the "seep" hoses marketed for the steady, gentle supply of moisture to borders or beds. Embed the hose in the filling mixture behind the cliff, routing it serpent fashion from end to end, with a vertical spacing of 60 cm (24 in) or there-abouts. Block the tail end of the hose to prevent escape of water and adapt the other end for connecting to a supply tap.

A season of tests, with a moisture meter equipped with a long probe, will provide a guide for how often the supply points need topping up, or how long to run the hose tap.

A tufa cliff
The lightness of tufa and its remarkable ability to sustain plants rooting directly into it make it uniquely suitable for cliff building. Construction is carried out in more or less the same way as for the rock-built cliff, but you can improve the fit between adjoining pieces by shaping the tufa with an old wood saw and an axe, to produce a cliff face free from gaps and holes and with improved stability (see page 67).

The cavity between the cliff and the supporting wall needs only coarse sand as a filling, as the tufa will provide sufficient nutrients to the plants. To be confident of a satisfactory water distribution use the hose system described above, in preference to the supply points system, which works less well in tufa constructions.

123

Beds under glass

a

b

1 Fix the uprights in place by either **(a)** digging a hole 45 cm (18 in) deep to take the bottom of the post; fill with concrete, using temporary supports made from scrap wood to hold the post steady while the concrete sets, or **(b)** using metal post holders.

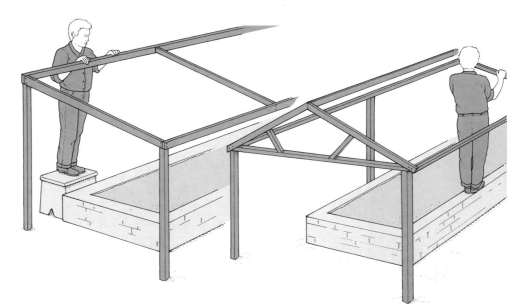

2 Make the roof flat and slightly sloped, or with an apex ridge.

This form of protection might be loosely described as a glasshouse with open sides and ends which, while giving cover from the rain, allows the maximum possible circulation of air to the growing area beneath it. It is indeed possible to convert an ordinary greenhouse in this way, but you should be aware that the structure is not designed to resist the abnormal wind loadings to which it will be subjected in this state – so it is best to consider it only for very sheltered locations.

There are no commercial products available for the purpose, so the structure must be designed and built around the bed that it is to protect. Make the bed to a simple rectangular shape, or the structure will be too complex, and work to a maximum bed width of 1.5 m (5 ft) to keep the span of the roof within practical limits.

Construction

It is usual for the roof to overhang the bed by a significant amount to minimize blown-in rain and also to give some protection to the gardener. Use strong timbers, treated against rot. The posts produced for wood panel fencing are ideal for the uprights.

Position the corner uprights 60 cm (24 in) out from the edge of the bed and the intermediates in line with them at spacings of not more than 2 m (6 ft 6 in). The uprights can be concreted into 45 cm (18 in) deep holes, or fixed by the specially designed metal post holders available from fencing specialists. Check them with a plumb line or builder's level.

The roof structure may be flat and inclined (like that of a bus shelter) or have an apex with a central ridge. The building of the roof requires a measure of skill in carpentry and if you are at all doubtful of your ability in this respect you should employ a professional for the work.

Some gardeners prefer to remove the roof glazing for the summer months, and consequently require it to be easily removed and installed. To this end the glazing is made up of self-contained units, very like traditional Dutch lights: a capping piece on the roof ridge secures one end of the light and the other is held down by a hasp and staple. The same arrangement can be utilized to hold shading units. All fittings, such as the hasp and staple, must be strong and rust-proof if they are to be long-lasting and reliable.

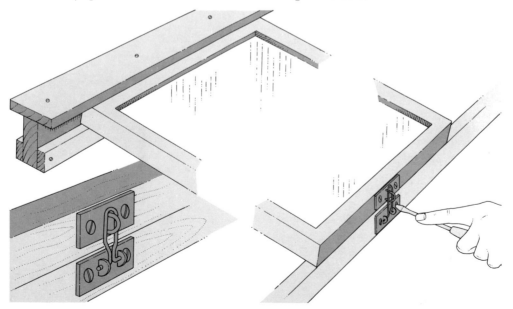

3 Cap the ridge to form a slot to hold the upper end of the glazing unit and fit a hasp and staple to the lower end. This enables glazing panels to be removed in summer.

Bulbs under glass

Constructing a bulb bed

1 Lay wire netting over the base of the bed, then cover this with a layer of gravel.

2 After spreading compost over the gravel, fill up the bed with a prepared soil mixture.

Many of the bulb-forming plants live in regions with a hot and arid summer and so have evolved to be active in the cooler months, when there are plentiful supplies of moisture, and to lie dormant during the months of drought. To grow these species successfully you need to simulate the natural conditions by cultivating them in houses and frames to provide the rain-free months to which they are accustomed. A further function of the glass cover is to shield the blooms from damage by the weather, which can be violent in the early and late seasons when so many bulbs are in flower. The natural bulbs lie far deeper, in many cases, than a plantpot will allow and so respond better to a specially prepared bed of generous depth.

The bulb bed
The construction of a bulb bed is the same for whatever type of protection is used. Start at ground level, by clearing the area of perennial weeds and making its surface level, then build a walled containment, as you would for a raised bed (see page 76). The walling material can be concrete blocks, frost-proof bricks (concrete commons), breeze blocks, or even railway sleepers. Make the wall 45–60 cm (18–24 in) high and if the bed is to be topped by a glass enclosure

make sure that the dimensions match up.

Mice and moles can be very determined pests in a bulb bed, so in order to thwart their underground entry, lay wire netting of the size used for rabbit hutches over the entire base of the bed. To fill the bed, first put down a 10 cm (4 in) deep covering of 0.5 cm (¼ in) gravel, then lay over this a similar depth of good-quality garden compost or spent mushroom compost, mixed with about one third of its bulk of coarse sand. Complete the filling with a soil mixture made up of: one part clean loam or sterilised soil, one part leafmould, peat or peat substitute, and two parts grit. If the latter is non-limy, add a half part of crushed limestone to the mixture. After treading this filling down it should be some 5 cm (2 in) below the top of the bed walling. Leave this as it is until after planting, when it should be topped off with grit or 3 mm (⅛ in) gravel.

Protection
If the bed is built within a greenhouse there is nothing further required, but if it is to be a bulb frame, then the next phase is the erection of the glazed enclosure.

In general, bulbs need plenty of light, so the sides of the enclosure, as well as its roof, need

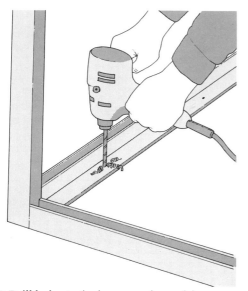

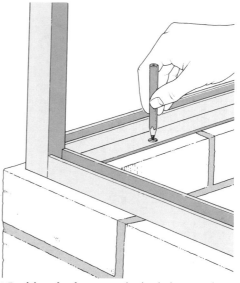

3 Drill holes in the base members of the frame, to take the anchoring screws.

4 Position the frame on the bed, then mark the screw hole locations.

to be transparent. While a normal glass-walled cold frame might be adequate you will be able to provide better ventilation and attend to the plants with greater ease if the structure has sides which can be opened. There are frames with this facility on the market, fitted with sliding glass panels, and a typical example is the "Access" frame which looks like a squat, miniature greenhouse. You can, of course, build your own from treated timber or aluminium. Whatever type is used, it must be very firmly anchored down to the bed and a reliable means of achieving this is with screws and plugs. Use rust-proof woodscrews, size 10 or 12, and the appropriately sized plastic plugs. Drill holes in the base members of the frame, to take the screws, and space these at 30–45 cm (12–18 in) apart. Set the frame temporarily in its exact position on the bed and mark the hole positions on the wall top. Remove the frame and, using a masonry bit to match the plug size, drill the wall top to take the plugs. After inserting the latter, replace the frame and drive in the screws. If the walls are of timber then it is only necessary to drill pilot holes for the screws, as plugging is not required.

Should the holes for the anchoring screws be in the channel along which the glass panels

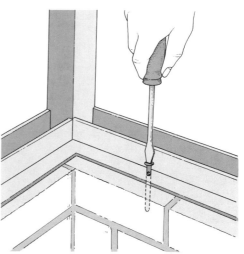

6 Drive screws into the plugged holes in the bed wall.

slide, use countersunk-headed screws, and countersink the holes accordingly to produce a flush seating for the screw head.

To complete the work, fit and secure the glazing in the frame, checking that the sliding panels are free to move and that the grooves in which they slide are thoroughly clean.

127

Management

All the moisture requirements of plants grown permanently under glass must be supplied by the grower. For the indoor cliff, hand watering with a can is impractical, hence the need for built-in watering systems, as described on page 122. Floor or bench-level rock gardens, however, can be hand watered, provided that this is done with care, but it necessitates frequent attention from the grower, especially during warm dry weather. If unavoidable absences, or other commitments, rule this out, then any device that will automate the supply of water in a controlled manner deserves consideration.

Watering by hand
The watering cans sold for general gardening use fall short of what is needed, being too short in the spout, and delivering a harsh, widely spread shower of droplets. The "Haws" pattern is much to be preferred, as it is easier to handle and control by virtue of its longer spout and the selection of end fittings. The latter give a gentler delivery with a limited spread, and the long-reach spout allows comfortable, two-handed watering right to the back of the bed. These refinements put the water where it is required without unwanted wetting of adjacent plants or washing away of the top-dressing.

Watering methods

Automated watering systems
The simplest of these relies solely on gravity for its operation. A header tank feeds a network of thin flexible pipes fitted with adjustable nozzles at their ends, which deliver the water in regular drips to gently soak the soil. The pipework is unsightly, but can be hidden to a large extent by burying it slightly beneath the top-dressing. Trials are needed, with various positions and settings of the nozzles, to achieve the desired amount and uniformity of moistness in the bed. It is possible to extend the automation of the system by adding a domestic cistern ball cock to top up the header tank. Direct connection of the pipework to a mains supply must incorporate a pressure-reducing valve, otherwise the system may be unsafe and work poorly.

If an electrical supply is available in the glasshouse, you can install more sophisticated drip-feed systems, fed by mains water through a fail-safe, electrically controlled valve. Kits of various size are commercially available for the DIY building of such systems, including computerized versions.

Overhead watering systems employ an array of sprinkler or mist-producing heads, which can be turned on and off manually, or by electrically controlled valves. They have the

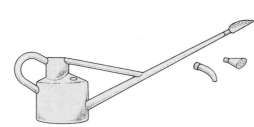

The "Haws" pattern of watering can, with long-reach spout and well-designed handles, is easy to use and control.

Try various positions and settings for the drip feed nozzles, in order to achieve a satisfactory spread of moisture in the bed.

disadvantage, however, of wetting everything beneath them and for many choice alpine plants this is detrimental, as it not only drenches them at regular intervals, but maintains an unwanted humidity within the house which is congenial to plant-attacking pests and fungi.

Shading

The air within the confines of an alpine house can be at a considerably higher temperature than that outside, particularly during sunny weather, subjecting the plants to harmful levels of heat. Generous ventilation will combat the effect, but it can become necessary to add shading at times. The painting of the glass with a semi-opaque colour wash is far too inflexible, as it remains in place when the weather turns dull, leaving the plants starved of light. Fine plastic netting stretched over light, portable frames allows you to put on shading as and when it is needed, by clipping the frames to the roof of the house. Roller blinds made from wooden slats are expensive, but give a high degree of control, and can stay in place throughout the hot months, lowered or raised as required. They are fixed to the roof ridge and rolled downwards or upwards to regulate the amount of shade cast within the house. They

do, however, inhibit the use of opening lights in the roof, whereas the netting frames can be shaped to leave these clear.

Fans greatly improve the atmospheric conditions within the house, expelling overheated air in warm weather and producing a beneficial circulation during dank, stagnant periods. When using fans for cooling, arrange them to draw in air from the outside and expel it through open doors and windows. When it is foggy or heavily humid, close up the house and let the fan circulate the interior air as there is no point in drawing in further moisture-laden air.

ELECTRICAL SUPPLIES

Fans, lighting and many automated watering devices require electrical power and in glasshouses these installations must conform to appropriate safety and operational standards, which are more demanding than those for domestic use. Make the relevant enquiries before undertaking such work, and if you are at all doubtful have the work done by a qualified electrician.

Shading

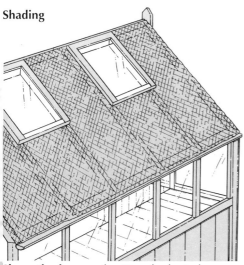

Shape the frames of netting shades to leave opening lights clear.

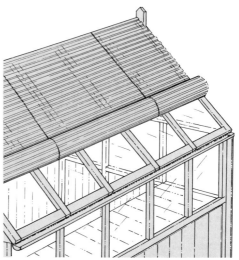

Slatted roller blinds are fixed to the house ridge and controlled by cords.

Planting 1

The transfer from nursery pot to rock garden is a shock to the plant and the operation needs to be carried out with care to minimize the distress caused. Also, as the plant is likely to remain in its allotted place for a number of years, it should be prepared and positioned with due regard to its long-term wants. Weather conditions at the time of planting can also help or hinder the plant's recovery and future progress.

The right place

If you find after planting that the spot chosen is unsuitable you put further stress on the plant by repositioning it, and if the error only becomes apparent after some time, you may be unable to dig up the plant for transfer without causing fatal damage. Give careful thought to the position that appears to be right and look for snags; there may be underlying rockwork that will be a barrier to root growth, or a nearby vigorous species that could over-grow its neighbours after a year or two. Mistakes often occur near pathways when the initially tiny plant is placed

at what seems to be an adequate distance from the edge but subsequently grows up to become an obstacle, hindering use of the path and suffering injury by doing so. By asking the supplier of the plant, or using reference books, you should be able to get an idea of its rate of growth and adult size. This foreknowledge is even more important for the planting out of a newly prepared area, when you are trying to envisage the result in a few years' time. For such plantings it helps to set out the plants, still in their pots, standing them in their intended places and considering how they will behave as they mature. By this means it is easy to swap plants around until a satisfactory layout is produced, without any harm to them.

The right time

As autumn approaches, rock plants slow down their activities, ceasing to produce new shoots and leaves, diverting their remaining energies to the ripening of seed and preparations for the winter rest. In this state they can do little to establish themselves in a new

Removing the nursery pot

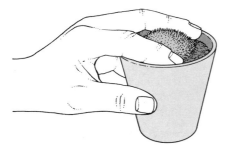

Spread the index and second fingers of your left hand to lie either side of the plant and across the top of the pot.

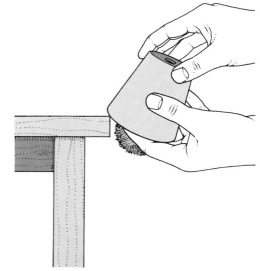

Holding the base of the pot in your right hand, invert the pot and tap its rim firmly on the edge of a bench, or similiar ledge. You should then be able to slide off the pot, leaving the root ball of the plant held safely in your cupped left hand. Left-handed gardeners should reverse the holdings given above.

home, as their root-making ability is at its lowest ebb. Also, as a consequence of reduced energies, their resistance to disease and recovery from injury are diminished. A further discouragement in these seasons is the cold, wet state of the ground, which defies satisfactory planting, and when frozen can heave an unestablished plant out of the soil in which it has been planted. In the cold dark months newly acquired plants are safer if kept in their pots in a sheltered part of the garden, or better still in a well-ventilated frame.

By mid-spring most of the plants are revitalized and busy forming flowers and new foliage, and by late spring their roots are on the move. This is the time when their urge to survive is strongest, helping them to recover from a change of place and to literally put down new roots. Of further benefit is the return to longer days and sunshine, and the recovery of soil from its wet state. This combination of plant vigour and encouraging conditions makes spring the best of the seasons for planting.

In summer the soil is warm and easily worked, which is kind to young roots. Also the plants are still eager to make growth above and below ground. The only hazard to planting at this time of year is the occurrence of a hot, dry spell soon after the work has been done. Diligent attention to watering and shading is then essential to reduce the stress caused by the parching conditions, and must be sustained until cooler, moister weather takes over. In prolonged drought, and even with the best attention, newly introduced plants may do little other than stay alive, making no progress until the climate brings relief.

The right method

Before a plant can be transferred to its permanent place in the rock garden it has to be removed from the pot, and unless done competently, this operation may cause damage. The method described here applies to all types of nursery pot, whether clay, plastic, round or square. First make sure that the root ball is thoroughly moist, but not soggy, then proceed as shown on pages 132–3.

TEASING OUT THE ROOTS

It is not uncommon to find an almost solid mass of root at the base of the root ball, in which case some teasing out is needed to liberate some of the larger roots. Do this with the tapered end of a plant label, or the point of a pencil, to disentangle without severing.

You will find it difficult to extricate roots in this way if the plant has been reared in a peat-based compost. If this is so, loosen the root ball by squeezing it between finger and thumb, then free as much of the root system as you can without breaking the strands. This requires patience, but does help the plant to adapt to a different type of soil mixture. Alternatively you can wash away much of the unsatisfactory compost by immersing the root ball in a bowl of water and gently loosening it away with your fingers. After removing as much as you can, lay the plant out on a pad of absorbent tissue to take away the excess water, following which it can be planted out or potted.

Planting 2

Planting beds

In a bed filled with a general rock plant soil mixture the initial step in planting is to scrape aside the top-dressing to clear a space sufficient for the digging of the planting hole. Use a garden trowel to dig out a hole which will comfortably accept the root ball of the plant, checking this by using the plant still in its pot. Make the depth of the hole equal to the height of the pot and save the excavated soil in a container. Having released the plant from its pot and teased out the roots, place it centrally in the hole and fill in with the saved soil, gently firming the filling with your thumbs. Take care not to push the plant lower into the hole during this operation; the neck of the plant should remain just above the finished soil level. Complete the work by returning the top-dressing, working it with your fingers to push it up to the neck of the plant, then smoothing outwards to blend with the general covering. Finally, insert the label and give a generous watering.

Planting troughs and containers

In troughs and containers the scale is smaller and the plants more closely spaced, which calls for more precision in planting. Each plant must be kept close to the desired position and guarded against damage while its neighbours are inserted. Begin by removing and putting to one side the top 7.5 cm (3 in) of the soil mixture

with which the trough has been filled, then mark each plant's position by inserting its label. Working on only one plant at a time, spread its loosened roots evenly, then cover them with soil mixture, firming with your fingers, until the root system is held in a cone-shaped heap, with its neck at the same level as the top of the trough. A straight stick laid across the trough will help you to check the plant's position. Work on the remaining plants, one by one, in the same way. Return the rest of the soil mixture to fill the hollows and top off with gravel. Label and water.

Planting cliffs

Cliff plants have to be persuaded into nooks and crannies, requiring their roots to be teased into these places, consequently the plant's soil ball must be completely broken down, even at the expense of some root loss. The result should be a loose tassel of root, which can be teased into cavities and crevices. Slim tools are needed for the work; a small fern trowel being ideal, but old kitchen spoons will serve. Having dug the soil filling from the planting place, lay the plant, with roots extended, on a slim trowel, or a piece of folded card, and insert them into the hole prepared. When the head of the plant is against the rockwork, slowly and carefully refill the hole with soil, pushing and firming it in gently with a blunt-ended stick. Use a hand spray to wet the finished planting.

Scrape out a wide crater in the scree and spread the plant's roots out over the bottom. Use a trowel or your gloved hand.

Holding the plant in position, push back the excavated material, being very careful not to injure the roots.

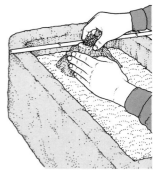

For trough planting, build up a cone of soil mixture over the roots, keeping the plant at the correct height with the aid of a stick.

Planting walls

It has already been recommended, in an earlier section, that wall planting is best carried out during construction. The planting is done in stages as the wall increases in height. When the soil filling has been packed behind a finished course of walling, plants can be introduced. First spread a 1.5 cm (½ in) layer of soil over the top surface of the stone(s) on which the plant will rest and add three or four pebbles, about 1 cm (⅜ in) diameter, to prevent squashing by the next course of walling. Prepare the plant as for the cliff planting described above, but lay its roots out over the stone and the soil packing behind it, then cover the roots with a thin layer of soil and moisten this with a hand spray. The next course of walling should then be laid immediately, to both secure the plant and prevent the roots from drying out. Exactly the same method applies to further plantings as the wall rises.

Planting in tufa

When a plant has grown to a size sufficient for sale, it is too big for planting in tufa. The technique requires small plants with root systems capable of being inserted into holes drilled in the tufa, which may be no more than 1.5 cm (½ in) in diameter. Seedlings with one season's growth, or rooted cuttings, are in the right order of size. Using an old woodworking auger or bit, drill the tufa to a depth of at least the length of the plant's roots and use the

blade of a screwdriver to remove the dust created. To insert the plant, wrap its roots in a fragment of moist tissue, then, holding the head of the plant, push it gently into the hole. Maintaining your hold on the plant, spoon sharp sand into the hole, pushing and tamping it down with a blunt-ended twig. To complete the operation, thoroughly wet the sand and surrounding tufa with a hand spray.

> ### PLANTING IN SCREE
>
> Scree beds demand a different technique, as a conventionally dug planting hole merely fills up again with shuttering stones. Using a trowel, scrape out a crater far larger than the pot's diameter, until it has the required depth, heaping the excavated material round the rim. Take the plant from its pot and remove as much as possible of the compost from the root ball, so that the roots can be spread over the bottom of the crater. Holding the plant in position with one hand, carefully push back the heaped material until the crater is filled. Throughout the operation you must maintain the plant at the right level, so that it sits snugly on the surface of the scree when the crater filling is complete. Label and water as before.

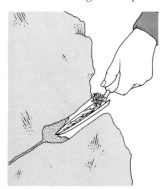

Use a narrow-bladed trowel, or a folded length of stout card, to insert roots into a cliff crevice or a hole bored into tufa.

In wall planting, spread the roots fanwise over the stone and the soil filling behind it. Note the pebbles for keeping the joint open.

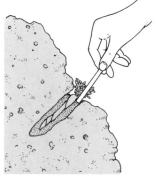

In tufa planting, tamp dry, sharp sand into the hole to firm-in the tissue-wrapped roots, adding sand a little at a time.

Buying plants

Many garden centres hold respectable stocks of "alpines", which in most cases are supplied to them by specialist wholesale growers working on a mass-production basis. Their range of types and species is, however, often somewhat limited. For variety and rarer species you will need to study the plant lists of nurseries specializing in rock garden plants, with the assistance of that invaluable guide, *The RHS Plant Finder*, which is updated every year. A few of the specialist nurseries still offer a mail-order service and most can be relied upon to provide good-quality plants, carefully packed, but if you can visit the nursery to see the plants before purchase, so much the better.

PROTECT WILD BULBS

Some bulbs and tubers are dug up in huge numbers from their natural habitats and exported for sale in gardening outlets. Such is the extent of this trade that several species are already threatened with extinction in the wild. Measures are being taken to halt this decimation and you can help by buying only those which bear a valid declaration that they do not originate from a wild source.

Looking for trouble

In choosing an individual plant from a sales display of dozens, or even hundreds, there are a few basic checks which will help you to select a good specimen. Look first for healthy growth, rejecting anything with yellowed or damaged leaves and weak, drawn shoots. Reject also those pots with moss, liverwort or other weeds overgrowing the top-dressing, and any which, when lifted, reveal tassels of root protruding through their drainage holes. These symptoms suggest that the plant is root bound, starved and possibly a left-over from old stock. If you are seeking scree or crevice plants, avoid if at all possible those grown in peat-based compost, as they will be difficult to transfer and adapt to the lean soil mixture you have prepared for them. Good specialist nurseries raise these plants in gritty, soil-based compost, thus producing the root system required. Make a close inspection for pests and diseases; white fluffy accumulations round the neck of the plant, or at the drainage holes, usually signal the presence of root aphids, and if the leaves seem limp despite the compost in the pot being moist, then suspect vine weevil larvae attack, or that watering has been missed earlier, leaving the plant permanently injured or dying. If the plants on display are standing in puddles or flooded trays, or if they are *inside* the garden shop or store, pass them by and go elsewhere to purchase.

Finding the right plant

Even in the best of nurseries and garden centres, labels can be lost, wrongly replaced, or illegible. If you think you have found the plant you want, but are not quite sure, seek advice. In all too many garden centres the sales staff may be unable to help, but at specialist nurseries you can expect to receive not only expert attention, but instruction on how the plant should be grown and cared for.

Certain rarities are often in short supply and are consequently not listed in the catalogues. It is well worthwhile telephoning nurseries which have either offered the plant in past years, or may hold a very small stock.

Good signs – healthy growth, clean surface on the pot, few roots emerging from drainage holes, good clear label.

Some species are notoriously variable in the quality and colour of their flowers. If you are seeking a particular clone or cultivar of such plants, then if at all possible try to see it in flower before you buy it. The same applies to certain hybrids.

When to buy

Being perennial, and of small stature, rock plants are usually raised and sold in pots and so can be bought at any time of year. A good proportion, however, are herbaceous, dying down in autumn and leaving little to indicate that the pot contains a living plant. Although some bulbs are also grown in this way, the majority are marketed in the dry, dormant state; the spring flowerers available in early autumn, and the late-year flowerers in spring and early summer.

It is wise to buy herbaceous rock plants when they are in growth, otherwise you might be unfortunate enough to obtain something which is dead, dying or diseased. The condition of evergreen plants can be judged reasonably well even in winter. In the case of pot-grown bulbs it is prudent to delay buying

Bad signs – stunted or weak growth, mosses and liverworts invading pot, excessive root emergence, faded or illegible label.

TRAVEL SICKNESS

Having bought your plants, treat them carefully for their journey back to your garden. The rear shelf of a car on a hot sunny day can broil a box of young plants, with terminal results; they are safer in the luggage space, even though it is dark and stuffy. If you make your purchase during a holiday do not leave the plants permanently in the back of the car, or in an hotel room. Take them out for a spell in the light and the fresh air as often and for as long as possible, not forgetting to give them water if need be.

until they are coming into flower, thus avoiding the disappointment of finding that they are too young to flower, or are of poor quality. A similar caution has already been recommended for particular named varieties, cultivars and hybrids of rock plants.

Buying in advance

Provided that you have somewhere to keep them, you can obtain plants before you have planting places prepared for them, retaining them in their nursery pots for a time, but they do need care and attention during the waiting period. Nursery pots can dry out surprisingly quickly and it is important to check on their watering regularly and to protect them from extremes of weather. If the young plants are kept in the pots too long they may become root bound, weakened and prey to disease. In spring and summer the delay in planting should not exceed six weeks, however, plants bought in autumn may be kept until the following spring, as their activity is very low during that period.

The bigger the better?

In garden centre stocks of rock plants, you frequently find a section containing much bigger specimens of certain species, usually in 15cm (6in) pots. These might give your planting a flying start, but only to a limited extent. Younger, smaller plants are easier to handle, and more likely to succeed where there are screes and crevices to fill, particularly where it is necessary to remove nursery compost.

Planting schemes 1

Unlike the traditional herbaceous border or annual bedding, the rock garden is not a place to be crowded with bloom. The carefully composed rock and stone features provide architectural forms, softened by the plants growing in and around them, but at the same time they display the plants to the best effect. This is true for an outcrop, a scree, a raised bed and even a trough. Again using the comparison with a border or bedding array, the rock garden does not lend itself to being divided up into compartments, each holding a designated plant, but there are guidelines and suggestions helpful to producing well balanced and interesting plantings. These are presented by looking at the various forms of rock plant and how they can be used.

Mat-forming plants

Mat-formers have a threefold value for planting schemes, being attractive for most of the year, useful as ground cover and acting as a background for other plants. There are quite a few rock plants with the natural habit of creeping over the ground and forming a dense mat of foliage, and many of them are transformed at flowering time into a carpet of colour. Some are vigorous and capable of covering an area the size of a dinner plate in a single season, and some take years to achieve that size. There is plenty of choice for various situations, with sun-loving types for dry, open places, easy-going species that will accept a range of conditions and those which prefer cool, moist environments. So dense is the blanket of stems and foliage produced by certain mat-formers that even invasive weeds are repelled, yet there are others sufficiently loose to allow underplanting with bulbs, whose flowers are then enhanced by the backcloth that the mat creates.

When selecting mat-forming plants check their rooting habits. There are those which need to root down from their creeping stems and so need to sit on a surface that will allow their roots to penetrate. Others rely on a central rootstock and will happily spread over bare rock.

Spot plants

These are plants with a vertical growing habit and are useful for relieving the flatness of a bed, especially if it is furnished mainly with low-growing species. One or two of the genuinely

dwarf conifers have the desired form, but for seasonal variation there are plants, such as irises, which put up blade-like foliage and some that flower in spikes or plumes, like the dwarf astilbes, all of which provide a vertical accent.

Domes and tuffets

The cushion plants are a speciality of the rock garden, with their unique, humped shapes, from tiny buns suited to nooks and crannies, such as thrifts, to large mounded tuffets like mossy saxifrages for the bed or scree. Being almost invariably evergreen they are an asset to the planting scheme, both in and out of flower – in fact some are grown principally for the shape and beauty of their foliage.

Wanderers

For the stonier soil mixtures and the scree there are plants which move from place to place, creeping along just below the surface and putting up growth and flowers here and there. They pose no threat to other plants with which they mingle as they never stay long enough in one place to be competitive. Some campanulas have this delightful habit, disappearing completely in winter and popping up unexpectedly during late spring and summer. More permanent are the crevice-hugging plants, which become a living "cement" between blocks of stone, following crevices and fractures in the rock.

Cascades and curtains

Aubrieta must be the best known of all rock garden plants – it spills out from walls and tumbles over rockwork, smothered in bloom during late spring. It serves well as an example for the character of those plants which give the cascade or curtain effect when grown in the right place, which is a raised perch that allows them to hang over the rockwork instead of straggling unhappily over flat ground.

Crevice plants

Another speciality of the rock garden, these plants have evolved to live in rock fissures and in many cases cannot be persuaded to live anywhere else, other than perhaps in scree. Their places need careful preparation, but once established the plants usually live for many years and, as most are almost as attractive out of flower as when in full bloom, they make their contribution to the display in all seasons.

Dwarf trees and shrubs

There are many imposters under this heading which when freed from the confines of the nursery pot will quickly exceed the size and vigour anticipated, but there are a few truly dwarf species and cultivars which can be used to great effect in planting schemes. The pygmy conifers offer a variety of shapes, from almost spherical to columnar, together with a fasci-nating variety in pattern and colour of foliage. In the slow-growing shrubs there are evergreen and deciduous types, with a bonus of flowers and decorative fruits for some.

Grouping

Small, slow-growing plants are seen as isolated specimens in the rock garden, lost among their lustier neighbours. A more natural and mature effect is created by planting them in groups of three, or even five. It does not matter if they eventually join up to form a single mass.

SAMPLE PLANTING SCHEME

Variety in plant form and habit enriches the planting scheme, making shapes and con-trasts just as important as textures and colours. The illustration is not a plan for planting, but an example of how the various types discussed can be brought together in a pleasing and interesting way.

137

Planting schemes 2

Planting for all seasons

Rock gardens are sometimes criticized for being "all over by summer", meaning that the flowering is concentrated in a period of about eight weeks spanning early to late spring, after which there is scant colour for the remainder of the year. Spring is certainly the time of peak blooming in the rock garden, but by making a planned selection of plants you can maintain a good follow-on of colour right through summer and well into autumn. The following are some suggestions for achieving a succession of interest.

A glance at the selection of plants on pages 178–187 will show you how, by taking into account the time of flowering, as well as other features, you can put together a collection which will give your rock garden colour for most of the year. To help you in this, here are some brief notes and examples.

Late winter – early spring

Some of the earliest to flower are the bulbs, particularly dwarf irises, such as *Iris reticulata, I. histrioides* and their hybrids, together with several species of *Crocus*. In a mild winter these can be expected to begin flowering before January has ended. Also reliable for bloom in this period are *Cyclamen coum*, which come in a range of pinks and carmines, and the tiny *C. intaminatum*, with its papery, white flowers. Another group of plants to begin flowering, if the winter is not too severe, are the Kabschia saxifrages, especially certain hybrids, such as 'Galaxie', 'Gem' and 'Karel Capek'.

Bear in mind that at this time of year conditions vary from winter to winter, and from region to region; consequently the flowering times given can only be approximate.

Spring

In these months there is an abundance of flower from a host of rock plants; too many to warrant specific mention. Also a wealth of bulbs come into bloom, including the deservedly popular dwarf daffodils and tulips.

Early summer

The "silver" or "encrusted" saxifrages, such as *S. callosa, S. cochlearis* and *S.* 'Tumbling Waters' and many others, are at the height of their flowering period at this time, accompanied by campanulas, potentillas, hardy geraniums

---

PLANNING A PLANTING SCHEME

Your aim in preparing a planting scheme is to even out the succession of flowers, so that at no time is the colour occurring in just one or two patches, but is present generally throughout the rock garden. This is by no means easy to accomplish, for while you might select three or four plants which follow on from one to the other, based on their flowering times, they may not all be happy with the conditions in the place for which they are intended. One may require light shade, another needs full sun, and a third could hate lime when the others want it. The selection thus becomes a matter of patiently noting the basic growing conditions required by each plant considered and matching these before separating into flowering groups. Even then you must still be alert to other pitfalls, avoiding colour clashes, or the mixing of slow- and fast-growing species. Let the preparation of your planting scheme be a leisurely fireside occupation for the winter, and enjoy it, with plenty of reference books to hand.

---

and the numerous "pinks" of the *Dianthus* genus. In bloom too are the *Edraianthus* (closely related to the campanulas), the choicest of which are *E. serpyllifolius* and *E. pumilio*, with their crowded blue bell-flowers.

Late summer

The earlier weeks of this period bring about a marked decline in flower, but the small poppies, like *Papaver rhaeticum*, will still contribute spots of colour to the scree or raised bed, and the penstemons show their value as flowers of high summer. Of the bulbous plants, *Merendera*, which is very closely related to the colchicums, puts up its bright, ground-level blooms before the leaves have even started to appear. Of similar behaviour is *Cyclamen hederifolium*. This plant first raises its pink or white flowers and only when these are fully developed does it proceed to spread out a carpet of beautifully patterned leaves which will last until spring.

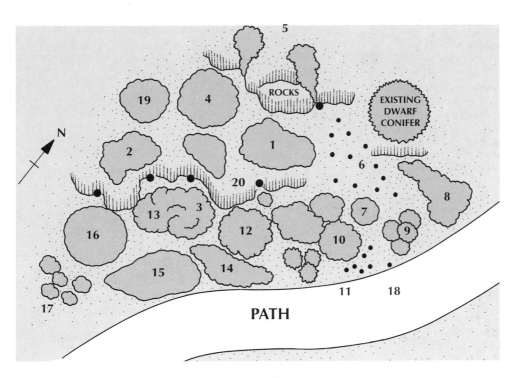

Autumn

As the season progresses the autumn gentians will take up the floral display with their blue trumpets and may be accompanied by the naked blooms of colchicums and autumn crocus species such as *Crocus goulimii* and *C. banaticus*. Such is the diversity of the late-flowering bulbs and tubers that it is possible to extend the blooming of the rock garden, at a modest level, right up to the onset of winter.

Sample planting guide

Prepare a rough scale plan of the area to be planted, including any major features such as rockwork, pathways and any plants already in place. Then mark in the positions and types of plants you want to have in the scheme. Use the marked-up plan as a guide for the selection of suitable species. If you already have firm ideas on the specific plants you would like to grow, the plan can be just as useful. List your choices and try them in various placings and relationships. Cut-out paper shapes labelled with the plant names will allow you to change plants around quickly.

Key

1 Mat-former with silver foliage.
2 Carpeter with plenty of flower.
3 Crevice plant.
4 Tuffet with plenty of flower.
5 Cascade plants, for sunny crevices.
6 Collection of spring and autumn-flowering bulbs.
7 Spot plant.
8 Low-growing, flowering shrub.
9 Group of cushion plants.
10 Mat-formers with successive flowering.
11 Group of summer flowerers.
12 Bushy, flowering shrub.
13 Mixed, low-growing alpines.
14 Dense mat with winter colour
15 Mat with bulbs under.
16 Domed, dwarf conifer.
17 Mixed alpines.
18 Autumn bulbs/tubers.
19 Dwarf deciduous tree.
20 Crevice plant for semi-shade.

Plants from seed

By comparison with other groups of garden plants, the raising of rock plants from seed is a relatively simple process, requiring little in the way of equipment or special skills.

Sources for seed

Major seed merchants have only a limited range of rock plant seed, but there are one or two specialist companies who do have a comprehensive "alpines" list. Organisations such as the Alpine Garden Society and the Scottish Rock Garden Club, offer their members excellent seed exchange arrangements wholly devoted to rock garden species. And, of course, you can collect from the plants in your own or friends' gardens, as many cultivated plants set good quality seed.

Seed composts

The make-up and condition of a seed compost are primary factors in the germination of seed and the healthy development of the resultant seedlings. Like all soil mixtures for rock plants the seed compost must have an open, free-draining structure, but needs also to contain adequate nutrient and moisture levels to sustain the infant plant. In addition, and very importantly, the compost must be free from harmful organisms, such as fungal spores, weed seeds and pests. To be certain that these enemies are absent the organic content of the compost has to be sterilized. The simplest solution to this is to use a good quality John Innes seed compost (already sterile) and to mix this with clean,

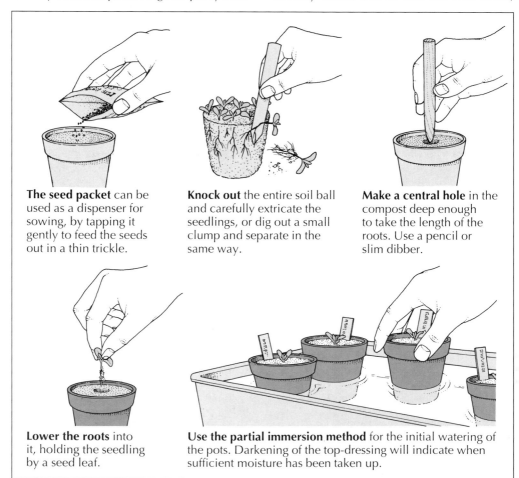

The seed packet can be used as a dispenser for sowing, by tapping it gently to feed the seeds out in a thin trickle.

Knock out the entire soil ball and carefully extricate the seedlings, or dig out a small clump and separate in the same way.

Make a central hole in the compost deep enough to take the length of the roots. Use a pencil or slim dibber.

Lower the roots into it, holding the seedling by a seed leaf.

Use the partial immersion method for the initial watering of the pots. Darkening of the top-dressing will indicate when sufficient moisture has been taken up.

washed grit, in the proportions two parts compost to one part grit.

Preparing for sowing

As you will probably want no more than a dozen seedlings to grow on, from each batch sowed, the container used need only be small. A 6 cm (2½ in) round, or square, plastic pot is ample in size. To aid the faultless drainage needed, cover the bottom of each seed pot with a shallow layer of 0.5 cm (¼ in) clean gravel, before filling it with the compost. Firm the latter with your finger-tips and give it a finishing settlement by tapping the base of the pot on a firm surface, to leave the compost about 1.5 cm (½ in) lower than the pot rim.

Sowing

In general, the seeds of rock plants are small, ranging from the size of a pinhead to almost dust, and require the right technique for sowing. With a steady hand and a little practice you can use the seed packet as the dispenser, squeezing it open by pressing its side edges and tapping out the seeds in a gentle dribble, moving this from side to side for even distribution over the compost. A modification to the method, which requires less skill and precision, is to put a half-teaspoonful of absolutely dry sand into the seed packet, hold the packet closed and shake it for a second or two, then spread the sand/seed mixture over the compost. The light colour of the sand makes it easy to see the coverage. All that remains is to put in a label and add a 0.5 cm (¼ in) of 3 mm (⅛ in) gravel top-dressing to the pot, and to water it by standing it in a tray or dish containing *clean* water 2.5 cm (1 in) deep.

Aftercare

The great majority of rock plants are fully hardy and there is no need to cosset the seed sowings; it is sufficient to stand the seed pots on a firm, clean surface in a sheltered spot in the garden, where they will benefit from regular wettings by the rain. Frost is not only harmless to the seed, but for some species promotes germination. When the first signs of growth appear make regular inspections for pests such as slugs and aphids, and treat them promptly if evident, or suspected. The pots of germinated seed can be left in place until the seedlings are ready to be pricked out for transfer to individual pots, but be sure that they never dry out by frequently checking their watering needs.

Potting up the seedlings

When the seedlings are showing the development of true leaves they are ready for transfer to individual pots. There are two methods of extracting these infants. The first, which causes least stress and damage, is to knock out the entire soil ball (see page 130) and to carefully separate out the seedlings one by one using the point of a plant label or a pencil. The second is to dig a small clump of seedlings out of the pot and then to single them out as above. Prior to carrying out the extraction the nursery pots should be ready-prepared and close at hand. Use the same size of pot as for seed sowing and fill them with the seed compost, or John Innes Potting Compost No. 1 mixed with an equal quantity of grit. While this compost is suitable for a wide range of rock plants, it is rather too gritty for ericaceous subjects and woodlanders. These will fare better in a mixture of two parts John Innes Potting Compost No. 1, and one part peat or peat substitute. To transfer a seedling, make a hole in the centre of the compost, using a pencil or small dibber, then, holding the seedling by its seed leaf (which is below the true leaves), lower its roots into the hole. Firm-in by gently pushing back the compost and then tapping the pot on its base. Finish off with a top-dressing of 3 mm (⅛ in) gravel and water as described for the seed pot.

Hardening off

To help the seedlings recover from their transfer keep them away from direct sunlight, but not in heavy shade, for a week. After this period they can be hardened off by gradually increasing exposure over a further week in a frame or plunge bed (see page 153).

Bulbs from seed

Bulb seeds require a variation of the procedure described. Instead of pricking them out as infants, you should leave them in the seed pot for the first year after germination, moving them on in the following year. This means that the spring-flowering types will be transplanted in autumn of the following year, and autumn flowerers in the spring of the year after.

Plants from cuttings

Not all rock plants can be propagated from cuttings, but a very large proportion will respond to this method. Although the commercial treatment of cuttings can involve fairly elaborate equipment, it is possible to achieve very satisfactory results with uncomplicated devices and procedures.

Taking cuttings
A very sharp knife, or scalpel, is an essential tool for the operation. Ideal are the smaller craft knives with replaceable blades, or those which extend in a series of snap-off segments. Small scissors and tweezers are also indispensable.

Success with a cutting is influenced by the time of year when it is taken, and a good rule-of-thumb for the optimum time is to wait until the plant has finished flowering, allow another two weeks, then take the cuttings. For dwarf trees and shrubs the timing is different, as generally it is half-ripened shoots that are required and these are usually ready in early to mid-summer.

The types of cutting fall into, more or less, three categories. The first of these comprises single rosettes or tufts from plants with dense, mounded growth, such as the cushion-forming saxifrages, drabas and some *Dianthus*. In the second category are shoots from the less congested types, with branched growth, such as the helianthemums, dwarf shrubs and many of the mat-forming species. In the third group are shoots from plants which send up growth from a crown or rhizome. Many primulas, gentians and geraniums belong to this final category.

Cushion plants

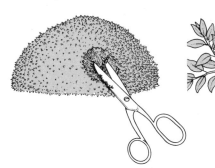

1 Take cuttings of basal shoots from cushion plants.

Branch cuttings

1 Use a sharp knife to take branch cuttings.

Crown cuttings

1 Choose outer shoots when taking crown cuttings.

2 Trim off lower leaves and excess stem.

2 Sever branch cuttings just below leaf joint.

2 Remove dead and damaged outer leaves.

Cutting rosettes or tufts

When taking rosettes or tufts from the cushion types, work around the base of the plant, selecting those shoots which are vigorous but compact. Sever the shoot where it joins another, or where it originates at the crown of the plant, using small scissors or a knife.

Cutting branches and shoots

Where branches and shoots are more obvious, choose youthful growth, severing them with a clean cut at the base of the selected shoot, using a knife.

Cutting crown shoots

Choose shoots at the outer part of the crown, slicing them off with a knife, flush with the rootstock from which they rise.

In all three cases you should put the cuttings into a polythene bag immediately after taking them from the plant, to prevent dehydration while they await treatment. Keep to a minimum the time between obtaining the cuttings and preparing them for rooting - preferably within an hour, and certainly within a day - whenever possible. When selecting shoots for cuttings reject old, woody growth and anything which is not in the best of health.

Preparing the cuttings

All cuttings require some preparation before they are set up in the propagator for rooting. Do this work on a clean smooth surface and in good light.

Preparing a rosette

The single rosette, or tuft, is likely to have dead foliage from previous years clinging to its stalk, which must all be removed. If these pull away easily without scarring the stalk, use tweezers to strip them off, but if there is resistance, use scissors, cutting as close to the stalk as possible. The length of the resultant bared stalk should not be more than twice the length of the leafy part of the cutting, and any excess should be cleanly sliced off.

Preparing a branch or shoot

Cuttings taken as branching shoots also require the lower two-thirds to be bared, which involves the clean removal of living leaves, with scissors or a knife. Additionally, the base of the cutting must incorporate a leaf node (where leaves sprout from the stalk), so always trim to length by slicing through immediately below the nearest node.

The shoots of some plants may be freshly grown each year and have only a very short stalk below the cluster of leaves making up the shoot. Preparation is limited to the removal of old foliage and perhaps one or two of the larger current leaves to reduce stress on the cutting.

Setting up the cuttings

Because any delay in transferring the prepared cutting to the safety of the propagator unit is harmful, all arrangements must be ready in advance. Just two items are required: the propagator and the rooting medium. At its simplest the propagator can be a plastic pot, capped with a piece of glass, or a polythene bag, but for ease of use and successful results an inexpensive propagator unit is hard to better. These are widely available and are made up of a seed tray (without drain holes) and a well-fitting, clear plastic cover.

There are various rooting preparations, but for rock plants sharp sand, with nothing added, works just as well as any. It is obtainable in a specially prepared horticultural grade, packed in sealed bags and ready for immediate use. The sand must have the right degree of moistness. Test this by squeezing a cupped handful. If a dribble of water emerges, it is too wet. If in its compressed form it falls apart when you open your hand, it is too dry. If it holds the form and sheds no water it is just right and ready to be put into the propagator tray. When filling the tray take pains to leave no cavities or soft spots, finishing off with a smooth, level surface, no more than 0.5 cm (¼ in) below the rim of the tray. Brush off any sand grains clinging to the rim, which if left will mar the close fit of the cover.

To insert a cutting, first make a hole with a matchstick, deep enough to take the bared length of the cutting's stalk, then lower the cutting into the hole and firm it in by pushing the sand with the blunt end of a pencil. When all the prepared cuttings have been inserted, put on the lid of the propagator, checking that it is properly seated on the tray. Stand the propagator on a smooth, level surface away from direct sun, but in good light. As it is possible for rainwater to seep beneath the cover to saturate the

Plants from cuttings 2

sand, which is very harmful to the cuttings, arrange some overhead protection. A lightly shaded cold frame is an ideal location.

Aftercare

Inspect the propagator weekly for signs of moisture loss. If the grains of sand on the surface become dry, take off the cover and apply a few squirts from a fine hand spray that has been filled with *clean* water.

Some cuttings will show that their roots have formed by producing new top growth, but others may give no clue as to the state beneath the sand. After the cuttings have been in the propagator for four or five weeks, and are healthy but unmoving, take one between your finger and thumb and very gently try to pull it out. If it comes up easily and has no or very little root, replace it and firm it in, then try again at weekly intervals. If the cutting resists the pull it is probably adequately rooted and ready for transplanting. Be vigilant for cuttings attacked by mould and remove them promptly, otherwise they can infect the rest.

Potting up

After carefully digging the rooted cutting out of the sand, follow the method described for the potting of seedlings (see page 141). The removal may disturb nearby cuttings in the propagator, but they are tougher than seedlings and will not be harmed if firmed back into the sand to continue their root development.

Rooting aids

Root-promoting hormone preparations have limited effect on rock plant cuttings. Tests with and without these substances have shown little difference in results.

Root cuttings

Only a very small number of rock plants, such as *Phlox ensifolia* or *Morisia*, can be propagated in this manner. These few have substantial, thong-like roots from which sections are sliced and potted up in a rooting medium, then kept in a propagator until new growth sprouts.

Leaf cuttings

This is of even more limited use than the root cutting, and is viable for just one or two plants with rather fleshy leaves, like the ramondas, which in any case can be more reliably increased by division. The method is to remove a leaf and insert its base into cutting sand. Tiny plantlets eventually develop at sand level.

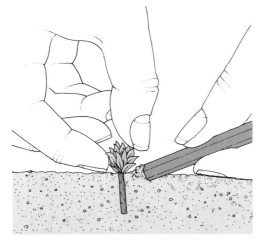

Firm the inserted cutting by closing the hole with the blunt end of a pencil.

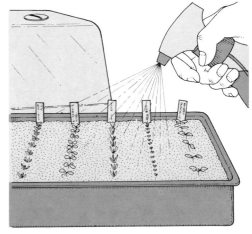

Replace lost moisture in the propagator sand using a hand spray.

Other methods

Division

Plants that have clumped growth, such as European primulas, and those which sprout from a network of underground stems, like the Asiatic gentians, will often lend themselves to this method of propagation. It should be carried out when the plant is starting to make spring growth.

First dig up the plant and remove the soil from the root mass, either by teasing or washing it off. You will see how the plant's structure is composed of a number of linked growths, each with its own set of roots. Choose the younger of these and separate them out, severing the links by cutting or simply pulling the plant apart. Discard old and poorly-rooted pieces. Cleanly cut off jagged ends. Pot up each piece as an individual plant, giving them the same aftercare as rooted cuttings. They should recover quickly and be ready to plant out within a few weeks.

HYGIENE

Whatever method of propagation you employ, cleanliness is vital to success. Wash all pots and trays in hot, soapy water before use. Never re-use old labels. Store propagating sand in sealed bags. Disinfect tools frequently, by wiping them with methylated spirit. Do not use stored rain-water, as it can harbour disease; tap-water is far safer.

Layering

This method applies specifically to shrubs with a branching habit like the daphnes, and it can be a successful alternative for species which refuse to root from cuttings (certain dwarf rhododendrons). Select a low-growing branch which can be bent down to touch the surrounding soil. At the point where this contact occurs, make a shallow slanting cut in the branch, about 2 cm (¾ in) long. Bury this wounded section in the soil, with some coarse sand beneath it, and anchor it down with a stone or a strong wire peg.

It may take one or even two years for roots to form, but you should make an inspection every six months, gently tugging the branch to assess the resistance. When, from the latter, you judge that a small root system has developed, use secateurs to cut the branch free from the parent plant, dig up the root mass and pot up for growing-on as a young plant.

Self-made propagation

Be ready to make use of offspring provided by the plants themselves. Seedlings may appear around a garden or pot plant in spring, and these can be carefully lifted out for potting up. Stoloniferous plants, such as sempervivums, can provide ready-rooted plantlets which need only be snipped off their stolon stalks and grown on. Runners from campanulas and other mat-formers can be similarly treated.

Separate individual growths, or plantlets, from the clump by pulling apart, or severing the linking stems or roots.

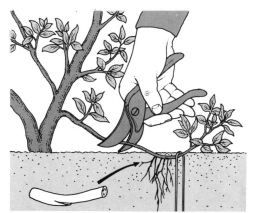

Cut the layered branch free when it has developed sufficient roots. Note detail of slanting cut, made to encourage root growth.

All about pots

Rock plants are grown in pots for a number of purposes. Exhibition plants need to be portable, for staging at shows and displays. Difficult species can more easily be given the constant attention and care that they demand, when grown separately in individual containers. The reasons for rearing young plants in pots are self-evident, when you consider the processes of propagation and growing-on, whether done by the amateur or commercially.

Pots in variety

The newcomer to pot culture will find a rather bewildering assortment of pots to choose from: they can be round or square, deep or shallow and formed from clays and plastics in several styles. Advice from expert growers may be of little help, as they differ in their personal preferences. No single type of pot is superior to others and your final choice will probably be the type that produces the best results for you and your conditions. A few facts about pots may, however, be helpful in reaching your decision.

Clay versus plastic

Clay pots are both strong and weak; strong in that they are completely rigid, and not distorted by weight of contents or handling, but weak in the sense that they are brittle and hence easily broken. They are also porous, and this property

can be used to advantage in certain growing methods. Some makes are vulnerable to damage by frost, but otherwise all clay pots are completely weatherproof. They are invariably round in shape and provided with a single drainage hole in the base.

Plastic pots vary considerably in strength and all are flexible. Their toughness in use depends on the nature of the plastic used in their manufacture. The lightweight and somewhat brittle types are intended for once-only use, but the heavier grades can last for several seasons, depending on how quickly they are degraded by exposure to sunlight. In this respect some makes will become unacceptably brittle after a year or so, but better quality products may serve well for several years of use. The square pattern of plastic pot allows edge-to-edge setting out of batches, with none of the wasted space produced in clusters of the round type, but the latter are still widely used. It is usual for plastic pots to have several drain holes in the base.

Some patterns of the plastic type have extra large drainage holes in the base. These are intended for capillary watering systems where the plants stand on wet matting and absorb water at the holes where the compost comes into contact with the matting. They are troublesome to use with normal potting techniques.

The relative advantages and disadvantages of the two materials, clay and plastic, are revealed when methods of pot culture are discussed later in this section.

Other materials

Pots made from compressed fibre or peat are less satisfactory. They both have a much shorter life than clay or plastic, and the peat-based type, as well as conflicting with conservation aims, needs to be permanently saturated, making the compost far too wet for the well-being of rock plants.

Pot sizes

The smallest size of pot you are likely to use is 6 cm (2½ in) diameter, measured across the rim of the pot. Anything smaller is liable to dry out so rapidly in hot weather that watering becomes necessary more than once a day and the volume is too little for adequate root development. Pots exceeding 25 cm (10 in) in diameter have a considerable weight when

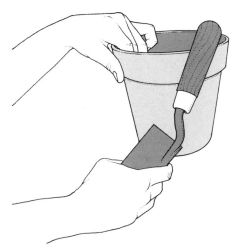

Before using a clay pot, tap it to check that it rings true and is free from hidden cracks.

Pots, half-pots and pans differ in their proportions.

filled with compost, posing handling problems for all but the fit and strong.

"Long Toms" and lily pots are much taller than normal, to accommodate plants with unusually long roots, or bulbs needing to be deeply planted. There is no firm evidence to support the belief that these lofty types are better for rock plants, even though they do have lengthy root systems.

Pans and half-pots are more squat than a standard plantpot. Whereas the latter has a height equal to its diameter, the half-pot's height is only two-thirds of its diameter, and that of the pan may be half or even less. In the larger diameters half-pots have ample depth for roots, are lighter to handle and much less liable to be knocked over. Pans are ideal for shallow-rooting plants like the dwarf rhododendrons and sempervivums.

Other considerations

Plastic pots can be used "as bought", but it is common practice to soak new clay pots by immersing them in clean water for an hour or two, to remove soluble minerals produced during the manufacturing process. The pots are then dried out fully before being put to use.

An apparently sound clay pot may have barely visible cracks which can cause it to fall apart at the most inconvenient times. Check each pot before use by tapping it with the handle of a trowel – which should produce a clear, ringing tone; a flawed pot will respond with a dull sound and should be discarded.

Pots should be washed before storing in clean, dry conditions, or they may become contaminated by dirt and pests. Clays stored in damp places attract algae and woodlice. An unclean pot is a threat to the health of the plant put in it, particularly if it is a seedling or a rooted cutting.

The drying of clay pots before use is important to future repotting; a pot used wet or damp causes the filling compost to adhere strongly to its inner surfaces. This adhesion brings problems when the time comes for the transfer to larger pot, the root ball resisting removal and breaking up in the process. More than half the root system can be lost in this way.

Hand thrown pots of the larger sizes may also cause removal problems in repotting if the inner sufaces are heavily grooved by the potter's fingers. The ridges formed act as barriers to the smooth sliding out of the root ball.

If you encounter undue resistance to removal it is possible to improve matters by inserting a thin blade, such as a pallet knife, between the root ball and the side of the pot. Work this all the way round, with a sawing action to break the bond between compost and pot, then re-try.

Pot repair for the larger, expensive clays can be worthwhile if the fracture is clean and simple. Use an epoxy resin adhesive, ensuring that the pot is absolutely dry beforehand. Hold the repair firm with a binding of twine or soft garden wire until the adhesive is fully set. For cheaper plastic pots, repairs are not worth the effort.

Potting composts

It is true to say that any plant suitable for the rock garden can also be grown in a pot. Furthermore, there are choice species which will not survive garden conditions, but can be coaxed into cultivation through pot culture. It follows that no one compost can be expected to satisfy such a range of plant types with their differing needs, but on the other hand it would be impractical to prepare an "ideal" mixture for each of the plants in a collection. Fortunately such precision is not necessary and the three *basic* mixtures given below should suffice for whatever you choose to grow.

"General" mixture

Suitable for the main bulk of rock plants and made up from equal volumes of John Innes Potting Compost No. 2, grit and peat or peat substitute. The latter should be put through a 0.5-cm (¼-in) sieve in order to remove lumps and stems.

"Lean" mixture

Has the extra sharp drainage necessary for scree and crevice plants, consisting of equal volumes of John Innes Potting Compost No. 2 and 3 mm (⅛ in) gravel. Alternatively, you can use sterilized loam in place of the John Innes compost, mixed with twice its bulk of grit or gravel, but the loam must be sieved, as specified for peat above.

"Ericaceous" mixture

Contains a high content of fibrous, organic material and is made up of the following, measured by volume: one part John Innes Potting Compost No. 2, two parts moss peat or substitute, one part sterilized leafmould and one part lime-free grit or coarse sand.

If you are able to obtain sterilized loam with a pH no higher than 6.5, then an even better compost for ericaceous subjects can be made up from: one part loam, two parts moss peat or substitute and a half part lime-free grit.

Variations

It must be emphasized that the three composts described are *basic* mixtures. As you gain experience in their use you may wish to adjust the proportions of their contents a little, to better suit your growing methods and the effects of your local climate.

LIME CONTENT

Tests have shown that mixtures with John Innes compost as the main element do not really need any addition of lime in order to satisfy species native to limestone habitats, although you will not cause harm by doing so.

For "lime-hating" species, such as the ericaceous plants, the use of limy soil, grit, sand or gravel can be very detrimental to them and even fatal. If you are doubtful about the level of lime in a prepared mixture (or for that matter garden soil), check it using one of the simple colour comparison kits, or a pH meter. For plants intolerant of lime the pH reading should be no higher than 6.5, but no lower than 4.0. The latter can actually be too acid for healthy growth, even in ericaceous species.

Good quality John Innes composts are prepared to exacting standards which include a required pH of 6.2–6.5. Where these composts are used in the ericaceous mixtures given their lime content is counteracted by acidic ingredients, such as peat, coir or leafmould. For plants other than lime-haters, crushed tufa makes an excellent alternative to the grit ingredient. Working on a hard, firm surface, use a wooden mallet or a smooth, flat stone to beat chunks of tufa into crumbs; then, with a sieve of the type used for flour in baking, remove the dusty fraction from the crushings.

GRIT ALTERNATIVE

Perlite is an expanded volcanic material which can, with confidence, be used as an alternative to grit in the potting composts described, without any alteration to the proportions. It is available as white, feather-light granules in graded sizes, the finest of these being the one for potting. Perlite is not suitable for top-dressing, as due to its very light weight it would blow away in the first strong draught.

Potting

The process of initial potting has already been dealt with under "Propagation" (see page 141), but whether acquired from a nursery or garden centre, or raised by yourself, young plants will soon outgrow their first pots and must be moved on to larger ones. In fact, purchased plants are usually ready for this "potting-on" when you obtain them. Tufts of root emerging from the pot's drainage holes indicate an urgent need for more space and compost. Another sign may be a loss of vigour in the plant, it having exhausted the available food supplies in the pot. Further moves become necessary in the life of a pot-grown plant, as often as once per year, and rarely can it remain in the same pot for much more than two years if it is to maintain healthy growth and good flowering.

If the move to a larger pot has not been delayed too long after the need has become apparent, the soil ball should be firm enough to handle, after knocking out (see page 130), but should not have roots so congested that they need to be teased apart. Handling of the soil ball during transfer to a larger pot should be kept to a minimum, especially where the compost is of the "lean" gritty type, which is prone to collapse. A useful technique for avoiding damage is to lay the soil ball in a curved trowel, with the plant at the handle end of the blade, immediately after knocking it out of its pot. This holds it safely while the new pot is being prepared.

To prepare the new pot, first ensure perfect drainage by putting a shallow layer of gravel in the bottom. It is often necessary to cover the drainage holes with fine plastic mesh to prevent the gravel from falling through. Next, partially fill the pot with the prepared compost and check its depth by sitting the old pot on it; the correct amount will bring the rim of the old pot level with that of the new one. You can then transfer the plant to its new home simply by tilting the pot and using the trowel as a slide to deliver the plant.

Complete the re-potting by filling the space between the soil ball and the pot with compost, then insert the label. After lightly firming this with your finger tips, surface the pot with a top-dressing of gravel. Water immediately using the partial immersion method (see page 140) rather than using a watering can, which is unlikely to saturate the compost fully.

1 Check the level of the initial compost filling by sitting the old pot on it.

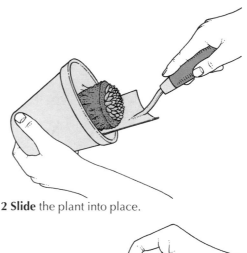

2 Slide the plant into place.

3 Fill the space around the root ball with compost so that the plant is positioned centrally, then top dress.

149

Where to house pots 1

The alpine house

This is the most popular way of housing a collection of pot-grown plants. Unfortunately, the word "alpine" has come to be misunderstood as applying to an elite group that is separate from rock plants, requiring specialized cultivation. As a result, the alpine house is mistakenly ranked with the orchid house and the cacti house, when in fact it is just a branch of rock plant cultivation. What the alpine house provides is a sheltered place where species vulnerable to bad weather can be grown. But this does not mean that only the vulnerable species are admitted; the shelter may also be used for tougher types, to grow them as specimens for exhibition, or for the very early flowerers whose blooms would be battered and soiled outdoors. The alpine house is also as much a place for the gardener as the plants, permitting work and enjoyment in reasonable comfort, whatever the weather.

The essential difference between an alpine house and a greenhouse is the amount of ventilation available. In a medium-sized greenhouse of conventional design the amount of glazing which can be opened up is no more than about 7 per cent and that includes the door. This compares with 30–40 per cent for a true alpine house. The vast difference is achieved with numerous opening lights in the roof of the alpine house, supplemented by side ventilators. The purpose of this extensive ventilation is to keep the air within the house as cool and fresh as possible for the well-being of the plants within.

The cost of an alpine house is considerably more than that of a similarly sized greenhouse, but you can improve the latter quite a lot with some modifications. Taking the commonest size of greenhouse as an example, which is nominally 2.5 m long by 2 m wide (approximately 8 ft by 6 ft 6 in), the introduction of a second opening light in the roof and one in each of the sides will almost double the available ventilation. The further addition of a door at the far end will treble it. Many manufacturers will include such extra features to order and there are also DIY modification kits available.

Setting up the pots

Pots can be set up at ground level in the alpine house, but for much greater ease of working and to display the plants most effectively, purpose-made staging is far superior. Simply stood on normal bench-like staging, clay pots can dry out quickly and plastic pots may heat up to harmful levels, when the weather is sunny.

Make a strong framework (staging) to carry the plunge bed using stout timber or metal.

Cut corrugated plastic sheeting to fit the staging with a hand or power saw.

Both types benefit from being sunk up to the rim in a bed of sand ("plunged"), which slows down moisture loss in the clay pots and acts as a buffer against heating-up (and freezing) in either case. To accommodate the larger pot sizes the depth of the sand needs to be 20 cm (8 in) and so requires a containment a little deeper. The resultant structure is a stout framework supporting a box-like container filled with sand. This is known as a "raised plunge" in rock gardening terminology. Aluminium versions of this are on the market, but you may prefer to build your own to the following guidelines. However, do bear in mind the great weight of the sand filling when you are building the support framework, and remember that this will increase further when the sand becomes wet.

Making the frame
Make the support framework from substantial timber sections, or metal, in the form of a skeleton bench. To keep working reach within comfortable limits the width "W" should not exceed 75 cm (2 ft 6 in). In 2 m (6 ft 6 in) wide houses "W" is limited to 60 cm (2 ft), otherwise it will obstruct the central access aisle. The height "H" is 60 cm (2 ft) and the length "L" is governed by the size of the house. Build in strong cross members, spaced at 30 cm (12 in) pitch, along the top of the framework.

Adding the base
Cut corrugated plastic sheeting, of the type used for roofing, to fit the top of the frame, but do not fix it in place with screws or nails.

Fixing the sides
Make sides and ends from lengths of 2 x 25 cm (¾ x 10 in) timber, rot-proofed with a non-toxic preparation. When these are in place the corrugated base is trapped in position, but may still be removed for maintenance, as it is simply a matter of lifting it out.

You will need enough sharp sand to fill the box-like containment to two-thirds of its depth. The subsequent setting in of pots will raise its level further. Some growers keep the sand moist at all times, but others prefer to water only the pots, leaving the sand more or less dry.

The finished structure
In the usual alpine house layout, staging of the type described runs along each side of the central access aisle and across one end. This end section often serves as a work-top and potting bench.

Fit the sides and the ends using rot-proofed timber and rust-resistant fastenings.

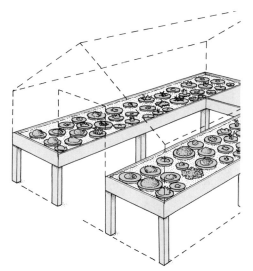

The usual layout of staging, incorporating a potting bench at the far end.

Where to house pots 2

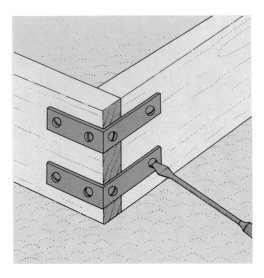

1 Check the squareness of the timbers after positioning them on the prepared site.

2 Use "L"-shaped brackets for ease of fixing the timbers at the corners.

Plunge frames

These serve as an addition, or as an alternative, to the alpine house, employing the same principle as the sand-filled containment already described for the alpine house staging. In its simplest form the plunge frame is built on ground level. Choose a site which is level, or if this is not possible, cut a level platform into sloping ground. The site must, above all else, be well drained and clear of deep shade and overhanging foliage. Access is also important as the frame will be visited frequently for the care of the plants it houses.

Construction

For the easiest and quickest construction, use timber, thoroughly treated with a non-toxic preservative. A suitable thickness for the timber is 5–8 cm (about 2–3 in) and it should be 20 cm (8 in) wide. Second-hand floor joists are relatively cheap and ideal for the purpose. An overall width for the structure of not more than 1 m (3 ft 3 in) will allow you to reach everything from one side, without over-stretching. The length has no actual limit, other than that imposed by the size of the site.

After cutting the timber to size and applying preservative, lay the pieces edge uppermost on

the site, checking that the ends are at right angles to the sides with a set-square. Galvanized "L"-shaped brackets make the joining of the corners an easy task. To anchor down the resultant framework drive two hardwood stakes into the ground against the outside face of each side piece. These should be about 5 cm (2 in) square. Alternatively, use a 2.5 cm (1 in) metal angle. Secure these stakes to the side pieces with a nut and bolt, after drilling through.

As you will need to put glazed covers on the frame, at least during the winter months, the structure requires a support feature. This must incline the covers and ventilation to create headroom beneath them and to shed rain. Start by fixing wooden or metal uprights to the rear timber of the frame, spaced at 60 cm (2 ft) intervals and with a height of 15 cm (6 in)., To these fix a wooden rail, about 5 x 2 cm (2 x 1 in) in section. Ordinary frame lights can then be placed with their front edges resting on the frame timber and their rear edges on the rail. Add a hasp and staple, or similar fastening, at the front and rear of each light to secure them against strong winds (see page 125).

Use sharp sand for the plunge material, but before putting it into the frame base you should

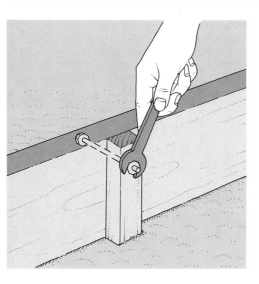

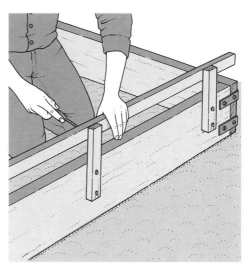

3 Join the framework to anchoring stakes with strong bolts.

4 Mount the support rail for the covers on uprights fixed to the rear timber of the frame.

lay porous plastic sheet over the earth to prevent the infiltration of worms, whose casts can cause problems.

Nursery frames

These are built in exactly the same way as the plunge frame, but are not filled with sand. Instead, the porous membrane is covered with a 5 cm (2 in) deep layer of 4–6 mm (⅙–¼ in) gravel. On this you can stand the small plastic pots used for seed and young plants, and propagators containing cuttings. The nursery frame is also an excellent place to hold purchased plants until conditions are right for their transfer to the rock garden.

Raised frames

The plunge or nursery frame can be elevated for easier use, or to aid disabled gardeners. One way is to utilize the construction for the sand-filled staging of the alpine house, and add covers. It is also possible to make a raised version of the plunge frame using a strong platform or table as the base. The structure is essentially a table bed (see pages 96–101) and just requires a facility for fitting covers, as described for the plunge frame. This can be constructed from metal (rust-resistant), or treated timber.

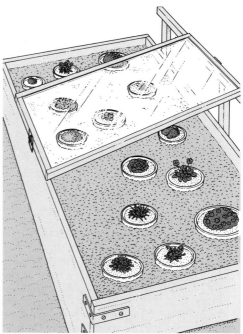

5 Add fasteners to hold the lights down in strong winds.

153

Aftercare

Watching the pots

Apart from watering, the work which takes up the largest amount of time in pot culture is re-potting. The procedure for this has already been covered earlier in this section, but it is important that during the months when the plants are growing you are always on the alert for the tell-tale signs of roots outgrowing their pots. Delay in re-potting checks growth, reduces the quality and quantity of bloom and weakens resistance to disease.

Watering

The mechanics of watering are the same as those described for "Indoor Rock Gardens" (see page 128). But knowing *when* to water is rather more difficult for pots than beds, as pots can become parched in much less time.

Where clay pots are used, a semi- or fully automated watering system may be installed to keep the plunge sand moist. The moisture then passes through the porous walls of the pots to the compost within them. By such means you can be reasonably certain that no plant will dry out completely and the system works well for the cooler, moister periods of the year. In dry, sunny weather, however, it is unlikely to keep up with the demands of the growing plants and must be supplemented with hand watering. You must also take into account the differences in moisture storing ability in large and small pots; the latter need more frequent topping-up. For hand watering, use a can fitted with a fine pouring spout and water round the plant, wetting it as little as possible.

When to water

To gauge the needs of pot-grown plants the most reliable, although seemingly crude method, is to physically check one or two sample pots. Choose a small, a medium and a large pot in the collection, then in each of these scrape away a small area of the top-dressing to reveal the compost. This should be moist, both visibly and to touch. If not, give water immediately. It is fairly safe for you to assume that the condition of the sampled pot is the same in others of similar size and hence that anything required by the sample is required by all.

Plastic pots need another approach, for although plunged in sand like the clays, no moisture can pass from the sand to the compost through the plastic. So the grower has little choice but to water by hand whenever the need is apparent. Furthermore, whereas clays are able to shed excess moisture through their porous fabric, the plastics cannot and consequently there is more likelihood of the contents becoming too wet than too dry, particularly during autumn and winter, when evaporation losses are very low. Automated drip-feed arrangements would have to deliver water to each individual pot and however slow the drip, would saturate the compost. The fingertip method of assessing water needs, using sample pots, is equally effective for plastic pots.

Capillary matting has been extensively adopted by commercial growers. In this system a blanket-like mat is laid over a bench and is permanently wetted, like a wick, from a water reservoir at the end of the bench. Plastic pots sit on the matting and take up water through their drainage holes, where the compost comes into contact with the matting. It is not possible to put drainage-assisting gravel in the bases of the pots, as they would then be unable to soak up water. Unfortunately, the moisture level sustained in the compost using this method is too high for the great majority of rock plants, as a permanent state. The system is, however, useful in short-term use, for instance during a holiday absence.

Heating

Unless some frost-tender plants are included in the population of the alpine house there is little purpose in providing winter heat. Indeed, most rock plants will be healthier without it. If it has to be installed then set it to maintain an air temperature of only a degree or two above freezing.

Ventilation

On most days of the year the alpine house should have maximum ventilation. Some of the opening lights may have to be closed for short periods to prevent snow or rain blowing in, but the only times when there is a need to close all the ventilators are during strong winds, exceptional frosts, or foggy weather. Electric fans, for recirculating the air within the closed house, or to supplement the ventilation on calm days, are a worthwhile investment.

Shading

Devices for tempering the heating effects of

summer sunshine in the alpine house or frame (see page 129) should never be left in place when the weather turns dull. So many rock plants need a high quality of light to prosper and bloom as they should.

Feeding
On the whole feeding is unnecessary if the pot-grown plants are in a well-prepared compost and are re-potted regularly. Bulbs are the major exception, for although they may be re-potted as often as other plants, they will benefit from a supplementary feed at flowering time and while they are making leaf. Use a liquid fertilizer of the type prepared specifically for roses or tomatoes, diluting it twice as much as for ordinary use and apply it every week or two in the watering routine.

Never resort to feeding as an alternative to re-potting, unless a move to a larger pot size has become no longer possible or practical, in which case you will have to feed them as for bulbs (see above).

Cleaning up
A pot re-used before it has been cleaned is a potential source of trouble; it may previously have held a diseased or pest-ridden plant. Wash all used pots in hot, soapy water and dry them thoroughly before re-use.

Clay pots can accumulate coatings of algae, or a crusty lime-like deposit. The algae is easily removed by normal washing, but the crusty deposit can prove very stubborn. An abrasive pad, of the type used for scouring pans, is often effective but if this fails you should use a medium grade of wet-and-dry abrasive paper, with plenty of water.

The surface of a sand plunge will eventually become contaminated with tiny mossy growths and, particularly in frames, liverworts. Although there are chemical treatments for these total removal is safer and long-lasting in effect. To carry out the clean-up, first remove all the pots from the plunge and put them to one side, then with a trowel skim off the top 2.5 cm (1 in) of the sand and dispose of it. Follow this with a general turning over of the remaining sand, using a hand fork. Return the pots to their places, bedding them in one by one. Towards the end of this re-plunging add new sand to make up for the amount discarded.

Water round the plant, using an angled, fine spout fitting on the watering can, to minimise wetting of the foliage.

Winter covers

Alpine houses, frames and raised beds fitted with lights can provide total overhead protection for the plants that they contain but in the open rock garden any protection has to be localized, temporary and come within practical limitations.

Tough as they may be, some rock garden plants need protection during the period when they are inactive. This is because the sheltering blanket of snow under which they naturally spend the winter keeps them more or less dry and at a constant temperature of just around freezing point.

Compare this state with the erratic garden winter which can bring alternating periods of cold and mild weather, persistent wetness and searing winds. Of course, there are mountain plants whose rocky perches are never snow-covered and fully exposed to the Alpine winter, but it is a dry winter where water exists only as ice. It is small wonder, then, that these spartans are distressed by conditions which are quite unlike those that they have evolved to endure and that they need a little help from the gardener.

Fortunately, although it bears little resemblance to snow cover, a transparent "roof" to keep the rain off the foliage is a sufficient survival aid for the plants which cannot tolerate winter wetness, even though this roof does nothing to improve the somewhat soggy state of the earth in which the plant is rooted. As it happens, the plants requiring winter "umbrellas" are mainly small, slow-growing and very often of the cushion-forming type, making it feasible to provide each plant, or small group, with an individual cover.

This can be made of glass or a reasonably transparent plastic and it is held in place by a firm support. There are various ways of providing these shelters.

The bent wire support grips a glass cover in clip-like loops and is anchored by pushing its legs deep into the soil. It is easily made from a heavy-gauge wire coat hanger, but may also be found at garden suppliers, albeit rather flimsy in some makes. Its merit is that it takes up virtually no space at ground level but its stability in strong winds is not always adequate.

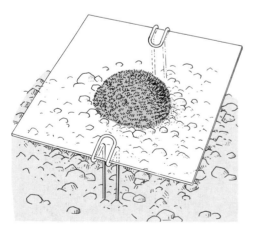

Wire supports are simple but not very strong.

Pegs and wire hold down the tunnel type of covering.

More stable in winds is the miniature tunnel type, made from corrugated plastic sheet. Long, slim metal pegs and a piece of wire provide the anchorage. This is a very safe and simple cover but needs some ground area beyond the plant on which to sit.

The simplest arrangement of all uses stones to position and anchor a pane of glass. It does take up a lot of ground space and may encroach on nearby plants, or be awkward to position in rockwork. Well weighted down with additional stones, its resistance to displacement by strong winds is good and can be reinforced with an extra (temporary) stone during gales.

Avoiding failures

Do not lay clear polythene sheeting over any part of the rock garden to serve as winter protection; not only will there be far from adequate ventilation beneath it, but it will also produce severe condensation, causing the very conditions that it is supposed to prevent. The spun-fleece covering material, used extensively in vegetable gardening, is equally unsuitable.

Whatever the form of cover you use, bear in mind that good circulation of air beneath it is vital to the well-being of the resting plants. Of similar importance is the security of the cover in strong winds; it pays to be a little pessimistice when assessing the strength of fixings, and to make them easy to apply.

Spot shading

Certain plants, such as the Kabschia saxifrages, need plentiful light, yet may be distressed by direct sun during the hottest part of the day. Overhead shading is not the answer to the problem as it robs the plant of good light for the rest of the day. What is needed is mid-day shadow and by positioning the plant at the base of a rock this can be achieved. Take note of the shadows cast by the rockwork in choosing places which enjoy sunshine at other times of day, but are in shade for an hour or two either side of noon.

Failing this you can deliberately position a rock next to the plant to contrive the mixture of light and shade required; the rock need only fit on the surface.

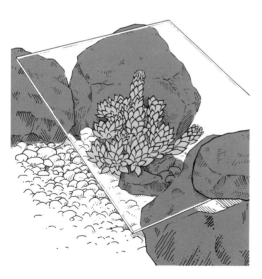

Stones can be utilized to support a cover.

Set a rock to provide shade at midday.

Plant welfare

Keeping a balance

No planting scheme ever works out perfectly. One or two species will find the conditions in your garden so much to their liking that they become "thugs", overgrowing their less robust neighbours, rooting far and wide to steal sustenance from others. At the opposite extreme will be those which fail to make progress because they, apparently, do not like the conditions provided. You can impose short-term control on any over-vigorous plants by pruning them back, but they will have to be removed eventually and the sooner this is done, the less will be the disruption caused.

There is no short-term treatment for those plants which fail to thrive; they have to be moved to other beds that might suit them better, before they are too far gone. But be sure that no hidden trouble is responsible for their lassitude by looking for localized bad drainage or soil pests when the plants are being dug out.

If you really must grow the species which have become "thugs", try them elsewhere, in harsher conditions, or in places where they can do no harm.

The removal of failures leaves empty spaces, but before you replant these with alternative species dig out the soil mixture that was around the roots of the removed plants and replace it with fresh mixture, for the benefit of the new residents. In the process of removal and replanting a quantity of top-dressing inevitably disappears and it pays to have a store of matching material to replace such losses.

Overcrowding

In a collection of rock plants there are often a few which self-propagate with great enthusiasm. Some will do this by scattering their seed around, producing a growth of infants in places where they are not always welcome, such as in the middle of a cushion or mat plant, or as a swarm that occupies every free space in the garden. If you are reluctant to dispose of these vigorous seeders, you must make sure you take the trouble to snip off their seed heads before they have ripened.

There are plants which spread excessively by stealth, advancing by hidden runners just beneath the top-dressing. By the time that they reveal their expansion, through the appearance of foliage, they have already formed a root system that is competing with nearby plants. Digging out these tendrils can badly disturb or injure the other residents in the vicinity and the only effective remedy is to eliminate the marauder by painting its leaves with a systemic herbicide. Use a small brush and paint carefully and with patience.

Bulbs, notably of *Crocus*, *Narcissus* and *Tulipa*, increase underground by producing bulblets. Certain species do this so well that in a few years a small group can grow to a tightly packed mass. This over-crowding reduces the vigour and flowering ability to an extent which can cause the whole lot to decline. Where such build-ups occur mark the spot and when the bulbs are dormant, dig up the clump. You will find it quite easy to separate them, just by pulling them apart with your fingers. After removing the soil from the spot where the bulbs were growing select the largest healthy bulbs for replanting, using fresh soil mixture. The surplus can be potted up, or planted elsewhere in the garden.

Clump-forming plants will often indicate

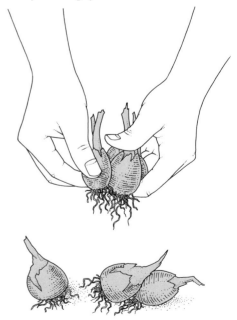

Break up tightly clustered bulbs by pulling them apart, putting aside the largest and healthiest for replanting.

congestion by dying out in the centre. The remedy is the same as that used for herbaceous border perennials, which requires digging up the entire plant and prising away younger, well-established growths for replanting. Again, as for bulbs, it is important to replace the soil locally, which will have become depleted.

Similar dying out of the centre can afflict cushion plants, but this is not due to congestion, as a cushion is by nature a crowded mass of growths. Inadequate supplies of moisture or nutrients, or simple old age, are the most common causes of this central die-back. Plucking out the dead foliage and filling the cavity created with a gritty soil mixture is a frequently recommended treatment that rarely succeeds with any but the most vigorous of cushions.

Good housekeeping

Withered shoots, spent flower heads and dead foliage all attract fungal diseases. Make a point of dead-heading plants after they have flowered and snipping away foliage which is less than healthy. Slugs love to hide away beneath mats of dead leaves and should be deprived of this comfort by pulling away or cutting off the autumn remains of herbaceous species. This applies equally to the foliage of bulbs, which, when it has begun to turn yellow, should be severed just above ground level and removed.

Make an occasional inspection of dwarf shrubs and conifers. At times they may throw out an unusually vigorous shoot that must be promptly pruned out, otherwise it is likely to dominate the growth and ruin its character. Dead or dying branches are also a threat as they may be infected with a disease which could spread through the whole plant. Cut these back to healthy wood as soon as you notice them.

Due to hard frost a recently created bed, particularly of the ericaceous type, may suffer from frost heave. This causes the upper layer of soil to lift, taking with it any plants which have not developed a firm root system. They can be partially, or even fully, jacked out of the ground by this action, so check new beds for this problem when the freezing has passed and gently push back into place any affected plants.

Remove dead flower heads, withered foliage and any sign of diseased growth promptly to keep the plants in good health.

Watering

Watering is a task that varies considerably from one region to another. In cooler, wetter areas it is an occasional need, brought on by the odd dry period, yet only a two-hour car drive away it may be a quite regular routine for much of the late spring and summer.

Where summer brings few dry periods lasting more than a week, a watering can may be all that is necessary for a modestly sized rock garden. For larger areas the addition of a hosepipe, for occasional use, completes the necessary equipment. By contrast, gardeners who expect summer to bring drought conditions are keen to find means of reducing the time and effort involved in keeping up with the moisture demands of the plants. The technical content of this section is likely to be of more interest, therefore, to those with "dry" gardens, but help with knowing *when* to provide water is common to all.

The need for water
A lot of time and water are wasted in refreshing gardens because they "look a bit dry", even though there are no actual signs of plants lacking sufficient moisture at their roots. Yet it is not difficult to determine the true state. The wilting of an otherwise healthy plant is a reliable indication of the ground becoming too dry and there is nothing wrong in waiting until this happens before you begin watering. Wilting is a natural defence against dehydration and the plant will recover, unharmed, provided that you rectify matters promptly. In woodland and ericaceous beds rhododendrons provide reliable warning of drying out by rolling their leaves inwards and allowing them to droop - this is another natural defence mechanism which, unless ignored, does no damage. A little observation will show which of your garden plants are the first to signal the shortage and from thereon you can use these as your early warning system.

Leaving watering until it is really necessary not only saves time, energy and water but encourages deep rooting, enabling the plants to tap moisture reserves that are inaccessible to plants which have not needed to root down because too frequent watering has kept the surface soil moist.

The foregoing does not apply where young and newly introduced plants are concerned, as these are not sufficiently established to withstand short-term water shortage.

Moisture measurement
Technology has now provided us with cheap and reliable moisture meters which give an instant reading when the probe is pushed into the soil. They can be very useful, but it is important to understand what they are telling you, as they are influenced by the nature of the soil. Even when quite wet, a very gritty soil may only register a medium level of moisture, whereas a denser, humus-rich soil can give a high reading when only moderately wet. Soil acidity also affects the working of these devices, but the variables can be taken into account by getting

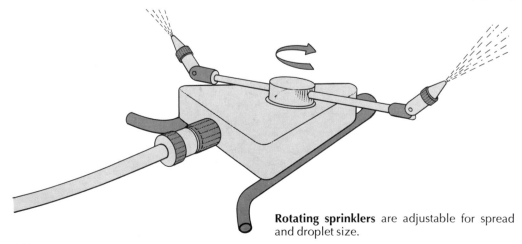

Rotating sprinklers are adjustable for spread and droplet size.

to know how they respond to your particular garden. After a heavy rainfall, when you are confident that the soil is thoroughly wetted, take readings with the meter in various locations. This will establish the maximum figure for each place tested. Make the same trials when the first signs of drying out are apparent (when wilting occurs), to obtain the "danger-level" figures. With these established you are then able to judge the moisture state at any time, from the reading obtained.

Watering systems
There are now hose accessories available which will deliver water to a desired pattern and in a variety of droplet sizes, through built-in adjusters. They can be linked to timing devices and even programmable controllers to operate when and for as long as you wish. The less sophisticated of them utilize the normal garden hose to supply water to a sprinkler fitting from a mains tap. Being unsightly if left in place, the hose and fittings have to be set up anew for each use. In-situ systems have permanent hose runs buried in the ground, serving a number of nozzles in fixed positions around the garden. These deliver the water as a patterned spread or as a pulsed and oscillating fine plume.

The "seep" or "dribble" hose, which delivers water along the whole of its length as a gentle seepage, is useful for ericaceous-type beds, where it can be hidden beneath the surface mulch. This type of hose can also be adopted for the scree bed, providing moisture below the

> **SAFETY NOTE**
> Regulations now require that all taps supplying garden hoses, of any type, should incorporate an anti-siphoning feature. This prevents possibly contaminated water in the hose from being sucked back into the domestic system.

surface in much the same way as natural screes are watered.

How much and how often?
A common mistake in providing water to thirsty plants is to give them a small amount frequently, during dry periods. A brief, daily wetting penetrates very little into the soil, never reaching the deeper roots which are seeking moisture. As a result the plants enjoy a series of short-lived revivals but for most of the time have insufficient water for growth and development, because the daily ration soon evaporates away. Consequently the plants are merely kept alive without further benefit.

When you decide that watering is needed, do it generously, making sure that it has done more than wet the top layer of soil. Wait until surplus water begins to run out of the bed, or until it forms puddles, before you turn off the supply. After a wetting of this extent you need do no more watering until your "early warning" plants signal a shortage, or the moisture meter indicates drying out; then you should give water again – plentifully.

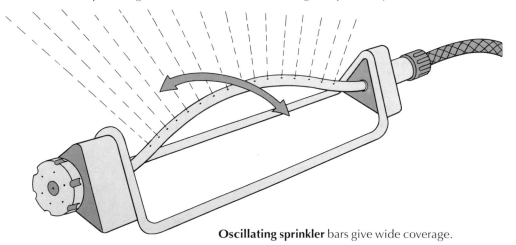

Oscillating sprinkler bars give wide coverage.

Feeding

For the first two or three years of its existence a rock garden feature will hold within its soil sufficient nutrients for the needs of its plants. Beyond that period, due to take-up by the plants and the leaching effect of rainfall, the sustenance levels become depleted and need to be supplemented. In doing this the aim should be to provide nutrients in a way that makes them available to the plants as a steady, measured supply, over a long period of time rather than as a short-term boost. Slow-release fertilizers function in exactly the right way and are obtainable in more than one form.

What to use

The granular type of slow-release fertilizer is a coarsely powdered product which dissolves slowly in moist soil, supplying an assortment of plant nutrients at a more or less constant rate, for several months. The release is only halted during times when the soil becomes dry. The coated type looks like small beads, each of which is a tiny ball of soluble fertilizers encased in a special skin or shell which governs the rate at which the dissolved nutrients can pass through it by the principle of osmosis. The simplest types release steadily while moisture is present, but there are also some which only allow this when the soil temperature is high enough for plant growth and so do not release nutrients when they would be wasted.

The granular type is better suited to rock gardens, where disturbance of carefully top-dressed surfaces is to be avoided wherever possible. (The coated type only works properly when incorporated in the soil and so to be effective would have to be forked in around the plant). The granular form can simply be sprinkled on the surface and left for the rain to take it

down to the underlying soil.

When buying fertilizer remember that rock plants on the whole resent high levels of nitrogen in the soil, so choose a "balanced" fertilizer with a low proportion of nitrogen, which is in the region of 5 per cent. The slow-release fertilizers prepared specially for roses or tomatoes have a suitable balance of ingredients.

When to use it

Early spring is the time to feed the rock garden, when the plants are becoming active and will need nutrients for several months to come. If applied as described below there should be no need for repeat feeding until the following spring.

How to use fertilizer

If you work to the metric system, weigh out 35 gm of fertilizer and make a simple measure by putting the amount in a small plastic container, such as a yoghurt carton. Mark the level to which the fertilizer fills it (see diagram, left), then use this quantity on each square metre of the growing area. Make the coverage by sprinkling evenly over the surface, avoiding contact with the plants as far as possible. If you prefer to use imperial measures the method is precisely the same, but use 1 oz of fertilizer for each square yard. These figures are not critical, but give a guide to the general quantity required. In fact, you will often have to guess the square metre or square yard when making the application around rockwork and awkward shapes.

Few troughs will have an area big enough to take even one of the above measures of fertilizer. A little arithmetic is needed to work out the trough area, and then to apply the relevant proportion required.

CAUTION

Fertilizers can irritate sensitive skin, so always handle them with gloves on. Avoid breathing in any dust created during their use and, if necessary, wear a nuisance mask. Store the fertilizers in cool, dry conditions, safely out of reach of children and pets. Never allow fertilizer to spill or leach into pools or other water features during application.

Weeding

The worst mistake a rock gardener can make in the control of weeds is to let them get too big before removing them. The pulling out of each well-developed growth disturbs the root runs of nearby rock plants and draws the soil up to spill over the gravel top-dressing, leaving the area pock-marked and in need of restoration. A further penalty, unnoticed at the time, is that the weed may have already scattered its seed, creating more work for the future. When really tough, deep-rooted invaders such as dandelions, docks and thistles have gained a firm hold, their physical removal entails extensive digging and even partial dismantling of the rockwork. Faced with such disruptions your only alternative is to use a hormone-based weedkiller on each individual. Follow the manufacturer's directions closely for "spot weeding" and to protect adjacent plants make a larger paper or plastic collar to fit around the weed while you apply the treatment.

Little and often
A great deal of work can be avoided if you take out the weeds when they are still small and can be pulled out easily. This is best done and causes the least disturbance when the soil is quite moist; in dry conditions they tend to snap off at the neck, leaving a stump which may regrow. Weed frequently, but for short periods of no more than 30 minutes, and you will be neither outpaced nor overwhelmed by your weeds.

Problem weeds
Marestail, bindweed and ground elder are some of the most difficult garden weeds to eradicate. Not only can their root systems be too vast and virile for eradication by digging out, but they are also unaffected, or only temporarily checked, by most weedkillers. There are systemic herbicides specifically formulated for these major nuisances which require methodical and repeated application to be effective.

Weeds on paths and drives
In gravel paths generally, and in the joints of paved surfaces, small but virulent weeds like pearlworts and speedwells, defy all attempts to eradicate them by hand pulling. They seed by the thousand and advance faster than the gardener can work. Chemical control may be achieved using weedkillers specially intended

for paths and drives, which as well as killing off current growth lay down an invisible inhibitor to prevent further germination for the rest of the season. The non-chemical approach is to use a flame weeder which operates like a giant blow-lamp to burn the weeds out of existence. The scorching usually has to be carried out two or three times per year but is certainly effective, and if used with care is safe, leaving no residue other than a tiny amount of harmless ash. The device is most efficient if used when the weeds are in the early stages of growth.

Weeding tools
All the tools manufactured for weeding disturb the soil to some extent. This ruins the carefully prepared surfaces of the rock garden.

You cannot scuffle with a hoe or fork up clumps of weeds as you would in the border or vegetable patch. The one implement which you will find invaluable is a very slim trowel, with a blade no wider than 2 cm (¾ in) and 10–12 cm (4–5 in) in length, with a curved section to give it strength. These are hard to find and most of those in use have been hand-made from a piece of thin-walled metal tubing. This is done by hacksawing away half of the tube diameter and filing the end to a point. If you use a piece of tube 20 cm (8 in) long and make the blade part 12 cm (5 in) long, the uncut length remaining serves as a handle. With this tool you can extract weeds with minimal disturbance and root them out of awkward spots.

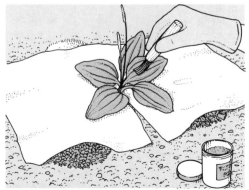

Put a plastic or paper collar round the neck of a weed to shield nearby plants, before spot treating with hormone killer.

Alpine houses and frames

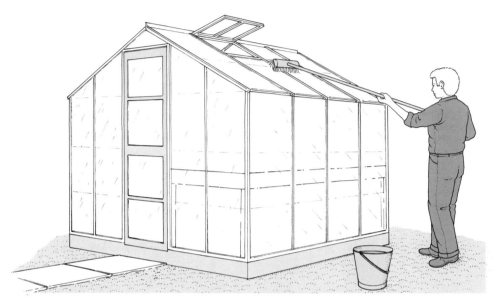

Use a long-reach brush to clean the exterior
of the alpine house.

Although it would not be tolerated on the windows of the home, the film of grime which builds up on glass is often unnoticed on the glazing of an alpine house or frame. This layer of dirt makes a significant reduction in the quality of light reaching the plants beneath the glass and should be cleaned off at least once a year, preferably in the early spring.

On frames the cleaning is a straightforward task, but on the alpine house it is not so easy. For the external surfaces a window brush, as sold by hardware stores, allows you to reach all the roof and sides, unless the house is very large, or you can use a hose-fed car-washing brush tied to the end of a broom handle. For the cleaning of the interior you will need to take precautions for the protection of the plants. Cover them with lightweight plastic sheet and leave this in place until all dripping has ceased after the work. Internally, a hand-held brush or sponge is sufficient as you should be able to reach all the surfaces. Lukewarm water, with a little washing-up liquid added, is an efficient cleaner and safer than preparations containing ammonia or other solvents. Avoid still, dank days for the work, as these will delay drying inside the house or frame.

Along with glass cleaning it is good practice to carry out a general clean-up, disposing of dead or sickly plants, used potting compost, cobwebs and the general litter that inevitably accumulates over the year. If pests have recently been a particular problem, take the opportunity to wash down all surfaces with a disinfectant recommended for garden use to kill off eggs and larvae that have overwintered.

Drips falling on to plants can very quickly harm or kill them. During a spell of heavy rain make a check for leaks. These may originate in faulty glazing seals, slipped or cracked panes, or warps in the framework. The remedy for some of these faults may involve some difficult work, including extensive removal of glazing and structural repairs. If you are unable, or unwilling, to go to such lengths, you can often make a satisfactory repair with the aid of silicone rubber sealant, of the type sold for bathroom and kitchen installations. This substance is strongly adhesive on most materials, including glass, is totally weatherproof, repels algae and mossy growths, and carries a 20-year guarantee. All surfaces involved must be clean and dry before the sealant is applied.

Modern aluminium-structured houses and

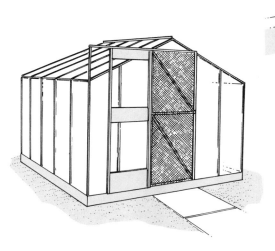

Door screens can be fitted to aluminium-framed houses.

Fix screens with self-tapping screws or pop rivets

frames are fitted with patent glazing devices which make glass replacement a quick and easy procedure, requiring only the removal of one or two clips to release a pane. Timber-built types no longer have their glazing sealed with putty, but have also adopted new glazing methods. Leaks in these are rare and if they do occur are usually the result of faulty assembly or misuse.

Door screens are a very useful addition to the alpine house, keeping out pets and also birds, which can harm themselves in trying to escape. In its most basic form the screen is merely a length of plastic or wire netting hung over the door opening, but a far more service-able unit can be made using roofing lath timber. Build a simple rectangular frame with the laths, just a little bigger than the door frame. Cover it with strong plastic net or fine wire netting and fit rustproof hinges to one side of the frame. When the hinges are also fixed to the edge of the sliding door the screen becomes a permanent part of the house. While the door is open the hinged screen takes its place to cover the opening, but still allows a full flow of air to the interior. When the door is closed the screen moves with it and can be hooked back to the frame of the house.

Cover the plants when cleaning the glass inside the house.

Materials

Peat or peat substitute if allowed to become dry is difficult to make moist again, and if incorporated in compost when dry may stay that way for a long time, despite watering. Keep these materials in closed plastic bags to maintain them in a suitably moist condition.

John Innes composts should be neither very moist nor very dry. If you discover either of these conditions upon opening the bag, return it promptly to the supplier as unsuitable for use.

Gravel is almost always in a wet state, from the washing process, when supplied in sealed bags. When obtained loose from builders' merchants it can be anything from saturated to bone dry, depending on the weather at the time. Wet gravel does not mix properly with other materials and should be dried to remove the bulk of the moisture before you use it in compost or as top-dressing for pots. Spread it out over a clean surface on a suitable day and it will quickly loose the water it holds.

Grits and sands are impaired by excessive moistness in the same way as gravel. Dry them off before blending them with other materials.

BUYING COMPOST

Take note of the storage facilities at your garden suppliers; some bagged materials are ventilated by small holes in the plastic which, if the bags are not under cover, allow rain to enter and saturate the contents. For the same reasons never accept a damaged bag.

Potting equipment
This should include a potting bench if you are to work comfortably and without wastage. It need only be a small, portable unit which will sit on any convenient surface. For the base of this use a 15–20 mm (½ – ¾ in) thick piece of plywood or blockboard, approximately 45 cm (18 in) square. To three of its sides fix a length of wooden board 15 mm (½ in) thick and 7.5 cm (3 in) deep, using woodscrews. If you then cover the top of the base with one of the plastics used for kitchen surfaces, it will be easy to clean after use. The side boards allow compost to be heaped without spilling over the edges of the unit and also provide a handy ledge for the knocking out of plants from their pots. Being portable, the unit can be used on the kitchen table, or other convenient work place. If there is no spare surface area in the alpine house make a pair of support pieces from 5 x 2.5 cm (2 x 1 in) timber. These need to be long enough to rest on the staging at either side of the central aisle. The potting unit can then rest on these bearers for use.

Labels
Where a label is supplied with a purchased plant it is often unsuitable for use in the garden, being either too big, too flexible or too colourful. For the rock gardener labels fall into two distinct categories: those for permanent use in the garden, or in pots, and those used in the short term during propagation and the growing-on of young stock. In both uses the label may carry information additional to the plant's

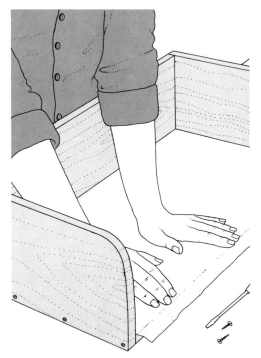

Make a portable potting bench from a square board, edged on three sides to hold heaped compost, and cover the base with plastic.

name, such as date of sowing or purchase, compost used, collection number (if wild seed) and so on. The loss of any such information, due to loss or failure of the label, can be a serious setback to the keen grower. For long-term use the label needs to be weatherproof, firmly anchored and legible, without being expensive. Three types that meet these requirements are: the aluminium label, which is still obtainable, but from limited sources. The metal is treated against corrosion and can be written on with pencil or ink. Some inks attack the metal under garden conditions, becoming illegible, but pencil lasts for years. The second type is the patent McPenny label, made from a tough and very durable white plastic, coated black on one side. The lettering is produced by scratching away the coating with the stylus provided, to expose the white beneath, and it stays legible indefinitely. Less durable, but good for two or three years, are the better quality plain white plastic types. These will take pencil or ink

inscriptions, which are preserved if the label is pushed almost entirely into the soil. As well as conserving the writing this anchors the label firmly, prevents curious birds from tweaking it out of the soil, yet allows it to be readily pulled up for reference. The other two types mentioned also benefit in the same way, and because the labels are virtually hidden from sight, your garden is saved from being blemished by a forest of name tags.

For short-term use, pencil or ink on the cheaper plastic labels is adequate, as by the time the writing is fading, or the material has become too brittle or discoloured, they have served their purpose.

Many so-called "permanent" inks perform poorly when exposed to the weather, dissolving or bleaching away to nothing in a few months. It is a matter of trying out various makes of marker pen until you find one which is durable on the labels that you use and in your particular conditions.

Pots, pans and other containers

Never store pots or other plant containers outdoors, whether clay or plastic. Rain-soaked clay pots can, in some cases, be damaged or completely shattered by a night's hard frost following a downpour. Plastic types, if stacked together, trap water between them which becomes stagnant and polluted. Pests such as woodlice, earwigs, slugs, snails and even mice can find cosy homes and breeding places in the nooks and crannies provided by a collection of containers.

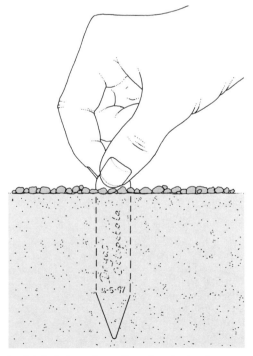

Push labels into the soil until only the tip remains to mark its location.

SAFE STORAGE

Fertilizers, fungicides, pesticides and weedkillers all pose a serious hazard to children and pets. Keep these substances in one safe store, returning them to it immediately after use. Aerosols and some light-sensitive liquids need to be kept away from direct sunlight, so bear this in mind when deciding upon the place to store. Always follow the manufacturer's directions and precautions exactly, always wear gloves and always wash all exposed skin as the final step in the procedure.

167

The rock garden

Carefully dig up plants which are to be replanted with as little damage as possible.

Work the extra top-dressing under mat-forming and cushion plants.

Revitalizing

After a number of years, even though given regular spring dressings of plant foods, some parts of the rock garden may begin to decline, failing to keep their resident plants in good health. The cause is usually a deterioration in the structure of the soil, where the numerous tiny air spaces become blocked by a combination of long-term settlement, dense accumulations of roots and the bringing in of soil by worms. Fortunately, the affected areas are often small enough to be given localized treatment, as opposed to the formidable task of rebuilding the whole bed.

Having identified the extent of the affected area, you should first determine which of the plants in it might be salvaged. Mature, deep-rooted specimens are unlikely to survive transplanting, but young plants and those with compact, fibrous root systems are worth saving. Dig these up with as little damage to their roots as you can manage, then plant them temporarily in a shaded patch of soil. With this rescue operation completed you can then dig out the affected area to a depth of 15 cm (6 in), removing old plants in the process. Refill the excavation with freshly prepared soil mixture, returning the salvaged plants as you do so, together with new stock to make up for those

discarded. Finish off with a top-dressing matching that of the surrounding surface and water generously. If hot, dry weather follows the completion of the work arrange some overhead shading until the plants have recovered from the disturbance (usually about two to three weeks).

Dealing with settlement

Despite every precaution having been taken during construction to prevent settlement, there will in time be some noticeable sinking of the filling in raised beds, more obviously in the deeper of them. Full-scale rectification involves topping-up and complete replanting, which is not something to be undertaken lightly. You can, however, disguise the effect to quite an extent by adding more top-dressing material. Work this under mat-forming and cushion plants as far as possible, without injuring them, so that their further spread will be over a slightly raised level. Other types of plant will soon adapt their growth to accommodate the changed level. The same remedy can be applied, on a smaller scale, to troughs and other containers.

Stonework repair

The movement of equipment around the garden is a common cause of accidental damage,

1 Mark each of the walling pieces to be removed, so that they can be rebuilt in the same pattern.

2 Clean off the mortar from the walling pieces that have been removed.

with dwarf walls high on the casualty list – they are vulnerable to knocks from wheelbarrows, trolleys and lawnmowers. These usually displace stonework in the top two or three courses. Severe frost may also cause similar localized damage.

Pushing the displaced walling back into place and patching up with a little mortar is a remedy that will soon prove unsatisfactory. To restore the appearance and strength of the wall properly, dismantle the affected walling to a little beyond the full extent of the damage, so that you will then be keying back the rebuilt section into a sound structure. Before you begin the dismantling make a note of where each walling piece should be returned to, if necessary marking them individually with chalked numbers. Clean off all the old mortar from the extracted pieces and also from the faces that they will join up with in the undamaged wall.

To give yourself working room and to prevent soil toppling in during repair dig out a little of the soil backing the affected length of the wall. Take care with the mortaring where the repair meets the sound walling to ensure that the joints are well filled. The rebuild employs the same technique as was

3 Make sure that the joints between the repair and the undamaged walling are fully mortared.

used in the original construction, and can offer the opportunity to introduce new plants (see page 133).

Path repairs

Even well-constructed paths may develop localized faults, where the surface either sinks or is lifted up to present a hazard. The sinking may be due to the presence of a soft spot in the base material upon which the path has been laid, overlooked during the process of tamping down. It is just as likely, however, that faulty drainage is the basic cause of the trouble. Persistently wet sand or grit can ooze away, leaving the surface material unsupported. Hard frost acts in a different manner, expanding the water and lifting whatever lies over it.

The first action in making a repair is to remove the path surface over the faulty area. If the surface is of crazy paving you should mark each piece as it is taken up, in order to regain the original pattern and fit when re-laying. Large paving slabs, whether symmetrical or otherwise, should be lifted methodically. Before attempting to move them dig out the mortar from the joints with a slim chisel and a small lever – such as an old, large screwdriver. To initiate the lift use a strong digging fork, pushing its tines under one edge of the slab and pressing down on the handle. This levering will raise the slab sufficiently for a piece of wood or stone to be pushed into the gap by an assistant. From this chocked position you will be able to obtain a good hold to raise the slab up to the vertical, and then to "walk" it (see page 24) to a temporary resting place to await re-laying. Gravel-surfaced paths are far easier to clear, requiring only a rake and brush to push a heap to one side of the repair area.

Having exposed the underlying base material you should then be able to identify and correct the fault. Replace badly draining hardcore with new material, ensuring while doing so that there is an escape route for the run-off water. Where straightforward settlement is the cause of the problem tamp down the base material more firmly, adding extra if necessary. With the fault corrected, restore the sand or grit overlay to the original level, making certain that it is thoroughly consolidated, then re-lay the surfacing. Where the latter is paving, you should mortar the joints, then leave the path undisturbed for two or three days before bringing it back into use. For the techniques of path laying see pages 114–115.

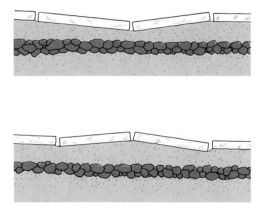

1 Path damage can take the form of a sinking or an upheaval.

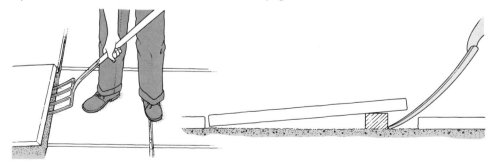

2 With a strong digging fork, raise an edge of the paving slab, and chock this open with a piece of wood or stone.

3 Use the gap created to obtain a good hold for the remainder of the lift.

4 After correcting the fault, restore the base material to the original level.

Pests 1

Sap-suckers

Aphids are by far the most prolific pests in this category. Although there are hundreds of different species, greenfly and blackfly are the major representatives. They are most obvious when clustered on young shoots, but can exist in similar densities unseen, hidden in the congested foliage of cushion plants. Besides weakening the plant that they attack, by robbing it of sap, they can also spread virus diseases from plant to plant by carrying the infection on the proboscis with which they pierce the tissue to draw up sap.

Root aphids are usually only discovered when a sickly plant is examined closely. They live on the roots and at the junction of the roots with the stem and produce a protective coating of a fluffy-looking, white, waxy substance. Very similar in appearance are the woolly aphids which attack conifers and congregate around the bases of the shoots.

Natural control of aphids occurs through predators such as ladybirds, lacewings, hoverflies, some parasitic wasps, and the larvae of these. Some birds also eat aphids, but all these foes combined are insufficient to combat an infestation and at times the gardener must employ additional means to literally save the lives of rock plants. No chemical used to kill off pests can be absolutely safe or harmless to all other living things, but systemic insecticides do at least approach the ideal. Once these have been absorbed into the sap system of the plant they will only kill the insects which feed off that sap. There are many "contact" insecticides, which rely on actually wetting the insect with the chemical, but these are indiscriminate, harming the good and the bad alike. One or two of the contact types are based on natural protective substances produced by certain plants, *Pyrethrum* being the main one, but even these will also harm some of the beneficial insects. Pirimicarb is a selective contact aphid killer which leaves most other pests *and beneficial* insects unharmed.

Scale insects look like tiny brown barnacles and cling to leaves and stems. The hard shell in which they live protects them from predators and contact insecticides, but they are vulnerable to systemic treatments. Fortunately they are less common on rock garden plants and far less

numerous than aphids. It is rare for them to be present in sufficient numbers to distress the plant that they inhabit.

Nematodes pose a problem for the rock gardener by being so small that they are difficult to see, even under a hand lens. They are wormlike in shape and live inside the tissues of the plant. Of the harmful types the stem and bulb eelworm is the most troublesome, attacking a variety of rock plants and bulbous species. Its presence should be suspected where distorted stems, leaves and flowers become noticeable and where growth is stunted and malformed. Chemical controls are not available to amateur growers, so affected plants must be removed and burned before the pestilence spreads to others. It is also wise to dispose of the soil that was surrounding their roots.

Red spider mite is not actually a spider, but a minute bug, so small that it is only clearly visible under a hand lens. Its presence is betrayed by fine, light grey freckling of leaves, which progresses to yellowing and wilting. The mite revels in the dry, warm atmosphere of a glasshouse. Because it dislikes cool, damp conditions it is far less prevalent in the open garden. Regular spraying with water, inside the glasshouse, does discourage the spread of this pest to some extent. If you feel it necessary to employ chemical control, there are products based on dimethoate or pirimiphos-methyl which can be effective, but there is also a biological control available, in the form of a predatory mite (*Phytoseiulus persimilis*) which is proving successful for amateur use.

Do not confuse this pest with the tiny, bright scarlet stone mite which hurries around on sunny surfaces, without apparently achieving anything. It is no threat to plants whatsoever.

Leaf-eaters

Slugs and snails are without doubt the most destructive of the rock garden's pests. Due to its relatively small size a rock plant suffers far more loss and injury from a night's grazing by a single slug or snail than does, say, a delphinium or cabbage. In combatting these menaces the first action is to deprive them of resting and breeding places, as far as possible, so avoid leaving around things like seed trays, pots and other items that offer cool, moist hideaways and clear up organic litter such as dead leaves and hedge clippings. Keep a look out for their eggs when weeding or planting; they are about 2–3 mm (⅛ in) in diameter, whitish and semi-transparent and are to be found in clutches in the soil, under stones and in rotting vegetation.

For a long time the most widely used method of control has been poisoned bait, in the form of metaldehyde pellets, but there are now growing concerns about birds, frogs and hedgehogs eating the stricken victims. Alternative preparations are on the market based on aluminium sulphate which claim to be much safer, killing by contact rather than by poison. If you do use pellets, then make them less accessible to other creatures by laying them in small heaps covered with pieces of roof tile or broken pots. Completely safe traps can be made from hollowed-out potatoes or halved oranges. Sit these, inverted, in various spots around the garden and leave them there overnight. You can pick them up next morning complete with "catch" and dispose of them. Also safe and completely certain is the "night attack" method. Go out after dark on a mild, moist evening armed with a torch, an old glove (or tongs) and a jar of very salty water. Pick up the slugs or snails as they are browsing in full view, drop them in the jar and seal this with a lid at the end of the hunt. A nematode is now available for slug control which is watered into the soil in spring or autumn. Less effective against snails.

Ground caterpillars are the larvae of certain moths. They are nocturnal feeders, inactive by day, hiding just beneath the surface of the soil or top-dressing. They can be up to 5 cm (2 in) long and are bright green to olive brown in colour. Poisoned baits are ignored by them; the only effective control is by "night attack", for which the jar of salty water is unnecessary as they squash easily.

Vine weevils have become much more prevalent since the great development of the container-grown plant industry. In its adult form the vine weevil is a wingless beetle, dull black in colour and 8–9 mm (⅓in) long. It makes notches in the margins of leaves when feeding but this damage rarely reaches problem status in the rock garden. Its larvae, however, are a different matter, particularly in pot culture.

Root-eaters
Vine weevil larvae are legless grubs of a dirty white hue, up to 10mm (⅜in) long, with a prominent brown head. They take up a "comma" shape when disturbed. They eat roots voraciously and live unseen below soil level. All too often the first hint of their presence is the sudden collapse of the plant on which they are feeding by which time it is already too late to save the plant. Chemical substances sold for their control have only limited effect, but there are now available biological control packs containing natural enemies in the form of nematodes. These can be used both under glass as a preventative measure, and in the open garden, in late summer and early autumn.

Wireworms are most troublesome where land has been brought into cultivation after being open pasture. They are not usually a significant problem in the gritty soils of a rock garden, but may cause serious damage in bulb beds.

Millipedes like the wireworms go for bulbous and tuber-rooted species, eating them from within. Both of these pests can be discouraged by soil fumigation or soil pesticides, but there are also certain plants, such as mustard (*Sinapis alba*), which exude a repellent.

Vine weevil and damaged leaves

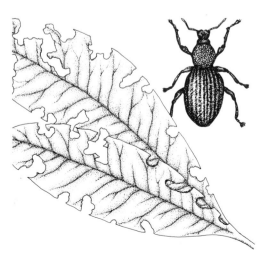

Pests 2

Other pests and nuisances

Ants can cause considerable damage in the rock garden by undermining plants with their nest building. *Dianthus* species in particular are prone to this trouble. The ants are not actually eating the plant but chewing through its roots as they tunnel and then making things worse by pushing up a mound of excavated soil onto the already injured specimen. There are powders for the extermination of these insects, requiring care in their use to avoid inhalation of the fine dust produced. Another proprietary control product is a sweet syrup laced with poison which the ants carry away to their nest and thus feed to others. For peace of mind you should hide this bait from the attention of other creatures with a sweet tooth.

Earthworms can disfigure the well-kept surface of a bed with their soil casts, but the good that they do generally far outweighs this annoying behaviour. The casts can be picked off in the dry state. The New Zealand flatworm is a new and deadly enemy of earthworms. This unwelcome immigrant has already become established in northern and western parts of Britain and is spreading. It resembles the earthworm in size, but is wider and ribbon-like in section with a slimy look to its smooth brown skin. Look for it beneath stones and other similar hideaways where it rests by day, coiled like a clock spring. In south-west England, the Australian flatworm, of similar appearance, is now established. It also preys on earthworms. A sure method of control has yet to be found for these scourges, but individual worms can be killed by putting them in salty water (page 173).

Moles can be a terrible nuisance in rural gardens and while there are traps and mole-smokes available to the gardener, eradication is really best left to an expert.

Birds are cherished by most gardeners, yet at times can behave badly, pecking lumps out of prized cushions, tearing newly opened crocus flowers to ribbons or flinging soft top-dressing material all over the place. Gentle discouragement can be arranged in simple ways. Black cotton stretched between pegs pushed into the bed does deter birds from landing, but it gets in the way of weeding and other work. You can achieve equally good results using the soft iron wire of the florists' trade. This material is dark brown in colour and is sold in bundles of 15 cm (6 in) lengths. Prepare each wire by bending one of its ends over to produce a safe tip, then push it into the soil to half its length, with the bent end uppermost. Space the wires about 20 cm (8 in) apart over the bed to be protected. Whether the birds are discouraged by seeing these obstacles, or touching them, is not clear, but the system works well. The iron wire is so soft and easily bent that it is not a hazard.

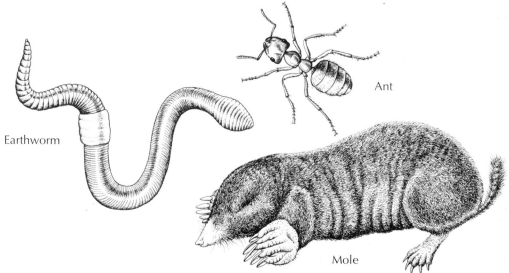

Earthworm

Ant

Mole

Diseases and other ills

Fungus attacks on rock plants are usually forms of *Botrytis*, appearing as grey, fluffy growth on shoots and foliage, or as yellow/brown blemishes on leaves and bulbs. There are other types, producing black blotches, or green, blue or white moulds. Poor ventilation and moist conditions encourage the initiation and development of these attacks, hence good management in frame and glasshouse culture is a major step in the prevention of fungal infections. In the open garden there is far less occurrence of fungal disease, as conditions are less favourable to them.

During lengthy spells of dank weather, when the air is torpid and the humidity high, keep a regular watch for the onset of moulds; they normally start on sickly or dead foliage. Remove promptly any leaves or shoots affected, by pulling or snipping them off and dispose of them immediately.

Good hygiene in cultivation will go a long way towards control, but it may become necessary to resort to chemical assistance if the attack is severe or recurrent. There are fungicides available which work on the systemic principle, applied as a spray, or for pot-grown plants can be included in the watering routine for take-up by the roots. They are most effective when the plants are in growth, and hardly worth using during the dormant period, as they are much less easily absorbed into the tissues of an inactive plant. Early recognition of fungal attack and prompt action to halt its development are essential to the success of any treatment.

Virus infections are complex, difficult to identify and impossible to cure. The symptoms can be yellowing, blotching or distortion of leaves stems and buds, but other ills can also produce these effects. If by eliminating possible alternative causes, such as root aphid, red spider mite, drought, bad drainage and others, you decide that virus may be present, dispose of the afflicted plant(s) immediately. In addition you should sterilize any equipment used in the pruning or propagation of suspect plants.

Chlorosis is a condition rather than a disease. It can be caused by drought, bad drainage, cold winds, excessive limyness, excessive acidity, pests, too much sun and too much shade among other things! The symptoms are yellow-ing of the foliage and a general lowering of vitality. If left untreated the affected plant will probably die, sooner or later, but the grower has the problem of first deciding what that treatment should be, before taking action. A bold approach is to move the victim to another part of the garden in the hope that the cause of the problem will be left behind. It really is a matter of making an assumption as to the cause, based on what you know of the plant's needs, correcting the suspected fault and waiting for the result. Excessive limyness is certainly a common cause of chlorosis in ericaceous species, but this is still not clear-cut, because excessive acidity can produce similar symptoms.

Mineral deficiencies may be responsible for poor flowering, retarded growth, leaf blemishes and generally poor performance. The presence and level of the predominant elements, such as calcium, potassium, phosphorus and nitrogen are easily checked using one of the soil testing kits available from most gardening suppliers. Trace elements, like zinc, iron, boron and cadmium require more sophisticated means for their detection and measurement. Some horticultural centres offer a soil analysis service. An alternative is to apply a chelated trace element mix. Balanced fertilizers usually contain all the essential elements in the correct proportions, although they do vary in nitrogen and potassium content to suit the particular application for which they are intended.

Blue mould on gladiolus

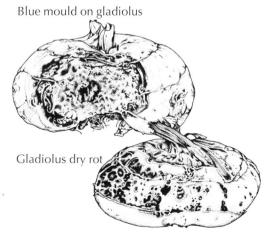

Gladiolus dry rot

Seasonal checklist

SPRING

Plant care
- Sow seed as soon as you obtain it
- Carry out a regular inspection of seed pots for germination and pot up seedlings as they develop
- Apply a dressing of balanced fertilizer to established beds and troughs
- Take cuttings from early-flowering plants (see page 142)
- Remove winter covers from beds, frames and individual plants
- Remove and replace with new stock those plants which have failed or have become invasive
- Prune back excessive growth on vigorous plants (see page 75)
- Divide congested clumps and replant or pot up (see page 145)
- Inspect generally for the onset of pest problems
- Move pot-grown plants on to larger sizes after flowering (see page 149)
- Make new plantings in the rock garden

Maintenance
- Replace any top-dressing which has become fouled by moss or other growths
- Store away winter covers where they are safe from breakage
- Spring-clean alpine houses and frames (see page 164)
- Wash and store any used pots after re-potting
- Replace damaged and defaced labels
- Removed dead leaves and other winter litter from beds
- Check that soakaways are functioning properly and that drainage systems generally are in good order. Improve drainage where rain has revealed inadequacies

SUMMER

Plant care
- Continue re-potting as plants complete their flowering cycles (see page 149)
- Inspect plants regularly for any sign of pests or disease, and take appropriate control measures promptly
- Take cuttings as plants finish flowering and shoots ripen
- Use cooler spells for any further planting of beds and troughs
- Remove spent foliage of spring bulbs
- Cover bulb frames for summer ripening (see page 126)
- Make layerings of dwarf shrubs (see page 145)
- Shade newly planted and newly potted stock from hot sun and pay regular attention to their watering needs
- Water thoroughly at intervals during dry periods, as necessary (see page 160)
- Use shading on alpine houses and frames during hot periods (see page 129)
- Watch out for ripening seed on early-flowering plants and collect when ready
- Dead-head flowering plants

Maintenance
- Carry out repairs to paths and stonework (see pages 169–171)
- Build new beds and features
- Compensate for settlement on raised beds (see page 85)
- Arrange for neighbours or friends to do basic caretaking during holiday absence

AUTUMN

Plant care
- Continue collecting seed as it ripens
- Dead-head and clean up summer-flowering plants
- Give a dressing of fertilizer to emerging autumn bulbs
- Continue the vigil for pest problems and watch out for the start of fungal diseases (see page 172)
- As the season approaches its end, fit winter covers to beds, frames and individual plants (see page 156)
- Open up bulb frames to let in rain

Maintenance
- Check frame and other covers for condition and clean up glass ready for use
- Make any necessary repairs
- Clean up plunge material, as necessary, in frames and alpine houses
- Always store collected seed in cool and dry conditions

WINTER

Plant care
- Keep a regular watch for fungal diseases on plants under cover (see p 172)
- Begin sowing seed
- Draw up plans and planting schemes for the coming year

Maintenance
- Check the security of winter covers periodically, and especially when strong winds are forecast

Plant directory 1

In compiling this list of plants the aim has been to offer a representative selection. It comprises only a fraction of those available; there are whole books devoted to a single generus. As regards the measure of skill and care required in their cultivation, those selected are slightly biased toward the easier species, but they do include a reasonable proportion of plants which present something of a challenge to the grower. The grading, in this respect, is made clear in the individual descriptions. Very difficult and very rare species have been deliberately omitted, as they fall beyond the scope of this book.

There would be little point in attempting to provide the "common" names of the plants as these, if they exist at all, not only differ from region to region, but are mainly in German, French, Serbo-Croat and a host of other languages, with no English version. You will find that almost all rock plants are identified and sold under their botanical names. Care has been taken to give the correct current names in this listing, but names are not static, and it is possible that one or two of those given in the following pages might have been subject to change between the writing of this work and its publication.

In each of the individual descriptions you can expect to find:
• The plant's general habit, with guidance on height and spread.
• Approximate time of flowering.
• Type and colour of flower.
• Suitable soils and situations.
• Brief notes on any special measures required, such as the need for winter cover, or intolerance to lime.

The dimensions given for plant sizes can only be approximate; plants vary (like people) in stature and are also affected in their growth by climates and soils. At the extreme, one grower's treasure may well be another's rampant weed!

A to Z of rock garden plants
Aethionema
Shrubby, free-flowering plants for scree or very gritty soils in warm, sunny positions.
A. schistosum bears clusters of rose pink bloom in June. Very compact and rarely above 7.5 cm (3 in) tall. A good trough subject.
A. 'Warley Rose' is an outstanding hybrid, with blue-grey leaves and abundant carmine pink flowers in early summer. 10–15 cm (4–6 in) tall and similar in spread.

Allium
The smaller of these decorative onions are ideal for raised beds and troughs in full sun, giving valuable summer colour.
A. cyaneum reaches no higher than 20 cm (8 in) with its sparse, narrow leaves and heads of tufted flowers, in shades of deep blue.
A. oreophilum has similar stature, but bears stiff umbels of little crocus-like flowers in a range of pinks, the richest of these being in *A. oreophilum* 'Zwanenburg'.

Androsace
This great genus of mountain plants contains a variety of forms and habits. The exquisite cushion-making species all require overhead protection during late autumn and winter, and are usually, but not essentially, grown in pots.

They require a "lean" soil mixture (see page 148) to grow properly. All androsaces need good light if they are to stay in character and flower well.
A. carnea has several sub-species, some of which grow more as tufts than mats. The late spring flowers are raised on short stiff stems 5 cm (2 in) tall, in umbels of pink or white. A gritty,but reasonably rich, soil produces the best results, particularly in troughs.
A. cylindrica is one of the least demanding of the cushion types. It forms a dense bun of narrow, dark green leaves which is smothered by a cap of snow-white flowers in spring.
A. lanuginosa has a trailing habit, with long stems up to 20 cm (8 in), clothed in silver-grey leaves. It flowers with almost spherical umbels of lavender blue, for several weeks during summer. A good subject for sprawling over rockwork or a low wall.
A. sarmentosa will often survive the winter without protection if grown in a scree or raised bed. It spreads by runners to produce an expanse of silky-leaved rosettes, which carry large umbels of pink flowers in late spring and early summer. A mature mat may spread to 60 cm (2 ft) across.

A. **sempervivoides** is similar in growth and flower to the above but has glossy foliage and is quite weather-proof. For the scree or raised bed.
A. **vandellii** (syn. *A. imbricata*) needs all-year protection from the rain. Its silver-grey dome of tightly-packed rosettes is completely hidden in late spring by countless yellow-eyed, milk-white flowers which sit tight on top of the foliage. It is a lime hater.

Aquilegia

There are several charming dwarf species of columbine for the not too hot parts of the rock garden. They like a gritty, but nourishing soil.
A. **bertolonii** is only 7.5–10 cm (3–4 in) tall, but for its size it bears huge, inky-blue flowers in late spring.
A. **flabellata** has an easy-going nature, seeding itself around, with restraint, when conditions are favourable. Similar in height to *A. bertolonii*, its equally large flowers are blue and white.

Armeria

Scree, very gritty soil, or a crevice will suit these sun-loving, tufted cushion plants.
A. **juniperifolia** (syn. *A. caespitosa*) is the species most often seen in rock gardens. Its dark green mound is studded with pale pink "drumstick" flowers in early summer. Cushions can attain a diameter of 30 cm (12 in) after several years.
A. **juniperifolia 'Bevan's Variety'** (syn. *A. caespitosa* 'Roger Bevan') is a selected form which has a richer tone to its blooms.

Asperula

Falsely regarded as needing alpine house treatment, the asperulas are in fact quite hardy in temperate regions, asking only for a well-maintained, sunny scree to be long-lived and generous with their flowers.
A. **suberosa** (syn. *A. arcadiensis*) needs careful handling because of its brittle stems, but is otherwise an easy plant. In early summer it puts forth a froth of soft pink narrow trumpets, over its mat of pale green foliage. There is often considerable die-back in winter, but spring brings a flush of new growth. An established adult will spread up to 35 cm (14 in) across.

Astilbe

Places with moisture-retentive soil and a little shade from the hottest sun will satisfy the astilbes. Their fluffy spikes of bloom arise in high summer. The following both die down in the autumn.

A. **x crispa** grows slowly and has a long life span. Worth cultivating for its curled and feathered foliage alone, it is even more eye-catching when the stubby, sugar-pink flowers are present. Only 15 cm (6 in) high and the same in spread after a few years. 'Perkeo' is the most popular form.
A. **'Silber Königin'** is almost as dwarf as *A. x crispa*, with white flowers and very dark green leaves with feathered edges.

Bolax

Grown mainly for their captivating patterned foliage, these tough plants are content almost anywhere in the rock garden provided that the soil is very well drained and not significantly limy. They resent shade.
B. **glebaria** (syn. *Azorella trifurcata*) spreads fairly vigorously to form an impenetrable mat of glossy, bright green leaf rosettes, over any stony soil or scree. The small yellow flowers are not very striking but add summer interest. There seems to be no limit to how far this carpeter will spread. It is long-lived.
B. **gummifera** is a cushion-forming species with beautiful rimed edges to its fingered leaves. Plant it in a trough and it will slowly increase its tight dome over the years.

Campanula

This is a large genus and difficult to honour with only a few examples. The campanulas are nearly all herbaceous with summer flowers, revelling in very well-drained, sunny places.
C. **arvatica** has blue- and white-flowered variants. It will creep over a scree bed with its tiny-leaved, prostrate stems, mingling with, but never threatening other plants. The dainty, upturned starry bells rise on 5 cm (2 in) stalks in summer and persist for weeks.
C. **carpatica** also has blue and white variants. It makes a low mound of heart-shaped leaves, over which crowds a mass of big, shallow bells on 7.5–10 cm (3–4 in) slender stalks in late summer. The plant can be 20 cm (8 in) across after three or four years. Ideal for a raised bed or hollow wall.
C. **cochleariifolia** is a little wanderer for the scree or any well-drained bed. It has charming tubby bells, in a range of blues from near white to Wedgwood. Never more than 10 cm (4 in) tall, and often less. Summer flowering.
C. **zoysii** is a connoisseur's plant, best grown in a pot, but can also be persuaded to inhabit a block

Plant directory 2

of tufa, in a trough or cliff. The cobalt blue flowers are curiously formed, their ends being winged and almost closed. The dark green leaves resemble those of birch. The whole plant is scarcely more than 2.5 cm (1 in) high and never attains any appreciable size.

Cassiope

No ericaceous planting should be without at least one of the cassiopes. Out of flower they are either an upright or a tangled mass of scaly-leaved stems. In the later weeks of spring numerous tiny, white, pendant globes light up the whole plant. Happiest in cool, moist conditions, but with plentiful light, they require a humus-rich soil with a pH of no more than 6.

C. lycopodioides grows as a mat of writhing branchlets and flowers very generously, beaded, in early summer, with little dumpy bells of purest white, each enhanced by its rusty-red calyx. Even more prolific in bloom is the hybrid 'Beatrice Lilley'.

C. tetragona is one of the upright species with a silky look to its tightly clinging leaves. The flowers hang from the upper part of each columnar stem and are more conventionally bell-shaped than most in the genus. Height and spread are about the same, at 15 cm (6 in).

Cyclamen

Quite distinct from the highly bred florists' cyclamens are the true species, some of which fall to frosts, but the following have, in general, proved hardy in temperate regions.

C. cilicium has a reputation for lack of hardiness, but given a warm, sheltered spot and really good drainage it will usually survive the winter. The rounded leaves are pleasingly patterned with silver, providing a lovely foil to the shell-pink flower petals with their crimson bases. This species blooms in the autumn. Height at flowering is 10 cm (4 in).

C. hederifolium has beautifully marked, ivy-shaped leaves, with no two plants being exactly alike in this respect. The pink or white flowers are formed in early autumn and persist for several weeks afterwards. The plant spreads by self-sown seedlings and is not too particular about soil or position. Height at flowering is 10–15 cm (4–6 in).

C. repandum is for the cooler woodland planting, loving dappled shade and a light, fibrous soil. It may be damaged by an occasional late frost if it is not given a snug place to live. The very pointed leaves can be a rather plain green, but there are lightly mottled forms and some with very striking yellow freckles. In mid- to late spring the elegant carmine flowers rise on 15 cm (6 in) stems.

Dianthus

A large and widespread genus with many species suited to the rock garden. The great majority are summer-flowering sun lovers from limestone habitats. Hybrids abound, but are no better or easier than the species. All enjoy a perfectly drained, but nourishing, soil.

D. alpinus builds small hummocks of deep green, strap-shaped leaves and holds its large flowers just above the foliage on stocky stems. The flower colour varies from a warm white, through pale pink, to deep blood red, according to cultivar. Not long-lived in cultivation but spectacular in its prime. Rarely reaches more than 15 cm (6 in) across.

D. microlepis competes with any of the flower-studded cushion plants. Its slow-growing little bun of grass-like leaves can be completely blanketed with sessile flowers of clear pink. A natural for trough, tufa or pot culture. The flowers come earlier than in most species, during mid- to late spring. Specimen plants have been grown to a diameter of 20 cm (8 in) and more.

D. pavonius (syn. **D. neglectus)** is another of the dwarfer species, producing a neat dome of its rather dull green foliage. The flowers are held on 7.5–10 cm (3–4 in) stems and have dual colouring, being pink on the upper surface, but fawn beneath. A quietly charming plant for a trough or pot.

Dionysia

This aristocratic breed of cushion plants has very few members which will survive without constant and highly skilled attention from an experienced grower, but there are one or two with lesser needs suitable for the indoor rock garden or pot culture.

D. aretioides is the most forgiving of them all, requiring only a gritty soil mixture and plentiful, but not scorching, sunlight. A contented specimen can attain the size and shape of half a football in seven or eight years. This plant is extremely generous with its bright yellow primrose-like flowers, which in spring completely hide the cushion.

D. tapetodes can be classed as one of the least difficult of the difficult-to-very difficult species. Grow it on indoor tufa, or in an alpine house pot or bed, using a "lean" soil mixture (see p. 148). From late autumn onwards give water very sparingly, until early spring when the plant bursts into flower with a host of little golden trumpets.

Draba

Another race of cushion plants, but one which has a lot of rather weedy members as well as some of real beauty. Of the best, one or two are tough enough for growing in the open garden, but generally they are plants for culture under glass.

D. dedeana is one that can be put in the rock garden, or an unprotected trough. The grey-green leaves cluster in a fairly tight mound which may eventually reach 15 cm (6 in) across. In early spring heads of white, four-petalled flowers jostle for space on their springy stems. At flowering time the height is about 10 cm (4 in) for a mature plant.

D. mollissima is a gem, with a downy appear-ance to the tiny leaves which make up the surface of the soft cushion. As spring advances the plant is transformed by a stand of shining yellow heads of flower, held on pliant and extremely slender stalks. A species for pot cul-ture in the alpine house or an "indoor" bed, it needs a gritty but sustaining soil mixture, such as John Innes Potting Compost No. 2 and grit in equal proportions. Can attain a diameter of 15 cm (6 in) in three years, but is usually slower.

D. rigida also has yellow flowers on delicate stems and also flowers at about the same time as *D. mollissima*, but it has a stronger constitu-tion and can be planted out in a sunny trough or on a tufa boulder. It grows at a steady pace to about 10 cm (4 in) across after three years, but is much slower in tufa.

Dryas

Very good carpeters for sunny scree or rock-work; extremely hardy and resistant to drought. The harsher conditions become, the better they seem to flower.

D. octopetala spreads a network of mahogany-coloured, creeping stems over the rockwork or scree surface. Its miniature oak-like leaves are silvery-white on their undersides. The pure white anemone-like flowers have a central boss of rich yellow stamens and rise on 10 cm (4 in) stems in late spring. A few weeks later the feathery seed heads develop to give the plant added appeal.

D. octopetala 'Minor' is smaller in all its parts and more suitable for use in the raised bed or trough as a compact mat.

D. x suendermannii has slightly pendant flow-ers which are cream in bud but pure white when fully open.

Edraianthus

These bell-flowers are closely related to *Campanula*, with similar preferences for warm, sunny places and lean soils.

E. pumilio grows as a compact, tufted hump of grassy, silver-grey leaves which die back in win-ter to resting crowns. In early summer a profusion of large, lavender-blue bells covers the whole plant. Not long-lived in cultivation, but a delight for three or four years, during which the tuffet may reach 10 cm (4 in) across. Easily propagated from cuttings to produce replacements.

E. serpyllifolius makes a mat of deep green, oval leaves, upon which sit clusters of rich vio-let-blue bells in early summer. Longer-lived than *E. pumilio*, it spreads slowly and steadily to 20 cm (8 in) across after several years. This species also dies back for the winter months.

Erinus

Only one species is favoured by rock gardeners and because it seeds around with great enthusi-asm it must be planted in a suitable spot. Use it to brighten up places with poor, stony soil, or to colonise the crevices of stone walls.

E. alpinus flowers in a range of pinks, with 5–7.5 cm (2–3 in) sprays of bloom, over small clumps of leaf rosettes little more than 7.5 cm (3 in) across at most. Short-lived, but permanent through self-sown offspring. There is an albino form with white flowers and paler foliage.

Fritillaria

Currently a very popular genus in frame and alpine house culture of bulbs. Many species require experience and skill to sustain and flower them, but happily, the less demanding are equal in beauty to the rare and difficult.

F. michailovskyi may be grown in a pot or bulb frame, but will also respond to a warm, perfectly drained spot in the garden; an excel-lent bulb for hollow wall planting. Rarely more than 15 cm(6 in) tall, it has narrow, grey-green leaves and normally produces more than one flower on a stem. The bell-shaped flower is deep mahogany-red with a purplish bloom, in the upper part, and golden yellow towards the mouth.

181

Plant directory 3

F. pallidiflora is a coolly elegant species for a humus-rich soil in light or dappled shade. About 30 cm (12 in) tall, with several large, pale yellow, pendant bells on each stem, complemented by blue-green leaves.

Gentiana

The gentians can be reasonably divided into two distinct groups: the spring-flowering and the autumn-flowering. Both are invaluable for the rock garden display. The only real difficulty in their cultivation lies in the amount of sunlight that they should receive. As a rough guide, in the more southerly parts of temperate regions full exposure to the sun is often too much for the autumn flowerers, and may even be excessive for the spring flowerers, whereas in the cooler, northern parts all can be grown in full sun. Both types require a generous amount of nutrients in the soil, with regular replenishment.

Spring-flowering gentians

G. acaulis is a variable plant and it also gives its name to a group of species with similar appearance and habit, including *G. clusii*, *G. kochiana* and *G. occidentalis*. All produce huge, spectacular trumpet flowers up to 7 cm (2.5 in) long in a range of blues. Mid- to late spring is their flowering time, when they rise to about 10 cm (4 in) in height. They grow as a slowly spreading mat of rather leathery leaves held close to the ground. There are white-flowered forms available of *G. acaulis*, but they lack vigour and stamina.

G. verna subsp. **balcanica** (syn. *G. verna angulosa*) is a delightful species for trough or raised-bed culture. It grows as a low clump of dark-green foliage, topped in mid-spring with intense blue flowers 2.5 cm (1 in) tall. Short-lived in cultivation, it usually begins to decline after reaching a spread of some 7.5 cm (3 in), at the age of three to four years. Good seed is often produced, from which replacement plants can be raised.

Autumn-flowering gentians

Although species such as *G. farreri* and *G. sino-ornata* are cultivated, the hybrids are more popular and easier to please, though no more beautiful than their wild parents. Give them an open-structured soil with plenty of fibrous content and a pH of not more than 6.0 (slightly acid). To maintain healthy growth, divide and replant autumn gentians every two or three years in spring.

G. 'Caroli' bears elegant, pale sky-blue flowers in mid-autumn, over a loose mat of fine-leaved growth. Height when in flower is about 7.5 cm (3 in) and the spread of a single plant reaches to about 20 cm (8 in).

G. septemfida fills the flowering gap between spring and autumn with its upright displays of slaty-blue blooms, in the latter half of summer. Can reach a height of 30 cm (12 in) and a spread of 15 cm (6 in).

G. 'Shot Silk' is a recently raised hybrid with an iridescent sheen to its deep-blue petals. Vigorous in growth and handsomely flowered it is at its best in mid-autumn. Height and spread are about 15 cm (6 in).

G. x stevenagensis is one of the most trouble-free, blooming generously during late autumn, with rich, almost violet-blue trumpets over long-branched clumps of leafage. Height when in flower is 10 cm (4 in) and its spread is similar to *G.* 'Caroli'.

Geranium

A few of the geraniums are sufficiently dwarf and well behaved for residence in the rock garden. They are sun-lovers and to flower well should be given a lean soil or scree.

G. argenteum as its name implies has a silver cast to its foliage. The bright-pink flowers have their petals veined, like a butterfly's wing, with a deep red and arrive in late spring. The plant grows to a height of some 10 cm (4 in) and after several years a spread of 30 cm (12 in).

G. cinereum flowers later, in summer, also with darkly-veined, pink petals. The leaves are deeply divided and blue-green in hue. Similar in size to *G. argenteum*.

Globularia

Several species are available, most of which form evergreen mats of overlapping leaves and bring quiet colour to the early summer display. They do best in sunny places with lean, limy soils or scree.

G. cordifolia will spread out over the rockwork from a crevice planting, to bear little 5 cm (2 in) high "lollipop" flowers of lavender-blue, over its blanket of shiny, heart-shaped leaves.

G. repens (syn. *G. nana*) is a very choice dwarf species, of similar, but scaled-down appearance to *G. cordifolia*. Ideal for a trough or miniature garden.

Helianthemum

This name translates as "flower of the sun", clearly indicating where it should best be positioned. A great deal of hybridizing and selection has produced a host of named hybrids from which to choose. Among them are:

H. 'Ben Heckla' – brick red.
H. 'Ben Nevis' – yellow, with a red eye.
H. 'The Bride' – pure white.

As to size, they can vary in height and spread from 5 x 30 cm (2 x 12 in) and 30 x 90 cm (12 x 36 in). All require hard clipping back after flowering to keep them compact. Summer is their time of bloom.

Helichrysum

These predominantly silver-leaved plants are always decorative, with their foliage alone, but add to their value with "everlasting" flowers in summer. Light, non-limy soil seems to produce the best results, provided that it receives plenty of sun.

H. milfordiae is a mat-former, for the scree or raised bed, with fluffy, silver-white foliage and stemless, white, daisy flowers. In regions with very wet winters it will probably benefit from a rain cover. Mature plants can attain a spread of 60 cm (2 ft).

H. sessilioides (syn. H. sessile) makes a splendid symmetrical mound of silver-edged leaves, reaching 30 cm (12 in) in diameter after only three or four years. In summer this perfect dome is studded with pearly-white buds which open to shining daisies on sunny days. Happy in any lean soil or scree which is not limy.

Hypericum

The hypericums are valuable for their summer colour and, in most cases, the ease with which they become established plants. Take care when choosing species for the rock garden as some so-called "small" species will soon grow too large or too vigorously.

H. cerastioides (syn. H. rhodoppeum) is a plant for the cliff or wall, where it will produce a cascade of grey-leaved shoots and a crown of huge golden flowers in summer. Not a subject for the smaller rock garden or trough, it arches to a height of 20 cm (8 in) and will spread to at least 45 cm (18 in).

H. olympicum is a plant for lighter soils and full sun. Its flowers are a golden yellow, with prominent tufts of shiny stamens and massed above delicate, grey-green foliage in summer.

nearing 30 cm (12 in) in height, its spread can be the same after two or three years.

H. olympicum forma minus (syn. H. polyphyllum) is more compact in growth.

Iris

This is an extensive genus, within which are many species suited to the scale of the rock garden. They range from the easy to the near impossible in cultivation.

I. innominata is a good-tempered plant for the general rock garden, as it is unfussy about soil or location. It has stiff blades of foliage and quite large flowers ranging in colour from buff-apricot to lavender-purple. These stand on strong 20 cm (8 in) stems in late spring. Divide the plant immediately after flowering, every three or four years, to avoid congestion.

I. reticulata flowers very early in the year in clear shades of blue, dramatized by an orange blaze at the throat. Its height at flowering time is around 12 cm (5 in), but the rod-like, narrow leaves, which develop after flowering, are twice as tall. Superb drainage is essential to the well-being of the species and it revels in sunny screes and hollow walls or raised beds.

I. winogradowii is similar in its character, stature and needs to I. reticulata, but has a flower of pure yellow. Its reputation for being very short-lived is undeserved; plant the bulb 15 cm (6 in) deep and it should last for years.

Jeffersonia

A genus of North American woodlanders with just two species in it. Most often seen as pot-grown specimens, but they can be planted out in cool, lightly shaded beds of humus-rich soil. Both species spread very slowly and in late summer die down to a resting crown.

J. diphylla has large white flowers, held on 20 cm (8 in) wiry stems, above double-lobed leaves, in early spring.

J. dubia is the more elegant of the two, with soft-blue flowers reminiscent of clematis and kidney-shaped leaves that change from purple to green as they mature. Less tall than J. diphylla, it approaches 15 cm (6 in) at flowering time, in spring.

Lewisia

Another North American genus, noted for vibrantly coloured flowers and, in some species, less than easy cultivation. Very limy soils are a problem, being unacceptable to most species. Winter wetness in the centre of leaf

Plant directory 4

rosettes is a major cause of loss.

L. cotyledon is a name now somewhat misused to embrace an ever-increasing crowd of hybrids and cultivars. But they are showy, vigorous and easier to please than most in the genus. In general habit the plants produce a rosette of rather fleshy leaves, up to 8 cm (3 in) long, which puts up multi-flowered heads in spring. Colours range from pink, through orange and yellow, to white. Shelter from winter rain is often necessary in wetter regions.

L. rediviva shrinks to a dead-looking crown after flowering and stays that way until the beginning of the following year, when it produces its dark-green, tubular leaves in a tuft. Only when these begin to wilt and wither in mid-summer do the glorious flowers appear as 4 cm (1½ in) wide saucers of clear pink, with a lovely metallic sheen to the petals. Although prized as an alpine house plant, this species is quite hardy and ideal for a hot, sunny trough or raised bed.

Meconopsis

A family of stately, poppy-like flowers which must have cool conditions for their well-being. Mainly from the foothills of the Himalayas, they respond to woodland plantings in temperate regions, needing dappled shade.

M. betonicifolia affectionately known as the 'Himalayan blue poppy', needs a well-drained, acid, woodland soil, and shade. It grows up to 1 m (3 ft 3 in) tall and bears a succession of slightly pendant, clear-blue flowers, through late summer. Ideal for woodland plantings.

Minuartia

These are the sandworts, undeservedly neglected or overlooked by rock gardeners. On very poor soils and screes, in full sun, they form dense pads of leaf clusters, smothered by starry flowers during early summer.

M. verna subsp. **verna** is typical of the mat-formers, growing no higher than 5 cm (2 in) and spreading to some 30 cm (12 in) across in four or five years. The essentially white flowers have purple stamens in the throat.

Narcissus

Dwarf daffodils are a must for any rock garden. As well as species, there are numerous hybrids to choose from, almost all of which are very easy to grow, accepting a variety of soils and tolerant of light shade.

N. asturiensis is a tiny, nodding species, only 5–7.5 cm (2–3 in) tall and can flower at the beginning of the year when weather permits.

N. bulbocodium has many varieties and subspecies. Aptly named the hoop petticoat daffodil, for its conical trumpets, it offers a colour range from pale lemon to golden yellow. About 15 cm (6 in) tall, on average, with grass-like, stiff foliage, it blooms in early spring.

N. minor is barely 10 cm (4 in) in height; a 'Tom Thumb' version of the common daffodil, with trumpets 2.5 cm (1 in) long, of clear yellow flowering in early spring.

N. watieri is a 10 cm (4 in) high miniature with white, jonquil-like flowers in spring.

Oxalis

Some members of this genus are pernicious weeds, yet others are models of restraint and exceptional beauty suitable for the rock garden. Give them a light soil or scree in full sun.

O. adenophylla produces clusters of fibre-coated, bulbous roots just at the surface of the soil. Its fan-like, grey-green leaves rise little more than 4 cm (1½ in), to match the height of the flowers. These are goblets of silky pink petals with a carmine eye, roofing the whole plant in late spring. A clump may spread to the size of a saucer after two or three years.

O. laciniata has much finer foliage, of a ferny appearance, and pearly-pink flowers with very striking purple-blue veining. It is also a flower of late spring like O. adenophylla. By means of pinkish tubers of worm-like appearance it spreads steadily outwards, with no apparent limit, but not invasively.

O. 'Ione Hecker' is a charming hybrid of the above two species.

Papaver

These are the true poppies and the little mountain species have delicacy combined with a surprising toughness. Plant them in your sunniest scree or raised bed, or in soil that is poor and well-drained. All the following flower in late spring to early summer and, although they are short-lived, perpetuate themselves with self-sown offspring.

P. alpinum is another of those names that is also used for a group of species, including P. burseri, which is 3–4 cm (3 in) high, with white, yellow-centred flowers, and P. rhaeticum, which is of similar height and has bright yellow blooms.

Phlox

The North American species make showy

plants and often have brilliant colour forms. Two contrasting examples are:

P. divaricata subsp. laphamii 'Chattahoochee' is splendid for a very well-drained but nutritious soil, in full sun. From a winter-resting crown rises a rather tangled mound of narrow-leaved stems, bearing loose sprays of pale-violet flowers, each with a carmine eye. This is a flower of early summer, with a height of some 20 cm (8 in) and a 30 cm (12 in) spread.

P. douglasii makes a neat, prickly pad of foliage, over which, in spring to early summer, it puts a mass of close-sitting flowers. The wild species is hardly in cultivation, but there is a wealth of cultivars in colours of mauve, pale blue, crimson and white. Not a plant for limy soils, but otherwise easily pleased in a sunny bed. Expect a spread of up to 30 cm (12 in) after three years.

Primula

Of this vast genus only a minute selection can be offered. Primulas are found in most habitats of the northern hemisphere, from seashore to mountain top and a great many of them are suitable for the rock garden.

P. allionii is a limestone cliff dweller for alpine house culture, needing midday shade and a gritty, rich compost. It very slowly builds a hump of sticky leaf rosettes, capped in very early spring by a complete covering of large, sessile flowers. Colour forms range from white through pinks to deep carmine. *Botrytis* (grey mould) is the great enemy, so remove afflicted leaves promptly.

P. bhutanica is just one of the lovely, low-growing Himalayan species, with powder-blue flowers in early spring, nestling among ruffs of soft, toothed foliage. Grow it as a pot specimen, or in a cool, shaded spot with humus-rich acid soil and give it winter protection. About 10 cm (4 in) high, it is unlikely to make a clump more than 15 cm (6 in) across and needs dividing every three years to keep it healthy.

P. frondosa is among the easiest primulas to please, happy in any not too hot location in the rock garden. This is a petite species, with 10 cm (4 in) tall umbels of lilac, yellow-eyed flowers, rising from rosettes of silvery-green leaves. Left to itself it will slowly spread to 15 cm (6 in) across after three years or so.

P. hirsuta in nature inhabits clefts and ledges of acid rock formations. Give it a lightly shaded nook in the rockwork, with a non-limy soil, where it will slowly increase its mat of saw-edged leaves. The plant flowers in loose umbels with a range of colours from rather pale pink to rich rose. Height at flowering is 10 cm (4 in).

P. marginata will accept a variety of soils and positions, provided that the drainage is excellent. It spreads gradually with creeping, woody stems, from which sprout tufts of attractively scalloped leaves and flowers in loose heads of blue to mauve, in spring. There are numerous cultivars. Size is variable, but average 10 cm (4 in) in height, with a 30 cm (12 in) spread.

P. rosea has vibrant deep-rose flowers in spring which stand only 5 cm (2 in) or so above the still emerging leaves. A plant for a cool, shaded place in the rockwork, or for a woodland bed, where the soil is moist and acid. Best divided every three years to prevent decline.

Pulsatilla

Elegant and lovely flowers, closely related and similar in appearance to the anemones, liking a rich, open-textured soil and a place in the sun.

P. vernalis has goblet-shaped flowers, steely blue on the outside and pearly white within, enhanced by a crowd of golden stamens. The rather ragged leaves are sparse and held close to the ground. The intensely hairy flower stem and calyx rises to a height of 20 cm (8 in). A contented plant may develop to a clump some 15 cm (6 in) across after several years.

P. vulgaris is lustier than *P. vernalis*, reaching 25 cm (10 in) in height and spreading to 30 cm (12 in) wide. The flowers nod a little, but open wide in response to the sunshine. Colours range from purple to wine red, with blues and whites also available.

Ranunculus

The mountain buttercups are not easy to cultivate, but given a deep, rich, open-structured soil, the following are well worth trying:

R. alpestris is a dainty, white-flowered species with glossy, divided leaves. No more than 7.5 cm (3 in) tall, it sends up branching stems to carry its blooms in spring. It spreads very little.

R. parnassiifolius has leathery, ground-hugging foliage and branching stems with a succession of large, white or veined pink flowers, each with a golden knob of stamens at its centre. About 15 cm (6 in) high at the peak of blooming. In late summer the whole plant disappears for hibernation, so mark its place carefully.

185

Plant directory 5

Saponaria

Plants for problem places, where the soil is poor, dry and broiled by the summer sun.

S. ocymoides makes a loose, 10 cm (4 in) high mound of dark green, narrow-leaved shoots which may achieve a spread of 30 cm (12 in) in maturity. The deep-pink, dianthus-like flowers open in early summer as compact sprays held close to the foliage.

Saxifraga

Like *Primula*, this is a very large and indispensable genus for the rock garden and it is only possible to give a few examples to show its diversity.

S. burseriana is one of the numerous Kabschia types, making a typically tight bun of compact, grey-green rosettes and topping this, in early spring, with a host of saucer-shaped, white flowers on 5 cm (2 in) stems. There are literally hundreds of named hybrids and cultivars, giving a wide range of colours, with almost everything except blue.

S. callosa belongs to the silver (or encrusted) group. It is a mound-forming species, with fairly large leaf rosettes beautifully patterned, or encrusted, with limy beading on their edges. The plant can be long-lived, reaching 25 cm (10 in) across after four or five years. In midsummer it puts forth plumes of countless white flowers, up to 30 cm (12 in) tall. For a limestone scree or crevice, in sun or partial shade.

S. exarata subsp. moschata (syn. *S. moschata*) is typical of the "mossy" saxifrages, and is very variable. The growth is a soft cushion of deeply divided leaves in rather open rosettes, and is capped during late spring with a swarm of white, cream or pink flowers on 5 cm (2 in) stems. There are numerous hybrids, some of which are too vigorous for all but the largest rock gardens, so take care in selecting. Plant in a light soil and a semi-shaded position.

S. oppositifolia deserves to be in every rock garden. It forms an extremely hardy, dense, creeping mat of tiny-leaved shoots and covers these, in early spring, with rose to purple flowers. Give it a sunny, but never parched, place in the scree or raised bed, where it will spread its carpet some 7.5 cm (3 in) or so each year.

S. stribrnyi enjoys limestone scree conditions and benefits from winter cover, although this is not essential. It is slow-growing, making a congested hump of leaf rosettes, from the centres of which, in late spring, rise 10 cm (4 in) tall flower stems coated in sticky hairs and stained rich red-purple from top to bottom. Recommended for growing in a trough.

Sedum

The sedums provide us with very useful and eye-catching plants for places with rather dry, poor soils. They are mainly summer-flowering, in bright, clear colours.

S. pilosum grows as a little globular rosette of crowded, silvery-grey leaves. It flowers in its second year with an almost sessile, dense head of starry, pink blossoms and then dies. But it leaves behind self-sown offspring to carry on the display in future years. Ideal for a sunny trough.

S. spathulifolium has spoon-shaped, fleshy leaves, enhanced by a coating of whitish bloom. It makes a dense, tangled mat and flowers with upright 7.5 cm (3 in) stems bearing golden heads, in summer. 'Cape Blanco' (syn. 'Cappa Blanca') has bluish-white foliage, whereas 'Purpureum' has a burgundy tint to its leaves. Tough and long-lived, this species has no real limit to its moderately slow spread.

Tulipa

As well as colour, the tulips provide valuable vertical form to the rock garden planting. They are particularly suited to the sunny raised bed, enjoying the acute drainage and warmth that it offers. The dwarf species are preferred for their appropriate size and habit.

T. batalinii has a flowering height of 10–15 cm (4–6 in), with goblets of cool, creamy yellow.

T. linifolia is of similar stature, but with brilliant scarlet blooms.

T. tarda makes a flat starfish-like rosette of leaves and has up to five white, yellow-centred flowers on its 10 cm (4 in) stem.

Viola

The mountain pansies are dainty, cheerful little plants, offering both easy and challenging species to cultivation.

V. calcarata has several colour variants, in blues and purples, blooming in late spring to early summer. The plant is compact in character, with a creeping root system. Rarely more than 10 cm (4 in) tall and short-lived, but generous with its seed. Plant in fairly rich soil, in sun or partial shade.

V. delphinantha is less easy to please than V.

calcarata, but in a sunny raised bed or trough it can prosper. It makes a loose, delicate array of fine-leaved stems, 10 cm (4 in) in height and spread, upon which hang rose-lilac flowers resembling those of a delphinium.

Zephyranthes

A family of bulbous plants, some of which are sufficiently hardy to survive in gardens not subject to long periods of frost. Worth trying for the beauty of their autumn flowers. Plant them at the base of a warm wall or boulder for the best chance of success outdoors, or grow them as alpine house specimens.

Z. candida is the species seen most often in gardens in temperate regions, growing to about 20 cm (8 in) high, with white, crocus-like flowers. Dormant in summer.

Z. rosea is slightly smaller and with broader leaves than *Z. candida*, with funnel-shaped, rose pink flowers.

A to Z of dwarf trees and shrubs

There are all too many trees and shrubs sold as "dwarf", but which do not remain so once freed from the restriction of the nursery pot. In the list that follows the selection has been made from species and cultivars which have proved reliable in maintaining their dwarf character as garden specimens.

As regards their cultivation, very heavy soils are not to their liking and should be improved with the addition of grit and organic matter. Otherwise the dwarfs will accept a variety of soils and situations.

Chamaecyparis obtusa 'Juniperoides Compacta' has many cultivars, such as 'Caespitosa', 'Compacta' and 'Nana', all of which make dense, globular growth of feathery leafage, in a range of greens. Very slow growing, typically 20 cm (8 in) in height and spread after ten years or so. Perfect subjects for trough plantings.

Daphne petraea, although usually seen as a pot-grown specimen for exhibition, is quite hardy and given a gritty but nutritious soil will make a dense, humped shrublet, smothered in sugar pink, sweetly scented flowers during late spring. After 15 years it might achieve a height and spread of 20–25 cm (8–10 in).

Daphne retusa (syn. *D. tangutica* Refusa Group) is an upright, evergreen shrub with twice the growth rate of *D. petraea* and responding to the same culture. In late spring the starry, white, perfumed flowers are generously produced.

Iberis sempervirens will spread its low mound of dark-green foliage over some 40 cm (16 in) in four or five years. It can begin flowering at the end of a mild winter and continue into the spring.

Jasminum parkeri is a miniature jasmine with typical pale-yellow, scented flowers. In time it makes an open shrublet 20 cm (8 in) high and wide. Not entirely hardy, it requires a sheltered, sunny spot protected from hard frost.

Juniperus communis 'Compressa' is the little church spire juniper so familiar in trough plantings. After ten years or so it may reach 70 cm (38 in) in height with its blue-green column of prickly foliage. Not fussy about soil or situation, but it can be injured by strong, cold, drying winds.

Picea abies 'Pygmaea' is a midget Norway spruce, attaining some 45 cm (18 in) in height after 25 years, with a spread of 30 cm (12 in). It has a conical form, with dense branches of broad-needled foliage.

Pinus mugo has had a lot of attention from dwarf conifer enthusiasts; there are dozens of cultivars, varying in colour and habit. Typically, it makes a mounded shape of crowded branches bearing "bottlebrush" clusters of needles, attaining a height of around 1.2 m (4 ft) and a spread of 60 cm (2 ft) after 15 or 20 years.

Rhododendron It would be folly to single out a particular dwarf species from this beautiful family. Far better that you visit a specialist nursery to choose from the fascinating forms and colours available, both in species and hybrids. All require a humus-rich, acid soil and must never want for moisture.

Salix 'Boydii' is a true dwarf willow; it has an upright habit, with rounded leaves and little catkins, all in perfect scale. Give it a rather moist, non-limy soil in the rock garden, where it may possibly reach a height of 60 cm (2 ft) after 15 or 20 years.

Sorbus poteriifolia (syn. *S. pygmaea*) makes an almost prostrate miniature mountain ash tree, spreading to 30 cm (12 in) across. It bears the typical white rowan blossom in spring, followed by bunches of white berries in late summer to early autumn.

Index 1

Index 2/Acknowledgements

Acknowledgements

Editor: Alex Bennion
Executive Art Editor: Mark Richardson
Designer: Victoria Harvey, Town Group Consultancy
Artists: William Giles, Sandra Pond

The Royal Horticultural Society and publishers have made every effort to
ensure that all instructions given in this book are accurate and safe, but they
cannot accept liability for any resulting injury, damage or loss to either person
or property whether direct or consequential and howsoever arising. The author
and publishers will be grateful for any information which will
assist them in keeping future editions up to date. We specifically draw
our readers' attention to the necessity of carefully reading and accurately
following the manufacturer's instruction on any product.

THE R.H.S. ENCYCLOPEDIA OF PRACTICAL GARDENING

A complete range of titles in this series is available from all good bookshops or by mail order direct from the publisher. Payment can be made by credit card or cheque/postal order in the following ways:

BY PHONE   Phone through your order on our special CREDIT CARD HOTLINE on 0933 410511; speak to our customer service team during office hours (9am to 5pm) or leave a message on the answer machine, quoting your full credit card number plus expiry date and your f name and address. Please also quote the reference number shown at the top of this form.

BY POST   Simply fill out the order form below (it can be photocopied) and send it with your payment to: REED BOOK SERVICES LTD, PO BOX 5, RUSHDEN, NORTHANTS, NN10 6Y SPECIAL OFFER: **FREE POSTAGE AND PACKING** (UK ONLY)

ISBN	TITLE	PRICE	QUANTITY	TOTAL
1 85732 976 7	GARDENING TECHNIQUES	£8.99		
1 85732 974 0	WATER GARDENING	£8.99		
1 85732 973 2	ORGANIC GARDENING	£8.99		
1 85732 900 7	CONTAINER GARDENING	£8.99		
1 85732 901 5	GARDEN STRUCTURES	£8.99		
1 85732 902 3	PRUNING	£8.99		
1 85732 903 1	PLANT PROPAGATION	£8.99		
1 85732 905 8	FRUIT	£8.99		
1 85732 904 X	VEGETABLES	£8.99		
1 85732 908 2	GROWING UNDER GLASS	£8.99		
1 85732 907 4	LAWNS, WEEDS & GROUND COVER	£8.99		
1 85732 906 6	GARDEN PESTS AND DISEASES	£8.99		
1 85732 774 8	GARDEN PLANNING	£8.99		
1 85732 775 6	ROCK GARDENING	£8.99		
			POSTAGE & PACKING	FREE
			GRAND TOTAL	

Name .... (BLOCK CAPITALS)

Address...

.... Postcode ....

I enclose a cheque/postal order for £   made payable to Reed Book Services Ltd, or:

Please debit my: Access ☐   Visa ☐   AmEx ☐   Diners ☐   account

by £................................Expiry date ....

Account no. ☐☐☐☐☐☐☐☐☐☐☐☐☐☐☐☐

Signature ....

Whilst every effort is made to keep our prices low, the publisher reserves the right to increase the price at short notice. Your order will be dispatched within 28 days, subject to availability. Free postage and packing offer applies to UK only. Please call 0933 410511 for details of export postage and packing charges.

Registered office: Michelin House, 81 Fulham Road, London SW3 6RB. Registered in England no. 1974080

THIS FORM MAY BE PHOTOCOPIED